Johnny Thunders:
In Cold Blood

Over the years, Nina Antonia has slogged away in solitude on numerous magazine articles and sleeve notes. She has also written several books, including:

The One And Only
the authorised biography of
Peter Perrett and The Only Ones
(Published by S.A.F. Books)

Too Much Too Soon
the makeup and breakup of
The New York Dolls
(Published by Omnibus Press)

Johnny Thunders

In Cold Blood

Nina Antonia

Originally published in the UK by
Jungle Books, 1987

Published in 2000 under license from Jungle Books by

CHERRY RED BOOKS
a division of Cherry Red Records Ltd
Unit 17, Elysium Gate West,
126–8 New King's Road
London SW6 4LZ

E-mail: iain@cherryred.co.uk

A catalogue record for this book is available from the British Library.

ISBN 1 901447 15 4

Typeset in Adobe Garamond by Strathmore Publishing Services, London N7

Printed in Great Britain by Biddles Ltd, Guildford and King's Lynn

This book is dedicated to the memories of
Johnny Thunders & Jerry Nolan
& Rock 'n' Roll

and the hope of the future
Vito, Dino & Jamie

Contents

(*Marcia Resnick*)

Acknowledgements

Original Cast List Bouquets (1986): Ann Arbor, Susanne Blomqvist, Leee Black Childers, Kris Dellanagi, Christopher Giercke, Bob Gruen, Alan Hauser, Tony James, Eddie King, Walter Lure, Jerry Nolan, Patti Palladin, Billy Rath, Marcia Resnick and Mr Johnny Thunders.

Update Appreciation: David Arnoff, Mariann Bracken and Family, Cherry Red Books, Tom Crossley, Jungle Books, Stevie Klasson, Freddy Lynxx, Maria McCormack, Pedro Mercedes, John Perry, Severina, Gail Higgins Smith, Phyllis Stein and everyone who agreed to be interviewed.

Technical Assistance: Sam and Aurora Lash.

Forewarned

Johnny Thunders didn't just flirt with death, he courted it. Even so, his eventual demise in New Orleans on 23 April 1991 still came as a terrible shock. All of the false alarms and embellished whispers of his passing over the years had somehow managed to make Johnny seem both vulnerable and invincible, until the dread inevitable was finally substantiated.

When I first began working on *In Cold Blood* in the early eighties, Thunders wasn't a memory and I wrote in the present tense, hope clinging to the ledge, Johnny nine-lives defying the odds. Now it's all consigned to the past.

Johnny Thunders created an almost unique situation, in that it was next to impossible to separate the man from his reputation. When reality had finished reporting on drug problems, police busts and deportations, rumour picked up the story, erasing the fragile line between cold fact and neurotic fantasy. Then you had to separate the man from himself: Johnny Genzale – the shy sweetheart, and Johnny Thunders – the sleepy-eyed gutterpunk.

Looked upon as the pale spectre of rock 'n' roll immolation, Thunders qualified his image every time he staggered into the mile-high headlines of the press. He lived a dangerous life and eventually came to represent what most people would rather forget when it comes to popular entertainment. Sure, they may want to read William Burroughs or go and see *Trainspotting* but media tourists rarely want to tangle with the real deal, choosing instead the darkness of the cinema or the printed word, so they can walk the same streets without having to cross through the shadows that exist there. Johnny didn't set out to be a dope fiend artiste ruling the roost of slum city rock, the needle haze as much a part of his performance as the guitar playing. He wanted to be as great as Presley before the army, or Sinatra in his prime, and sometimes he was.

Sadly, and perhaps obviously, for a great many of Thunders' 'fans', one of the main pulls seemed to be the progression of the guitarist's mental and physical anguish, the tolerance of his body and the levels of his nihilistic, self-destructive motivations. As the condemned man of rock 'n' roll, Johnny wasn't always as oblivious as casual observers might have believed or critics presumed but he wasn't strong enough to escape, either.

He once said, on stage: 'OK. You got it. I'm gonna die tonight. I'm gonna die up here …'

And the audience cheered.

In time, the junkie mythology overshadowed Thunders' innate abilities; the unique rock 'n' roll sense of finesse, sharp wit and a singular guitar style. A legion of musicians have attempted to emulate his stance and attitude but haven't come close and never will. It's not too hard to play the way that Johnny did and guitarists have tried and will go on trying but they can't make it sound

the same: a pact between persona, warmth and power that built to an extra-
ordinary crescendo. When Johnny was on form, he could charm a snakepit of
a crowd, snapping out of drugged lethargy to deliver all that rock 'n' roll ever
promised to be: Freedom, Subversion, Style and Release. Johnny Thunders was
the last embodiment of a broken perfection that was true rebel culture before
commerce married creativity and stifled the bride. A miniature classic that
assumed legendary proportions, Johnny Thunders had a way of moving
through it all that told you he knew everything, even though there were some
things he'd rather forget.

NINA ANTONIA

August 1999

Johnny Thunders:
In Cold Blood

Hollywood '73. (*Bob Gruen*)

1
A Jukebox Made Of City

Before the fifties died of an exquisitely painless form of cancer and fear, blood cells tingled to Dion and stolen Lucky Strikes. Leather jackets boasted turf designs stitched on the back like pirate flags as warnings to wanderers in the wrong parts of town. Baseball bats swung in alleys, while high above the shadows someone played a Paul-and-Paula tune. Drive-ins became the official shrines for swift sex, popcorn and B-movies, and Sal Mineo turned capped-sleeved vests into an art form.

On the outskirts of the city, where ivory was still the colour of soap not the polished handle of a switch-blade, a little kid with heavy black hair lay in bed listening, when he should have been sleeping, to the music that came dancing across the landing from his sister's room. The teenage romance and ruin of The Shangri-Las, The Crystals and The Angels seeping into his dreams. 'I grew up listening to music. My sister Mariann was five-and-a-half years older than me and she played all those girl groups, that's how I heard all that stuff.'

John Anthony Genzale was born in Queens, one of New York's outer boroughs, on 15 July 1952, a heady mix of second-generation Neapolitan and Sicilian heritage. His father, Emil, should have been proud but he was prouder still of his lady-killing charm and good looks, leaving his wife Josephine to fend for the family. Mariann Bracken: 'We lived in East Elmhurst, Queens. It was always just the three of us, my mother, Johnny and I. My father was a woman-iser and he left when Johnny was an infant. We had little or no contact with him. He never gave my mother any support, financially or otherwise. She had to work at whatever she could and while she worked I took care of Johnny. We had a hard life but no matter what, Johnny had everything.' Except a guitar. By the time Johnny Genzale was four years old, he'd seen Elvis Presley personify what rebellion was on television and wanted some. He hadn't had to plead too much for his Ma to bring home a plastic guitar from the toy store, and although no melody could be plucked from the strings, it felt right. A year later he had his first brush with the law and audience approval. Mariann: 'He had to have his tonsils out and he kicked and screamed all the way to the hospital. He wasn't going in. We walked in one door, he ran out the other. A police officer brought him back. Although it was only one night in the hospital and home the next day, we were worried sick. When we went to pick him up the nurses told us that he had entertained them, he'd been imitating Elvis Presley the whole night!'

Although little Johnny Genzale was usually shy outside of his impromptu performances, he was a live wire and all of the esoteric disciplines of the Catholic church and his role as an altar boy did little to curb the wild streak

Little Italy. Mariann and Johnny.

that ran through him. It was baseball that mopped up his energy, hitting the ball as high as the stars, and even though he was kind of petite, he was strong enough and fast enough to make the neighbourhood team. 'I used to play baseball from eight in the morning till eight the next night and loved it.' Queens, after all, does boast Shea Stadium, where the legendary Mickey Mantle, the sporting hero of Johnny's childhood, brought the New York Yankees to baseball glory.

If Johnny Genzale progressed through his schooling in a deluge of bad be-haviour reports that followed him from Our Lady of Fatima in nearby Jackson Heights, to New Town High, his passion for baseball remained a constant fea-ture, something to excel in. Eventually scouted by the Philadelphia Phillies and several other teams including the Boston Red Sox at the age of thirteen, a future in the sport might have been on the cards for Johnny except for one Little League ruling that insisted upon the presence of the junior hopeful's father. Johnny Thunders would later tell journalists that he quit baseball after a coach demanded he cut his hair, evading not the truth but the hurt.

While baseball lost a star in the making, rock 'n' roll gained one on the re-bound when Johnny traded his bat for a bass guitar. Mariann Bracken: 'After he couldn't play baseball, he really started on his music. He formed a band with a bunch of kids in junior high school. I'd got a job in a small catering firm and they'd play there for bar mitzvahs and things like that. My mother says that at one time Johnny worked in the candy store on the corner, in the ice cream parlour, but the only thing I ever remember him doing was playing music.' Starting out as smart little princelings in their matching nylon no-crease suits covering the lat-est chart hits, they soon abandoned both the uniformity of their clothes and ma-terial, evolving into a short-lived rock band called The Reign. As they developed over the course of some nine months, Johnny began oscillating between playing bass and guitar. In the winter of '67, when the group entered Associated Studios in NY to cut a track with a psychedelic pop slant entitled 'Zippered Up Heart', little Johnny Genzale was credited as the lead guitarist, alongisde vocalist Don Bruce, drummer John Pisapia, organist George Boyd, and bassist Frank Sardelis. However, once Reign disbanded, little Johnny seems to have reverted back to bass.

Even though a place at Bryant High, a regular neighbourhood school, awaited Johnny, he managed, in what was by all accounts a heart-rending turn, to persuade his mother that he would be better suited attending a private, liberal establishment called Quintanos. Tucked behind Carnegie Hall and with-in easy reach of Central Park, Quintanos aimed to groom their students for suc-cess in the performing arts. However, no form of education, no matter how laid

---

An asterisk [*] after a quote denotes that the interview, originally conducted by the author, first appeared in *Too Much Too Soon – The Makeup and Breakup of The New York Dolls*, Omnibus Press, 1998.

'He believes in God.' Johnny age 11.

back, was going to corral Johnny Genzale and he bolted at the age of sixteen, to play in a city shaped like a million stone jukeboxes. Becoming familiar with the wash of noise and neon, he started hanging out at Nobody's Bar on Bleecker Street, a groupie haunt and pitstop for English bands passing through town, and the Fillmore East, renowned for its live rock acts.

It was quite a drive from their respective homes in Long Island, but the journey to New York City signified the start of the weekend for Janis Cafasso and her cousin, Gail Higgins Smith: 'When the Fillmore East opened in New York, we used to go there every Saturday night. In between acts we'd hang out in the lobby and Johnny was always there with a gang of boys. This was about 1967, when he was living in Jackson Heights. I don't remember how he came up to us but I do remember that by the end of the evening, he and Janis were sitting on the floor talking, which started this great romance. From that point on we'd go to the Fillmore with Johnny and whoever the boy was that I was seeing. The three of us even visited California together. After that, Janis and I were going to live in San Francisco but after New York we felt there was no night life, so we came back and decided that we would move into the city. We went over to John's house, got the *Village Voice* and found an apartment in the East Village and the three of us moved in. I took a job at Gimbel's department store. Was Janis working? Was John working? I can't remember them ever working while we lived there but we were all chipping in on the rent. I do remember Janis and John fighting, and Janis moving in and out, but in between the craziness, it was great fun. We all used to go to our parents and come back with shopping bags full of food. John would bring these big roast beefs from his mother and we'd cook these huge meals, but we had to eat really fast because John would eat everything that was on the table so if you didn't eat faster than him, you wouldn't get any. He used to sit in the other room with his bass guitar and try to play and sing. I would scream: "Give up John, just give up!" The first song he ever wrote was "Dirty Dusty Dungarees". We went to Coney Island where they have these little recording booths and we said: "Let's go in and make a record." He sung "Dirty Dusty Dungarees", then we sang the "Duke Of Earl" together.'

Costing less than a dollar to make, 'Dirty Dusty Dungarees' has gone the same sad way as the little novelty recording booths, simply vanishing with time. Johnny's future was still misty, but he had already chosen the direction that would engulf him. Gail Higgins Smith: 'Me, Johnny and Janis were big rock 'n' roll fans. We went anywhere to see a rock 'n' roll band and to meet rock 'n' roll people. Somehow, because we were brazen, we'd always end up meeting them. When we went to the Newport Jazz festival we ended up sitting in a hotel room with Rod Stewart, drinking beer. We met Janis Joplin, and the MC5, who were Johnny's heroes. He was so excited when he met Keith Richards. He would talk about him all the time. We met him at a bar on 5th Avenue and 13th Street. People like Jagger, Richards and Lennon used to go there and one night Keith Richards was there. We sat around this table, having drinks and meeting Keith. Johnny used to say: "I want to be a pop star, I want to be like Keith Richards." He even kept Keith's cigarette packet.' *

In 1969, Johnny and a girlfriend (almost certainly Janis Cafasso) took a three-month trip to London to check out the English music scene. Wielding a borrowed press pass, the young couple hustled their way into a plethora of gigs but the stand-out event of their vacation was seeing Tyrannosaurus Rex at the Roundhouse, in the period when Marc Bolan switched from acoustic to electric guitar. Johnny returned home ready to pursue a future in rock 'n' roll. If the finer details of his career were still somewhat vague, he already looked

(*Bob Gruen*)

every inch the part with his long, dark, teased hair – akin to Ronnie Spector donning a tiara of raven's wings. Although his quiet manner ruled out any form of verbal self-promotion, his decorative appearance which had been further accentuated by Janis, who would find a future in fashion, drew the attention of most of the boys who would become The New York Dolls.

By the end of the sixties, Central Park was no longer a rallying point for hippy experimentation and the nudity and headbands were scorned by a new generation of kids who flocked to the park's Fountain landmark on Sunday afternoons, dressed to the nines. In July 1991, Jerry Nolan told the *Village Voice*:

> Out of the hundreds and hundreds of people you'd see at the Fountain, where everyone was profiling, Johnny and Janis stood out the most. You could see them ten miles away. She looked like a Doll, very heavy rouge, wild socks, platform shoes, lots of colours. He was really young then, 15 or 16. I was older, 22. Janis got Johnny into his look. He was wearing high heels, and you remember that teased-hair look, that Rod Stewart look? Johnny's was like that, but even more dimensionalised and exaggerated, teased all the way up in like a crown. It was so long. He would have a

platinum blond streak down the back. He would have a girl's blouse on,
and on top of that a sparkling girl's vest. And then maybe a cowboy scarf.
Mixing in cowboy stuff with glamorous forties girls stuff ... and he wore
make-up which really set him off.

Originally hailing from Brooklyn, Jerry Nolan had been bounced back and
forth between army bases in Oklahoma and Hawaii, after his mother married a
military man. At the age of ten, Jerry and his sister went to see Elvis at a local
roller derby arena. Already a little too hep to display outright enthusiasm,
Nolan was nonetheless deeply impressed by both Presley's original band and his
early sartorial splendour. After being taught to play the drums by a young black
soldier, Jerry put into practice all that he had learned at a high school assembly
talent contest in Oklahoma. The boy who had such a tough time in class suddenly acquired status in the eyes of his fellow students. 'That changed my whole
life. I wasn't ashamed anymore. I could finally do something real good.'
However, when the family moved back to Brooklyn, Nolan found a new status
when he joined a gang called the Young Lords. It wasn't morality or cowardice
that made him hold back from full on fighting but the thought of a rumpled
suit and the dry-cleaning bill. Violence was a formality but style was everything.
It could be said that playing drums eventually got Jerry off the street, but his
hard-knock brand of rock 'n' roll was not about salvation. Nolan's career had
been as choppy as the bumps and grinds of the strippers, whose routines he'd
backed with a heavy hitting flourish after leaving school. By the time he set eyes
on Johnny in Central Park, Jerry had just returned from Detroit, where he'd
spent the summer playing in Suzi Quatro's band Cradle. Although Johnny was
pretty young, Jerry Nolan could spot rocker credential from a million miles,
and knew that one day they would be in a band together.

If Jerry Nolan was sure of the future, Arthur Kane, a blonde from the Bronx
who could have been tagged Marilyn Morose, and his best buddy George
Fedorcik, were more hopeful than certain but equally impressed by Johnny's
sense of style. George: 'We used to see Johnny at the Fillmore every time there'd
be a British band playing. We were totally into the English scene – The Stones,
The Yardbirds. We never really spoke to Johnny but we'd always say "Hi"
because of the way he looked. We thought he was the coolest thing in the
world.' * However, the nascent core of The New York Dolls was formed when
Johnny started jamming with Sylvain Sylvain (née Mizrahi) and Billy Murcia.
It wasn't like Johnny had to audition to play bass with them; Syl and Billy
already considered him to be something of a local legend. Sylvain: 'Now this
was the time when *Gimme Shelter* was playing. Me and Billy were in love with
that movie and Johnny is in it. He's fooling around with his hair, sitting on one
of his friend's shoulders. It's in the sequence when the lights get turned on the
audience and Mick Jagger says something like: "New York, let's look at you,

now." We used to see it every other day and we'd go "Hey man, there's that fucking guy we used to go to school with!"' *

In spite of the fact that all three had been raised in the same neighbour-hood, and had attended New Town High and Quintano's, it actually took Syl and Billy longer to hook up with Johnny than might have been expected, due to a detour into the fashion industry. Although Sylvain's family had been forced to flee from Egypt during the Suez Canal crisis of 1956, while the Murcia clan made a similarly hasty exit from Colombia after Billy's father got embroiled in a business deal that turned hostile, both boys looked as if they'd been cut from similar cloth, sharing the same wilful corkscrew curls and slight build. They cemented their friendship after a playground scuffle in junior high, and became virtually inseparable. It seemed only natural for Billy, who had once been described as 'a cool drink of water with a hot head', to start playing drums, while Syl reached for the guitar. By 1968, they'd joined forces with an older, more accomplished guitarist called Mike Turby, who had gained neigh-bourhood notoriety with The Orphans – Queens' retort to The Rolling Stones. Declaring themselves to be 'The Pox', the trio whose influences included The Who and The Stooges, cut a demo for Harry Lookofsky who had been responsible for the grandiose production on The Left Banke's stateside top-ten single, 'Walk Away Renee'. Unfortunately the public remained immune to The Pox and Turby quit. Having failed to make a significant gesture with their music, they devoted themselves to what was then rock 'n' roll's second-in-command: fashion. As they began to weave psychedelic sweaters on hand looms, Sylvain learned the details of retail when he started working at a trendy men's boutique called A Different Drummer on Lexington Avenue and 63rd Street. Across the road in an old brownstone building was a hospital, yet no ambulances ever screeched to a halt outside. The victims might have been too small for stretchers but they were better cared for than the peeling façade over the entrance which read 'The New York Dolls' Hospital'. Billy thought it would make as great a name for a band as Sylvain did. As their fashion outlet, Truth & Soul, expanded, orders started coming in from Betsey Johnson's ultra-happening boutique, Paraphernalia, and they began to receive press attention. After being made a lucrative offer by a large knitting mill in Brooklyn, they sold their designs and went to Europe for the best part of a year. Like a down payment on their future, Sylvain purchased an impressive stack of Marshall amps while in London, which were shipped back to New York. Gathering dust in Billy's mom's basement, the amps lay dormant until the dandy duo returned from their travels, nabbed Johnny and finally activated The Dolls as 1970 drew to a close.

With all the pent-up energy of a freshly lit fire-cracker, Johnny Genzale was not cut out to be a bass player. Recognising this, Sylvain began to pass on some of Mike Turby's guitar licks. 'When it really started between us three, we became like a family. Johnny started coming down to the basement and I taught him all the riffs I had learned from Mike and the things that I had picked up on my own. I basically said, "Look, if you know those scales and you go like this, instead of doing the whole fucking bar chord, just hold it with two fingers and you make a little power chord." Johnny took to that, baby! We'd all sit on the bed with these cheap guitars and do Marc Bolan songs, as well as some blues and instrumentals.' * However, the opening phase of The Dolls lurched to a full stop after Syl went back to London.

Even if Johnny had in fact closed the door behind him, it always felt like it got slammed in his face when it came to girlfriends. Although he was never short of female attention, his closest relationships were doomed by his volatile neediness and by the age of nineteen, he had already written the song that many consider to be his finest moment, 'You Can't Put Your Arms Around A Memory'. Inspired by Janis, with whom he was embroiled in a typically intense saga of reunion and despair, the song takes its title from a throwaway line in one of his favourite television shows, *Jackie Gleason and The Honeymooners*, and plunges the depths of dejection. Gail Higgins Smith: 'Before he started taking drugs, his adrenalin level would make him high. I remember one time he got so crazed because of a fight with Janis, he started banging on this steel door that we'd had built because the flat was on the ground floor. It moved two feet out with the sheer force of him. It was emotional turmoil, not temper, that made him like that. The drugs didn't make John crazy, he was like that before he started taking them. He was still insecure.' While they would remain life-long friends, the overwrought nature of Johnny's relationship with Janis, combined with a disregard for boring stuff like coming up with rent money, led to Gail penning a polite 'Dear John' note in which she asked him to move out.

After finding and losing a place on Avenue A, Johnny resorted to crashing at the Chelsea Hotel, before he got back together with Janis. If life wasn't already crazy enough, they turned their new 14th Street apartment into a mini-zoo. Aside from Johnny's dogs, Pretty Girl and Onion, they installed a snake and a pet monkey. Mariann, who had by now married her boyfriend Rusty Bracken and just started a family, got a typically frantic call from her little brother after the monkey escaped. A chase ensued on rooftop and fire escape until the runaway monkey was talked down from doing something desperate by Johnny and Rusty.

With an unruly menagerie to feed, Johnny began making a buck or two selling acid and pot. Given that potent hallucinogenics can rip the lid off the in-secure, he only occasionally dipped into his stash of LSD. While under the influence, however, he managed to summon Arthur Kane into his orbit. Gail Higgins Smith: 'I remember meeting Arthur because Johnny and I were tripping. We'd gone to Nobody's and there was Arthur with these huge platform boots on. He looked like a six-foot tall blonde Frankenstein. Johnny and I both stared at each other as the same thought crossed our minds : "Why do they send people like this when you're tripping?!" '

Outside of being a surreal figment of acid-tinged reality, Arthur had recently been deported from Amsterdam, where he and George Fedorcik had unsuccessfully attempted to get a band together. Back in the city, Arthur found work at the telephone company while George began a stint at the post office. Before New York got its post wired and its lines mailed, they got serious about their music, Fedorcik reinventing himself as Rick Rivets to denote his rock 'n' roll aspirations. Late one evening, in the course of an impromptu attempt to steal a motorbike, they spotted Johnny outside a pizza place on Bleecker Street and decided it was time to get properly acquainted. Arthur: 'We were across the street and I said, "OK, here's that guy, why don't we go over and find out what's going on with him?" I went over and said, "I hear you play guitar or bass or something, do you want to get together?"' *

Arthur Kane's indecisive quest to ascertain Johnny's instrument of choice was more prophetic than he could have grasped at the time. Although Johnny turned up for rehearsals with his bass, he was still getting a handle on playing rhythm guitar. After a couple of sessions, Arthur made the crucial decision to swop with him. It was during this period that Johnny Genzale sought a new identity which would reflect his final transformation as a guitarist. While he couldn't have wished for a first name more loaded with rebel connotations than Johnny, an alter ego was required, something that suited the elemental and distorted quality of his guitar playing. After toying with calling himself Johnny Volume, he settled on Thunders, after the DC comic-book cowboy hero, *Johnny Thunder – Mystery Rider Of The Wild West.* Splendid, childlike and stormy, Johnny Thunders was created. With a drummer in tow, they booked some studio time and riffed through a selection of covers including material by The Yardbirds, Chuck Berry and The Rolling Stones. At Thunders' suggestion, their original sticksman was ousted in favour of Billy and the band began rehearsing in the Murcia's family basement. As Johnny became increasingly adept, Rick Rivets switched to rhythm guitar, allowing Thunders to take over the lead position. Johnny's waning enthusiasm for the journey he had to make from the city to Queens every time the band got together, prompted a search for a more central rehearsal space. They found one in the dingy store room of a cycle shop off Columbus Avenue and 82nd Street. The owner, Rusty, who the band nicknamed 'Beanie' owing to the funny little knitted caps he always wore, took their money but not their word. Fearing that they would liberate his stock if he allowed them to roam free, Rusty locked them in for the duration of their rehearsals. Faced with nightly incarceration, the band members chose their provisions with care, Arthur and Rick making a ritual out of picking up a quart of vodka which they shared with Billy, while Thunders, who wasn't particularly partial to liquor, supplied downers and pot. He also started to bring in some of his own material.

Although this stage of The Dolls' development is usually referred to as their 'Actress' phase, after a suggestion by Janis Cafasso, the band never officially adopted the title. On 10 October 1971, Rick Rivets captured their unruly blues cacophony when he bought his cassette player down to a rehearsal. The Actress session which was released over twenty-five years later as *Dawn Of The Dolls* is a crucial artefact, almost entirely comprised of Thunders' numbers. Unlike most early recordings of musicians and songwriters, where a glimpse of nascent style might be heard or the glimmer of technique discerned, Johnny is absolutely formed. He is of course very young and the thicker-than-bubblegum New York intonation would lessen over the years, but the nasal mewl of his voice would remain just the same. The unique brand of the painful married to the melodic already infuses his guitar playing while the core of the songs would be scattered through his repertoire for the majority of his life. 'That's Poison' is an undeveloped blueprint for 'Subway Train'; 'We've Been Through This Before' would eventually metamorphose into the elegiac 'Sad Vacation'; while 'I Am Confronted' is a rough sketch for the epic sob story 'So Alone'. Similarly 'I'm a Boy, I'm a Girl' would also be revived. Perhaps the most staggering aspect of *Dawn Of The Dolls*, aside from the band who probably were, is the sheer sense of loss in Johnny's material, which belies his age.

As Thunders was more interested in being the lead guitarist than the front-man, the band started looking for likely candidates, and found David Johansen. The product of a working-class Catholic family from Staten Island, presided over by a Norwegian insurance salesman and his Irish wife, David Johansen had grown up with a tantalising view of the New York City skyline that seemed like a stage set of miracles to him. Biding his time dreaming of a glittering debut, he poured his frustrations into writing poetry and lyrics which came in useful when he started singing with a local outfit called The Vagabond Missionaries before he made it to the city as part of an art rock band, Fast Eddie and The Electric Japs, who played around the Greenwich Village area. Quick-witted and fast-mouthed, David Johansen combined a love of music with theatrical ambitions and would later tell journalists that he had appeared in a couple of skin flicks prior to joining The Dolls, notably *Bike Boys Go Ape* and *Studs On Main Street*. While his porno past was just another put on from his lightning repartee, Johansen landed a walk on part as a spear carrier in one of Charles Ludlum's avant-garde Ridiculous Theatre productions. Gravitating to the artistic underground, he met and moved in to an apartment on East 6th Street with a former model called Diane Poluski. Part of the Andy Warhol scene, Poluski had played Holly Woodlawn's pregnant sister in *Trash* and introduced David to some of the participants in the world of Warhol, all of which put him in good stead when Billy and Arthur made a house call. David Johansen: 'There was a Colombian

Johansen & Thunders. (*Leee Black Childers*)

guy who lived in my building and he was friends with Billy and me. He told me that he knew these guys who were looking for a singer in their band. One day Billy and Arthur came to my door. I'm kind of exaggerating here, but Billy was like four feet tall and Arthur was eight feet tall and they both had these really high boots on and were kind of dressed like Marc Bolan. I just saw them standing there and liked them right away. I thought "Oh God, this is great, what a pair of lunatics!"' *

Possessing a voice that could sandblast a city and a contorted harmonica technique, Johansen passed his audition and brought to the band a flagrantly dramatic edge partially copped from Warhol's drag queen muses, Candy Darling, Jackie Curtis and Holly Woodlawn. When she later described the essence of drag as 'it's not a man or a woman, it's fabulous', Holly Woodlawn could have been introducing The New York Dolls. The band finally reactivated The Dolls' moniker as the end of 1971 loomed, Arthur tagging on the New York prefix: 'I wanted to add the "New York" because in New York you would always be hearing on the radio and television like: New York Jets, New York Yankees, New York Vets, New York this and that – and I thought we'd get an immediate local following if we called ourselves The New York Dolls, and also it sounded like something from a 1930s Broadway show.' *

When Sylvain returned from Europe he was understandably piqued, for not only were the band up and running without him but they were also using the name he'd originally suggested. Fortunately, harmony was restored with heels. Sylvain: 'I'd come back from London with all these boots from Johnson & Johnson. There was one particular pair, knee high maroon suede lace-ups with a layered leather platform heel. Johnny went nuts for them. They were a little bit small but he traded half his house for those fucking shoes. Whenever Johnny would move into a new apartment, which he seemed to do all the time, me and Billy would help him cos we had a car. He had so many clothes, it would be like a party.' One party that Syl missed out on was The Dolls' debut at a city-sponsored beggars' banquet. The welfare workers in charge of the Endicott Hotel, a crumbling refuge for the homeless across the street from Rusty Beanies, had been left high and dry when the group they had booked to play at the residents' Christmas bash reneged on their promise. Unable to miss the nightly racket issuing from the cycle shop, one of the welfare workers approached the band. On Christmas Eve, The New York Dolls got a bedraggled crowd up and dancing to a fine selection of R & B covers. However, their official launch was not enough to keep the necessary momentum going for Rivets, who had begun to slack off. The situation was remedied almost instantly. Johnny: 'Rick Rivets started fucking around, coming to practise late and stuff like that, so we canned him and got Sylvain in.'

All Dolled Up. (*Ian Dickson*)

2

Cursed, Poisoned and Condemned

Freed from the restraints of reality or inhibition, The New York Dolls became their own fantasy of how they imagined life in a band would be; a fabulous delirium of a party where the music never stopped, the joints 'n' pills 'n' liquor 'n' sex were always in plentiful supply, and the purgatory of morning was banished forever. Extravagantly erotic, The Dolls projected their dream world in a neon-coloured thrift-shop burlesque, wearing clothes that looked best after midnight and tawdry in natural light, a hybrid of straight baiting semi-transvestism. Although their shimmering plumage and high heels, which lent a tottering feminine gait to the proceedings, were a terrifying violation of natural order to most hetero males, the boys in the band knew that girls liked nothing better than to play with Dolls.

Everything was exaggerated, the gesture, the drama, the lyrics, the dirty R & B throb that kept the momentum in their music. As estranged from convention as The New York Dolls were, they retained all the best traditions of rock 'n' roll and reinvented whatever they couldn't quite grasp, creating a uniquely dyslexic approximation of The Stones, Bo Diddley and The Shangri-Las, combined with their own highly idiosyncratic style. What The Dolls lacked in refinement they made up for with a streetwise sophistication, yet remained tenderly oblivious to just how subversive they were until they tried to transcend their immediate domain.

In their gestation phase, The New York Dolls got further acquainted with playing live in front of a small crowd at their loft on 119 Chrystie Street. Situated above a Chinese noodle factory, the loft became the band's central HQ, after Johnny, Janis, Billy and Sylvain moved in. Mainly surviving on shoplifting sprees, the band threw parties whenever the rent was due. Sylvain: 'One of Johnny's friends would be at the door collecting $2 from each person that arrived. Janis was in charge of the lights. We performed in the kitchen area cos it was a step or two up, behind us was the refrigerator and the sink. There would be guys selling drugs and girls selling sex and we'd play rock 'n' roll. "Human Being" and "Frankenstein" came from one of those long, rent party nights.' * Mindful of their fabulous destiny, and living in almost continuos performance, The New York Dolls quickly developed a set list. Aside from the grotesque glory of 'Frankenstein' and the wry assessment of mortal frailty that is 'Human Being', 'Jet Boy' also took its first steps in the Chrystie Street loft. Sylvain: 'Johnny was playing the opening riff and I said, "Wait a minute" and did my little baby chords which were a D and a G. We jammed it at rehearsal and David said he had some great lyrics for it. Then we added the background

An Early Soundcheck. (*Leee Black Childers*)

oohs and ahhs.' * The Dolls were all Jet Boys, cartoon kids of the jet age flying around New York, and by the spring of 1972, they were ready to descend on the city.

Before The New York Dolls even had a reputation, they managed to confound the critics when they played their second gig on 29 May, in the Palm Room of the Diplomat Hotel. Running adjacent to the X-rated crossroads that was then Times Square, the Diplomat was a suitably seedy setting for an 'Invitation Beyond The Valley', which also featured Jackie Curtis who had been immortalised by Lou Reed in 'Walk On The Wild Side' and a band called Shaker, whose drummer Jerry Nolan particularly impressed Billy Murcia. If Jackie Curtis and Shaker were at the opposite ends of the spectrum, The Dolls were less easy to define and garnered a couple of lousy write-ups by local journalists who couldn't quite decide whether they were a theatrical turn or a rock act, or both. The response of the patrons at a bath house in Brooklyn where The Dolls played their next two dates, again with Jackie Curtis in support, might have erred toward the pernickety but the band eventually won out. Arthur Kane: 'It was like there was no audience because all the guys stayed in their cubicles having sex with someone, so we didn't know what to do. Everyone in the group had taken MDA, I think I was selling it at the time. It was kind of like LSD without the heavy thinking but it makes you stumble around, hallucinating. We weren't sure how to dress for the bath house, so the first night we

David and Johnny at Max's, Kansas City. (*Bob Gruen*)

went feminine, I wore hot pants. They didn't seem to appreciate the *femme* look, although we had a lot of fun on the MDA. The next night we came back in leather and chains and got more interest, everyone came out of their little cubicles to watch us.' *

What The Dolls wanted was to get the whole glittering island of Manhattan out of their little cubicles and dancing, but oddly enough there were very few venues where they could start to establish some sort of following. Many of the clubs that had flourished in the previous decade had fallen into dereliction and although Max's Kansas City would have been an appropriate place to start, The New York Dolls were initially considered to be upstart urchins in the hierarchy of the underground firmament that gathered there. Like most innovators, The Dolls were left to blaze their own trail, a journey that led them to a theatre complex one block west of Broadway, called the Mercer Arts Center. Attached to the crumbling Broadway Central Hotel, the Mercer Arts Center was a contemporary venue that housed several different sized theatres named after various authors and playwrights. The Dolls might have been considered a little freaky by the Center's booking agent, but he agreed to let them play there, designating a tiny room in the back of the complex so they wouldn't scare off the regular patrons of the arts. Used to the language of the theatre, the Mercer Arts Center advertised the forthcoming gig as 'The Dolls Of NY' which sounded more like a Busby Berkeley musical than a rock band.

In Johnny's Closet – The Original New York Dolls. (*Leee Black Childers*)

In readiness for the big night, the band put in some extra practice. It wasn't a question of perfection, they just honed what they did best: alienated rock 'n' roll roughly punctuated by 'Killer' Kane's cavernous sounding bass lines and the Flintstone shudder of Billy Murcia's drumming. Probably the most accomplished musician out of the bunch, Sylvain Sylvain constantly resuscitated the faint melody under Thunders' fractured, squawking riffs, while David Jo's full strength unfiltered vocals flayed the lyrics. As the band developed, Johansen and Thunders emerged as the main song-writing team, penning the profoundly sexy 'Bad Girl' just before they began their legendary residency at the Mercer Arts Center, the lead singer's astute mini-melodramas in a turbulent alliance with Johnny's wildly careening guitar maulings.

Tired of the lock-ins at Rusty Beanies, The Dolls moved to Talent-Recon, a more accessible rehearsal place run by a fire-eater called Satan. In the less obscure location they came into further contact with Shaker, who also rehearsed there and managed to inspire a denim clad cowboy band who plugged away night after night in another room. Knowing they could never be as pretty as The New York Dolls, the cowboy band eventually took the guise of glam animals and emerged as Kiss. However, the group with the highest local profile at Talent-Recon was Eric Emerson and The Magic Tramps, their frontman having once shared a scene in *Chelsea Girls* with Nico and danced in Andy Warhol's live multi-media event, *The Exploding Plastic Inevitable*. When The New York Dolls finally made their debut at the Mercer Arts Center, it was as support to The Magic Tramps (minus Emerson) and Satan. Perhaps it was a

Busby Berkeley musical after all, the one where the little known starlets unexpectedly dazzle the audience. As David Johansen later told *Circus* magazine: 'It all came together at the Mercer Arts Center. We were opening for the The Magic Tramps, but we were so good that they booed The Tramps off stage, so we opened and closed the concert.' After the resounding success of their opening night, the band were given access to the larger Oscar Wilde Room. While the staff at the Arts Center were unused to dealing with the mutant Mardi Gras that started to turn out in force for The Dolls' shows, they drank like a return to prohibition was imminent and tripled the bar profits.

On 13 June 1972 The New York Dolls kicked off a seventeen-week, Tuesday-night residency in the Oscar Wilde Room. With several floor-to-ceiling mirrors that reflected The Dolls from all angles, the 200-capacity theatre became a narcissistic playroom, the crowd almost as much of an event as the band. The Dolls' seduction of New York's decadent *demimonde* was swift, melting ice and hearts into one glorious pink cocktail, they quickly became the toast of the town.

Suddenly everyone had an opinion on The New York Dolls. Lou Reed thought they were cute, while some wry social observers christened them The Velveteens, the junior oracles of Manhattan poised to take the baton from Reed's former band. Andy Warhol came a-courting and David Bowie infiltrated their scene, then staggered away with a harder look, higher heels and a rockier sound. At each successive gig, the celebrity guest list expanded. Alice Cooper checked them out, his girlfriend, model Cindy Lang, began an affair with Johnny Thunders, while Cooper's manager, Shep Gordon, showed an interest in The Dolls' career. Rod Stewart's manager, Billy Gaff, also made a business overture to the band but all bets were cancelled after he got them a gig supporting Long John Baldry out on Long Island. Although Gaff supplied a limousine to take The Dolls to the club, they had spent the day snacking on a cheap form of powdered acid which was rolled up in a cigarette paper then guzzled down with a liquor chaser, and they arrived too late and too addled to go on.

News of The Dolls started to filter into the local press and this time there were no misunderstandings over where they were coming from, as Ed McCormack writing for *Andy Warhol's Interview* magazine noted: 'On stage in the Oscar Wilde Room of the Mercer, they generate a futuristic energy that gets people up off their asses and dancing. The lead singer, who looks like Mick Jagger's skinny kid sister, stands there all knock-kneed and plaintive, throwing his arms out palms-up in a gesture of helpless horny adolescent frustration and growling and moaning in this surprisingly gruff voice, singing these great teenage torture rack blues-rock sock-hop type of rock 'n' roll songs about how he has personality problems that no one else understands, and the lead guitarist with the green-streaked hair and the hermaphrodite leg is leaning into the mike to back up him with the harmony on vocals, and the drummer is pounding away, and the big tall skinny goldylocked blond bassist is looking a little shy in his lipstick and pink pantyhose.' For a group with no record deal it was quite a coup when *Melody Maker's* New York correspondent, Roy Hollingworth, went to interview them, accompanied by the flamboyant photographer, Leee Black Childers. The finished article, and Leee's picture of The New York Dolls posing inside Johnny's closet in the Chrystie Street loft, confirmed to *Melody Maker's* English readers just what growing up in Gotham could do to a boy.

As well as attracting the attention of the art and rock crowd, The New York Dolls also drew in kids from Queens, the Bronx and Brooklyn who began to root for them like a home team. Yet for all their new-found adulation, the shy lead guitarist had only just started to play facing the audience and beyond their once a week residency, little had changed for the band aside from the acquisition of soundman and all round helper, Peter Jordan. What The Dolls needed was someone who could represent their interests, someone who could make the party bigger and better.

Marty Thau or the 'Mighty Thau' as he was known by his buddies in the upper echelons of New York's music business circles was in an expansive mood. Celebrating his decision to resign from his position as the head of A & R at Paramount Records to run a singles-only label, Marty and his wife Betty had hit the town. With a solid gold reputation, Thau had always been on the winning team. At Cameo Parkway Records he'd nurtured along some twenty-eight hit records in one year, then repeated the Midas routine at Buddah, overseeing a run of successful singles in the bumblegum vein, before Paramount eventually snapped him up. After dinner, Marty and Betty took a stroll through the Village where they spotted a tiny flyer advertising a gig by The New York Dolls that very evening, and decided to check them out. Wilting in the hectic whirl of the Oscar Wilde room, Thau turned to leave as The Dolls trooped off stage at the end of their set but something pulled him back, the sudden clarity of a hunch. Maybe The New York Dolls could launch his new label. Marty Thau: 'They were so entertaining, so visual, so animated and full of life but on the other hand, they were almost out of tune. They weren't playing that good but it almost didn't seem to matter. We got to the door to leave, when I said, "Let's go back, I want to talk to these guys."' * A trifle incongruous in his safari-suit, Thau pushed his way through the lost tribe of Shangri-La to find the band, and arranged a meeting with them for the following week at Max's Kansas City.

No longer on the fringes of the scene at Max's Kansas City, The Dolls had stormed the notorious red-hued back room of the club, where they regularly held court at the round table, the most sought after spot in the joint. Although the band's frequent high jinx had not endeared them to the generally liberal owner of the club, Mickey Ruskin, they were somewhat better behaved than usual for their first date with Marty: 'David emerged as the spokesman, Johnny was a little withdrawn but didn't hesitate to give his two-cents worth at any given moment. He was more along the lines of a traditional rocker. Arthur was without anything to say, although he was the funniest of of all them and probably the most intelligent. Billy and Sylvain were bubbly and extroverted, full of life, interested in bedding down as many women as they could and looking great in as many clothes as they could buy. None of them had any knowledge of the music business and nor did they care, they were really quite naive about all of that. They just seized on the possibilities of getting a manager, playing around the world and becoming rock stars.'

So smitten was he by The Dolls, Thau scrapped the flimsy proposition of a one-off single deal and became their personal manager instead. While he appeared to have all the trappings of success, Marty lacked the kind of funds it would take to hoist The Dolls' star into a prominent position but he did have the phone number of Steve Leber and David Krebs, two booking agents from the powerful William Morris agency who had set up on their own. A business alliance had been mooted by Leber and Krebs during Thau's stint at Paramount and now it was time to call them on it. After Marty invited them to see the band, they joined forces. It was a fairly unusual set-up, Thau taking a paternal role to Leber and Krebs' traditional suits. Peter Jordan: 'Leber and Krebs were strictly attracted to one thing, the potential for lucre. I got along with Leber and Krebs, but they are both sharks in the true showbiz sense. Marty isn't a shark, he's more like a dolphin.' * Of the three, David Krebs had the least input in The Dolls' career, spending most of his time with their other new act, Aerosmith. Later, when the managerial trinity split back into its original factions, it would be alleged that The New York Dolls and Aerosmith had been pitted against one another as part of a boardroom wager. However, when The Dolls signed on the dotted line in the summer of 1972, they were tipped as the hot favourites. If being in love means never having to say you're sorry, then 'In Perpetuity' means having to say you're sorry forever, but the nuances of business eluded The NY Dolls. After all, being kept in the dark was where all the fun things happened, wasn't it?

Before the contracts were sealed and delivered, Marty Thau whisked the band in to Blue Rock Studios for an evening. While The Dolls knew how to move, preening and teasing like the fairest of them all in front of the mirrors in the Oscar Wilde Room, they hadn't had the same chance to reflect on their music in such detail. Although the Blue Rock recording was never meant to be anything other than a test run for the band, it was later released as *The Mercer St Sessions* and reveals them in confident mood. Aside from nailing gritty versions of 'Bad Girl', 'Jet Boy', 'Human Being' and 'Frankenstein', The Dolls laid down 'Looking For A Kiss', a grimy revamp of Marc Bolan's 'Get It On', which pitches desire against drugged doom. Who wants to waste time waiting for the man when you can have a kiss instead of a fix? If only the band had taken their own advice. They also recorded 'Personality Crisis', a wonderful portrayal of social disintegration that captures their fetchingly awkward musical dexterity, each instrument seemingly on the verge of collision, yet managing to swerve away just in time. It's often been said that The New York Dolls didn't play so great at first, but they never aspired to being polished or polite which aided their affinity to raw rhythm and blues. Right from the start, the band incorporated cover versions in their repertoire. Accordingly the Blue Rock session would not have been complete without souped-up revisions of Bo Diddley's 'Pills', Sonny Boy Williamsons' 'Don't Start Me Talking' and Parker, Floyd and Croppers' 'Don't Mess With Cupid'.

As the summer gave in to autumn, The Dolls continued to put the life back into the nights of a devoted coterie of followers. Aside from regularly playing at the Mercer Arts Center and Max's Kansas City, they also put Kenny's Castaways on the Upper East Side of Manhattan and the Coventry in Queens on the rock 'n' roll map, establishing a club circuit that many other bands, including Kiss, would traverse in their wake. Despite the ensuing furore that The Dolls' gigs generated, the record companies failed to take the bait as Johnny T. noted in an interview with journalist Lisa Robinson. 'The record company people who have come to see us have been freaked out, and we're not really doing anything except standing there playing.' Following on from Thunders' comment, David Jo concluded: 'I think we turn them on. Their wives get drunk and start dancing and they go crazy. But then they think about their kids ... y'know ... and that's what stops them.' The Dolls had become the hostesses at the biggest bash in town but nobody wanted to get serious at the end of the night. Marty Thau: 'A & R people would come to see them but they couldn't see past The Dolls' exterior. They were such repressed times, people today wouldn't believe it. You couldn't even say "Goddamn" on television. The issues of women's rights and gay and lesbian liberation had been put on the table, but they weren't put into practice. The music business perceived The Dolls as a bunch of degenerate queers. It was all down to homophobia.' *

One man, however, had got the strings of his heart well and truly strummed by the band. The captivated Paul Nelson, a well-respected former rock journalist, who had landed a position in A & R at Mercury Records, began a solo campaign to get them signed. At Nelson's behest a series of scouts from the company regularly attended The Dolls' shows through August to mid-October. The subsequent feedback was rarely unanimous or flattering and on one particularly spectacular night when the band were only an hour late for their scheduled appearance at the Mercer Arts Center, Johnny Thunders in his platform basketball shoes managed to kick holes in the stage and Arthur Kane failed to notice that his bass had come unplugged for four songs. While Nelson prevailed and Mercury prevaricated, the New York Dolls' managerial trinity changed tactics. Steve Leber: 'The Dolls' time had not yet arrived here, so therefore we decided to go to England in order to get a record deal. We thought that the timing, their image and the excitement they could create would be incredible. I paid for the entire group to go.' * Assisted by Roy Fischer, a London-based promoter, Leber organised a handful of dates for the band. The crowning glory of their strategy came when they got The Dolls a support slot to Rod Stewart and The Faces at the 8,000-seater Wembley Pool. In return for Fischer's services, it was agreed that the band would record a couple of songs on his behalf, once they arrived in England.

Roy Fischer, who had a thing for transport stunts and had once orchestrated a car smash in a shop window lark for Alice Cooper, arranged for a horse and carriage to collect The New York Dolls from Heathrow airport. Hung-over and jet-lagged, the band perched as prettily as they could for a small group of photographers before giving way to nausea, the antique wheels of the carriage amplifying every bump in the road. Eventually they were ushered into a Mercedes and driven to Escape Studios in Kent. Quarantined in the former oast house which had been converted into a studio with accommodation, The Dolls recorded new versions of 'Personality Crisis', 'Looking For A Kiss' and 'Bad Girl'. The old Actress number 'That's Poison', which had been reincarnated as 'Subway Train', was also captured. Like the Flying Dutchman transported on to the IRT, the lovelorn protagonist of the song can't understand why he has been 'cursed, poisoned and condemned' and is fated to ride on a subway train, the screeching crescendo of guitars like failing brakes.

After fulfilling their obligations to Fischer, the band headed for London. Steve Leber had already settled into his suite at the Dorchester while The Dolls and Marty Thau had reservations at a somewhat less salubrious hotel in Holborn. The New York Dolls made their UK debut at the Speakeasy, as starry in its own way as Max's Kansas City, but their performance was hampered by an inadequate PA system. On 26 October The Dolls supported The Groundhogs at the Alhambra Rock in Birmingham. Before going on stage the band were presented with a couple of crates of Newcastle Brown ale, most of which Billy Murcia violently regurgitated during their set. It was nothing unusual, Murcia didn't have the hardiest of constitutions, especially when it came to alcohol. While getting loaded was almost mandatory for most rock bands in the early seventies, The Dolls went beyond the call of duty, never knowing how or when to stop. Everywhere they went, people were keen to give them party favours and England was no exception. Why, at the Speakeasy that model chick, Marilyn, had offered Billy her phone number and a generous helping of mandies (Mandrax). He guessed they were like downers or 'ludes or something cos they gave you the same kind of fogged-out numbness.

On Sunday 29 October The New York Dolls played the biggest gig of their entire career at The Wembley Festival Of Music. After the confines of the Mercer Arts Center, the stage at Wembley looked bigger than an airport runway but they created their own little maelstrom, refusing to yield to the collective smirk in the dark of a largely hostile crowd. Journalist Mark Plummer captured the moment for *Melody Maker*:

> The New York Dolls played what was possibly one of the worst sets I've seen. Their glamour bit brought wolf whistles and shouts to go before a note had been played, and by the time a string had broken on Johnny Thunders' Plexiglas guitar they had lost what audience sympathy they had. Musically their set was dire and failed to gel, their two guitarists play all the old tired licks. And who really wants to know about 'Pill City'? Wembley didn't for sure.

One artful kid who had broken into the venue to see The Faces and The Dolls, vehemently disagreed with Plummer's dour assessment. Future Sex Pistol Steve Jones: 'The Dolls played rock 'n' roll music how I liked to hear it, kinda sloppy. I was a real big fan of The Faces but they were a bit more controlled, more like good time music but The Dolls were seriously crazy and I'd never seen anything like that. I don't think anyone had. The audience hated them and started slinging shit at them but they kept on playing. They were great, wild.' *

As a special treat for the band after their appearance at Wembley, Kit Lambert, The Who's manager and the boss of Track Records, hired out an expensive restaurant for their use only. Of all The Doll's potential suitors, Kit Lambert was the keenest and wooed them from the moment they set foot on British soil, inviting them to party with The Who and introducing them to a social circle where the aristocracy mingled with new rock money. Aside from Lambert, representatives from Virgin and Charisma Records also made their interest known, as well as Mick Jagger who flew in from Ireland to see The Dolls when they played at Imperial College with Status Quo and Capability Brown. Although it was never official, The New York Dolls were effectively auditioning for Rolling Stone Records, and while Jagger deigned to talk to them after the gig, he later told the press 'Yeah, I've seen The New York Dolls. We were almost going to sign 'em up at one point. I went down to the Imperial College gig and – uh, their lead singer – I saw 'er and I just didn't think much of it all.'

On 4 November, The New York Dolls opened for Argent at the Mile End Sundown in East London before travelling to Liverpool where they had a support slot to Lou Reed at a former boxing ring called The Stadium. The Dolls didn't even make it as far as round one, Reed sending a message to their dressing room threatening to cancel if they set foot on the stage. Suddenly Uncle Lou didn't think they were so cute anymore. Rebuked by the main draw, the dejected Dolls left the venue. Returning to London the band made good use of their free time before the next date on their itinerary, 9 November, with Roxy

Music at Manchester's Hardrock. In the background Steve Leber and Marty Thau continued to negotiate with Kit Lambert, drawing ever closer to a deal with Track Records, but on the evening of Tuesday 7 November everything changed forever.

Nearly three decades later, the memories of the surviving protagonists from The Dolls' camp have faded, like the ink on the death certificate, while the outside catalysts have remained silent. What is irrefutable is that Billy Murcia died sometime between the hours of 8 and 11 p.m. at Brompton Lodge, on the Cromwell Road. Marty Thau has always maintained that Billy met his fate because of a telephone coincidence. At a loose end in his room, Murcia apparently took a call from a wrong number but got talking anyway and after admitting to being a NY Doll, was invited to a party. Before leaving he picked up some pocket money from Marty, who suggested he get a lift in the chauffeur-driven managerial limousine which was waiting outside the hotel. Once the hired limo returned from dropping Billy at Brompton Lodge, Steve Leber and Marty Thau sped off to impresario Tony Secunda's apartment, where Kit Lambert and his business partner Chris Stamp awaited them. Several hours later, and a breath away from signing the band to Track Records for £100,000, the meeting was interrupted by a phone call for Marty. The caller, whose identity has never been revealed, told Thau that Billy Murcia was dead. Steve Leber, however, recalls being at the Dorchester when Scotland Yard contacted him and broke the news. Leber then dashed over to The Dolls' hotel, filled them in on what little details he had been able to glean, and told them to ditch any drugs in their possession. Unable to register what was happening but wanting to be near their friend, the band quickly made their way to the Cromwell Road where Marty Thau had already fulfilled the unhappy task of identifying the body.

The following day the stricken band members were sent home on the next available flight, while Leber and Thau stayed in London to help the police with their paperwork. Needless to say, negotiations with Track were never resumed and aside from letting the music papers know that the band would no longer be supporting Roxy Music and had left the country due to the demise of their drummer, Marty engineered a press blackout: 'I suspected that this could grow into a big rock 'n' roll scandal. It was certain to be ammunition for *Melody Maker* and *NME* and I wanted to spare the band, and the Murcia family more than anyone, the pain and the anguish. Their son was dead and he died under such a grey cloud, or at least that would be the way it would be manipulated and portrayed.' *

At the inquest held on 24 November 1972, in West London, it was revealed that Billy Murcia had in fact called Speakeasy Marilyn and been invited to her apartment on the Cromwell Road. In a statement to the coroner, Marilyn Woolhead claimed that he arrived in a reasonable condition, 'He didn't seem absolutely sober, but he didn't seem that drunk.' Also at the flat were two of

Woolhead's friends, James Owen and Malcolm Raines. Aside from Raines, who went out for a short while, James Owen, Marilyn and Billy shared a bottle of champagne. By the time Raines returned, Murcia was lying on the bed, incoherent, a result of mixing Mandrax and alcohol. If the drummer had been left to sleep it off, he probably would have recovered with adequate supervision, although calling an ambulance would have been the safest bet. In the escalating panic, the two men employed second-hand drug folklore in an effort to bring Billy round, submerging the unconscious Doll in a cold bath, simultaneously managing to hold ice against the back of his neck, while trying to give him black coffee. Both denied that Billy's head had tilted back into the water. A verdict of accidental death was recorded, caused by drowning in a domestic bath while under the influence of alcohol and methaqualone (Mandrax).

In the immediate aftermath, The New York Dolls retreated to mourn their friend. Beyond the funeral they had no plans. A badly shaken Johnny Thunders would later admit: 'I just couldn't describe how I felt about Billy dyin', how I still feel. He was a close friend and you never get over a thing like that.' When the Grim Reaper sneaks up on a band, the gravity of the situation imbues a fatalistic authenticity. Suddenly, The New York Dolls were taken more seriously than they ever had been before, on an international scale. Eventually they started auditions for a new drummer. Disbanding would have been akin to a second death for Billy Murcia, but the tragic implications of his passing haunted the next phase of The New York Dolls. Leee Black Childers: 'Instead of sobering them up it made them crazier. It affected Johnny a whole lot. He'd had a real innocence about him but when Billy died he started to plunge into self-destruction. The death of Billy Murcia was the death of The Dolls, as we had loved them.' * A decade and a half after the event, Johnny T. was still trying to come to terms with what had happened when he attempted to write a song for Murcia, but the lyrics were never completed and the number was released as the instrumental 'Billy Boy' (*Que Sera Sera* – Jungle Records). However, two of the unrecorded verses survived and conclude with the sentiments:

> Why did he take you away
> And make our lives that way?
> I'm crying.

*

As for a new drummer, the only real contender was Jerry Nolan. He already knew the guys, had even lent his kit to Billy once or twice. After Shaker, he'd notched up some gigs with Wayne (Jayne) County's group, Queen Elizabeth, and wound up playing the same circuit as The Dolls. The audition was pretty easy for Nolan, it was the band that had to jump to keep up with him. Jerry

Nolan: 'I respected The Dolls' ideas very highly. They didn't play so well and being a little older, I was more advanced as a musician, so a lot of my friends would say "How can you play with those guys? They don't play so good." I said, "Hey man, you're missing the whole point. And nobody plays so good at first, what they've got, what I see in their approach and music, is magic."' Following the audition, Jerry was welcomed into The Dolls over a round of drinks at Max's. Early the next morning, Johnny met Nolan on the corner of 14th Street and 3rd Avenue, and took him up to the apartment he now shared with Sylvain to present the new drummer with some assorted Dolly finery from the communal wardrobe.

Jerry Nolan made his live debut with The New York Dolls on 19 December 1972, in the Sean O'Casey Theater, one of the largest rooms in the Mercer Arts Center. Unfortunately, the gig was more like a record industry convention. David Johansen recalled the night for *Creem* magazine:

> Someone had invited down Ahmet Ertegun, Clive Davis, Joe Polydor and these other crazy people. Out of an audience of five hundred, there were maybe twenty real kids who were there to rock. The rest of 'em were record company people, and if you mess up ... well, goodbye, and the trap door opens and you fall into the snake pit. We came on stage, and all we could see were these balding old relics with their polished heads, snorting coke and thinking that they're so outasite. And I'm supposed to get a record contract out of these people?

The top brass went home disgruntled. 'Hadn't those boys learned to mind their manners yet? Others shook with rage. Or was it excitement? Clive Davis, the president of CBS at the time, was rumoured to have said that if you wanted to keep working in the music business, you didn't admit to having seen The Dolls. Such a *faux pas* was likely to bring one's sexuality into disrepute. Nothing had changed within the industry and that included Mercury, who still couldn't make up their minds. Ever loyal, Paul Nelson put his career on the line as he continued to petition the company to sign them. Eventually he succeeded and on 20 March 1973, The New York Dolls were officially taken on by Mercury for a two-album deal. It was a daring move for the conservative second rung label whose biggest selling act was Rod Stewart minus The Faces. However, just because The Dolls were now on board, it didn't mean that their detractors within the company were prepared to put on a happy face.

The hunt began for an appropriate producer to work with The Dolls on their all-important debut album. Phil Spector was briefly considered while David Bowie declined their advances. Todd Rundgren wasn't an initial choice but he was accessible and had plenty of prior studio experience. Peter Jordan: 'There was a lot of oddball ideas as to who should produce. We wanted to try

Ladies and Gents: The New York Dolls. (*Bob Gruen*)

and get Roy Wood, Wizzard were brilliant and Wood could duplicate the style
of Dion or The Ronettes. He had pink hair and a two necked guitar and was
pretty crazy, well too crazy actually because it turned out he was having a
nervous breakdown, so we nixed him. Leiber and Stoller, who wrote 'Jailhouse
Rock' and had worked with The Coasters and produced some great records,
didn't like us. The reason why we got Todd Rundgren was because apart from

producing The Band and Bad Finger, he was available, lived in New York and was young. Although he looked pretty outrageous and had a large purple streak in his hair, he was a very straight guy.'

According to an interview he gave *Creem* magazine, Todd Rundgren's decision to produce The Dolls was based on geography rather than musical compatibility:

> The only person who can logically produce a New York City record is someone who lives in New York. I live here and I recognise all the things about New York that The Dolls recognise in their music. It doesn't necessarily mean that I testify to that stuff; it doesn't even mean that The Dolls' music testifies to that stuff. The only thing that it testifies to is that they're punks!

The divisions between Todd, who looked the part but wasn't, and The Dolls became apparent once recording started in Studio B of the Record Plant on 44th Street. Rundgren was a remote taskmaster, while the band larked around with their entourage and girlfriends between takes, extending their seven-day weekend ethic to the maximum, which is roughly how long it took to make the album. For those familiar with The Dolls' live sets, there were no surprises when it came to the choice of material: 'Jet Boy', 'Frankenstein' and 'Bad Girl' rowdily jostling for attention alongside the adorable confusion of 'Trash', Johansen's voice in direct competition with the seismic drumming and jarring guitars. The only vaguely gentle number 'Lonely Planet Boy' has all the restless containment of a noisy fidgety child who has just been told to hush up. In spite of the disparities between the band and Todd Rundgren, he managed to capture the frantic rush of The Dolls' music and also emphasised their backing vocals which recalled the glory days of the sixties' girl groups from The Shangri-Las to The Dixie Cups. Unfortunately, Mercury unduly hastened the mixing process while Rundgren's production did not endear him to all of the band, particularly Nolan and Thunders. In Europe, later that year, Johnny told the *NME*'s Nick Kent:

> He [Rundgren] screwed up the mix really bad. Everytime we go on the radio to do an interview we always dedicate 'Your Mama Don't Dance And Your Daddy Don't Rock 'n' Roll' to Todd.

The New York Dolls' eponymously titled debut album was released in the US on 27 July 1973 to a typically mixed reception. Most of the critics gave it a standing ovation, including Nick Kent who wrote:

> The New York Dolls are trash, they play rock 'n' roll like sluts and they've

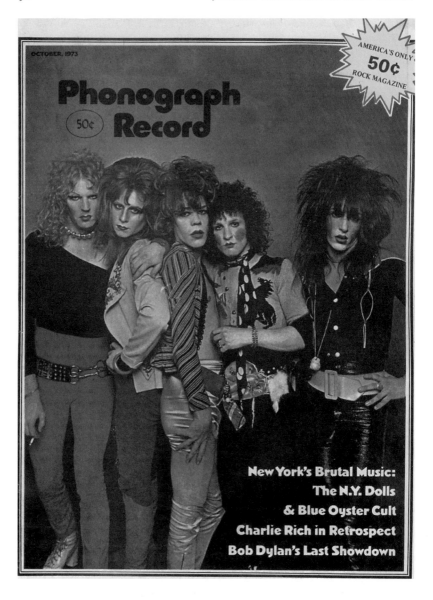

just a released a record that can proudly stand beside Iggy & The Stooges' stupendous *Raw Power* as the only album so far to fully define just exactly where 1970s' rock should be coming from.

Outside of their own realm, the legendary 'kids' that David Johansen had predicted would love the band, turned the other way and bought The Rolling Stones' lukewarm *Goats Head Soup* instead. Paul Nelson eloquently addressed the issue in the *Village Voice*:

They [The Dolls] were unquestionably brilliant, but finally too spare, too restricted, to reach the hidden places in suburban, small-town hearts. In the end, they rode on real rather than symbolic subway trains to specific rather than universal places, played for an audience of intellectuals or kids even further out than they were: and when they eventually met the youth of the country, that youth seemed even more confused than captivated by them.

The record's infamous drag cover proved even more contentious than the music. Some were intimidated by it, others were repulsed, too few understood the sense of humour beneath the lipstick and mascara, and took it at face value.

Between picking up bouquets and dodging missiles, the band stepped out on their first American tour, sharing a couple of the dates with Mott The Hoople. While they were away, the Mercer Arts Center collapsed after the adjoining hotel fell down. Maybe it was God's wrath, or maybe he was just missing them. In mid-August The NY Dolls returned home and before the start of a week-long stand at Max's Kansas City, Sylvain invited Johnny, David and Arthur to a fashion fair. At one of the more outrageous stands, Syl introduced them to Vivienne Westwood and Malcolm McLaren, whom he had met during his solo trip to London back when The Dolls were just getting started. McLaren was immediately intrigued, perceiving them as the very essence of the seamy allure of New York but he didn't fall head over heels until he listened to the album: 'I thought "My God, this is so bad, how could they make a record like that?" I was absolutely shocked and it made me laugh. It made me laugh so much that I suddenly thought you can be brilliant at being bad and there were people loving them for it. I loved them from that moment on. I was sold hook, line and sinker, and I loved the photograph of them on the album cover, sitting on the couch. I loved that asexual or bisexual look which in many ways had a direct correlation with much of what had happened in English pop but Vivienne and I liked it much better because we thought it was somewhat cruder and tougher. They were in many respects inspiring for us.' *

Following the block booking at Max's, the band had two days off before they were due to fly out to Los Angeles for a five-night stint at the Whisky A Go Go. Things should have been peachy, but miffed at being told she couldn't go to LA for financial reasons, Arthur's girlfriend Connie Gripp, went for him with a kitchen knife. While trying to disarm her, Kane got his hand filleted. The incident left the bass player in plaster and unable to play for the next two months. Although Peter Jordan deputised, Arthur was still taken on tour. Left to his own devices, Kane's unstable lifestyle and alcoholic tendencies put him at risk. After Billy Murcia, no one was taking any chances.

The New York Dolls' run of gigs at the Whisky became the stuff of legend, and had a lasting impact on LA's rock scene. The English musicians who had

Maximum Factor: The Doll's Debut Album.

once reigned supreme on the Sunset Strip were well and truly trounced by The Dolls. Finally, tinsel town started living up to its reputation. Lisa Robinson, writing for *Creem* magazine, reported on what happened when New York trash met Hollywood sleaze:

> The line at the Whisky A Go Go is, indeed, up the block. Kids who can't be more than twelve years old, boys with lipstick smeared on their faces, girls with all those kitschy, clutzy shoes, hot pants and feathers. Like some kind of fungus, it's slowly creeping across the country, but it's at its best in LA. I'm talking about sleeeeze. Sabel Starr is there of course, the undisputed Queen of the Strip – and she's holding on tightly to Johnny Thunders.

Within days of meeting Johnny T., the beauteous Miss Starr (née Shields) announced her retirement from groupiedom. One of LA's most celebrated rock courtesans had found true love at last. Hailing from the exclusive

Hollywood High. (*Bob Gruen*)

neighbourhood of Palos Verdes, Sabel and her sister Corel had canoodled with a string of bands until Corel started going steady with Iggy Pop. After seeing a picture of The Dolls in *Creem*, Sabel set her sights on Johnny Thunders. When the band finally rolled into town, Sabel was waiting for them at their hotel but her heart was reserved for Johnny. It was valentines all around once he took her up to his room. Janis Cafasso had faded from the scene after Thunders' insecurity spilled over into unpredictability, but to the besotted Miss Starr, The Dolls' cute lead guitarist was the embodiment of all her rock 'n' roll fantasies. If The New York Dolls really were the junior Stones, as some of their more affable critics reckoned, then Johnny and Sabel became teen world's Keith and Anita, exuding a damaged glamour. Aside from the gigs, Miss Starr and Mr Thunders spent every waking and sleeping moment together, Johnny phoning home to tell his mom he'd just met the girl he was going to marry. Naturally they started hanging out with Corel and Iggy, but the innocence of double-dating evaporated when Pop found an initiate in Thunders. Sylvain: 'Johnny was a big Iggy Pop fan and the four of them were always together and one thing led to another.

True Romance:
Mr T. and Miss
Starr. (*Bob Gruen*)

Johnny's the kind of guy, you turn him on to one joint and the next day he's got a whole pound, so they fix together and that's when that started. Johnny began using, not regularly at first, just a little bit here and a little bit there. It turned out to be the worst thing you could ever introduce Johnny to.' *

Before the band headed down south, Johnny packed Sabel off to New York for safe keeping but, unbeknownst to Miss Starr, her mother called out the National Guard. In the confusion, David Johansen's pretty blonde girlfriend, Cyrinda Foxe, was mistakenly apprehended by the Texas Rangers while she waited for The Dolls at the next stop on the tour. Sabel: 'Marty Thau was out-raged when Johnny sent me back to New York to wait for him on my own for the next three weeks. I'd just turned sixteen but I was very mature for my age. When I realised what my mom had done, I phoned her and told her to call off the police cos it really was quite scandalous.' Further castigation awaited The Dolls when they hit Memphis with Iggy Pop. Despite warnings from the local police department who had been whipped into a frenzy by a group of moral vigilantes known as the Mothers Of Memphis, the band went ahead with their gig at the Ellis Auditorium. The rioting began when a boy broke through the

police cordon around the stage and planted a kiss on David Johansen. As the
cops started beating up the kids in the crowd, The Dolls' frontman attempted
to calm the situation but was hauled off stage and charged with inciting a riot,
which was later bolstered by a lewd behaviour rap. After an uncomfortable
night in the slammer, David Jo was bailed out and the band beat a hasty trail
to Detroit. The tour climaxed on their home turf, with a Halloween bash in the
Grand Ballroom of the Waldorf Astoria. It was the major event of NY's autumn
season, featuring a fancy dress competition, the winner looking forward to a
night on the town with The New York Dolls, the second and third prizes being
a weekend for three at the Newark (New Jersey) Motor Inn and a bottle of New
York State Champagne. However, the band's characteristically late arrival and
the Waldorf's reticence to open the doors of the ballroom to the children of the
night who had shown up in force, resulted in fractious scenes and some two
thousand party goers were turned away. Although The Dolls missed their midnight stage cue by two hours, they swiftly revived any flagging spirits in the
audience. But as the *New Yorker's* Ellen Willis noted:

> To know The Dolls' repertoire is to love it, but I've already heard it live
> half a dozen times and some fresh material would have been nice. The
> Dolls' next album according to Johansen, is tentatively titled *Too Much Too
> Soon*. I hope so, but one new song per set is more like too little too late.

Since Billy Murcia's demise, allegiances within the band had changed. While
Syl and Johnny had been very close, Jerry Nolan had a profound influence on
the lead guitarist. Older and more streetwise, Nolan knew how to handle the
diminutive firebrand: 'The first time we went on tour together, we got into a
big fist fight in the back of the limousine and I kicked the shit out of him. Ever
since that day Johnny was like my son. He loved me for it. Every once in a while
he would push and I would let it get so far then I'd say "No more, boy, no
more." For some reason I happened to know Johnny real well; I knew his type.
Maybe it was the neighbourhood I grew up in. I taught Johnny everything he
knows, he got the blame for it all, but I actually did it all.' * Independently of
Johnny, the drummer had started chipping away at heroin, not so much that it
would detract from his playing, for Nolan was a stickler when it came to pro-
fessionalism, but the gradual alignment of their habits was a further bond.
However, at the half-way mark of The Dolls' short career, Johnny was still more
partial to heroin's opposite number, speed. Arthur Kane, meanwhile, was left
out on a limb when Syl and David buddied up. The knock-on effect of the new
loyalties estranged the band's main song-writing team, who hadn't been all that
prolific. 'Babylon', The Dolls' sprawling answer to 'New York New York', didn't
really qualify as a new number given that it had nearly made it on to their debut
platter, while 'Who Are The Mystery Girls?' had also been kicking around for

some time. Aside from the camp and catchy 'Lone Star Queen' and the rollicking 'Puss 'n Boots', which considers the plight of a shoe fetishist, there wasn't much evidence of fresh material for the second album. Matters were not helped by an extensive touring schedule that took them right up to the end of the year.

On 20 November 1973 The New York Dolls returned to England. Apart from a couple of university gigs, the first key moment of their trip came when they appeared on *The Old Grey Whistle Test*, a television programme that took its music seriously and expected the bands to do the same. The Dolls' inclusion on the show was a miraculous aberration. When Bob Harris, the *Whistle Test*'s presenter, mocked their brilliantly gauche performance of 'Jet Boy' and 'Looking For A Kiss', he earned the collective wrath of the upcoming punk generation. The Sex Pistols' drummer Paul Cook later told authors Fred and Judy Vermorel:

> I saw them [The Dolls] on the telly and I was fucking knocked out by them. It was mainly their attitude – I couldn't believe it, they was just all falling about all over the place, all their hair down, all knocking into each other. Had these great big platform boots on. Tripping over. They was really funny and they just didn't give a shit, you know. And Bob Harris at the end of it went: 'Tut, tut, tut, tut, mock rock' – just cast it off in two words.

Up in Manchester, Steven Morrissey was so galvanised by The Dolls, he wrote to Leber-Krebs' office letting them know of his intentions to start a fanclub for the band. The live high point of The New York Dolls' English jaunt came when they played two nights in the Rainbow Room, a huge art deco lounge and bar on the sixth floor of Biba's, the most decadent department store that London had ever known. Unfortunately, Arthur Kane was nabbed by security when he switched the price tag on a jacket he wanted, but couldn't afford. Barbara Hulanicki, the shop's creator, recounted the incident in her biography, *From A To Biba*, and stumped up the charges.

> The day they were due to appear we were watching their roadies setting up the equipment when the head of our security arrived, gripping two bedraggled looking creatures who had been caught shoplifting dresses and who claimed to work for us. They were part of the group and reluctantly we had to let them off. The Dolls did not go down very well with our audience either.

Like a crowd scene from *The Great Gatsby*, a gathering of sultry sirens and lounge lizards sipped their cocktails while pretending not to look at the assembled celebrities, who included Paul McCartney, Brian Eno and Elton John. Whatever they were expecting from the band, it wasn't what happened. Melody

Another
smash hit.

and harmony flew out the window as The Dolls tore into their set, breaking the sound barrier and the audience's ear drums. It had not been a good idea to borrow The Rolling Stones' PA system, which was intended for stadium use. On each consecutive night, only the die-hards like Malcolm McLaren stuck it out until the end: 'It was fantastic. They were like the worst striptease rock act you can imagine. I loved their awkward, trashy vibe. We became a part of their entourage and like groupies we followed them to Paris.' *

The NY Dolls' arrival in France became infamous, Johnny taking over from the late Billy Murcia when it came to throwing up in public, but the assembled ladies and gentlemen of the press were not amused and neither were the European representatives of Mercury. Only the *NME*'s Nick Kent, no stranger to decadence himself, failed to take umbrage.

> Five minutes off the plane in Paris, walking up towards the airport entrance, and Johnny Thunders throws up. Bl-a-a-a-a-a-g-g-h-h! God knows how many photographers are there: *Paris Match*, *Stern* magazine – all the European rock press and the nationals. The record company folks have arranged a special little welcome. Bl-a-a-a-a-g-g-h-h! The members of the band look stone-faced and wasted, wondering if he's maybe going to fall into his vomit.

Aside from being sick, Thunders and Nolan seemed to be sharing the same malady. Peter Jordan: 'I noticed that Johnny and Jerry were acting a little funny. That was the first time I became aware of their abuse of narcotics. When Jerry joined The Dolls he didn't even smoke cigarettes, he didn't do any kind of drugs, he didn't drink. If he did go out and have something to drink, it'd be something really corny like whisky and soda. It was a surprise to me that either of them had gotten into heroin. Johnny was a hip guy and he'd been around the block, even though he was very young. Frankly, there was enough aggravation already going on, so the last thing I expected anyone to do was to get strung out on heroin.' * The next day the band had a chance to make up for lost ground at a press conference in the bar of the Ambassador Hotel, where they were staying. Unfortunately, the question and answer routine was supposed to start at noon, normally the time the band would just be tumbling in or out of bed. While a harassed Marty Thau attempted to round up his unruly charges, the foyer started to fill up with journalists. Attempting to stave off any ill feeling over the band's tardiness, Thau threw the bar open. As the day turned to dusk, The New York Dolls finally assembled and the interviews began. While Marty's cordiality eased the situation, Mercury were aghast at the $8,000 bar tab run up by the press. Later that evening The Dolls went off to play a live concert at Radio Luxembourg. Sozzled to the point of near collapse, only Nolan's hard-hitting backbeat kept them bouyant. The broadcast was later released as *Paris*

Around and a round. (*Courtesy of Charlotte Nolan*)

Burning or *Paris Le Trash*. Sylvain: 'If you listen to that recording you can hear what condition David was in. He was a drunken mess. His ego had gone completely overboard and he couldn't do no wrong in his own eyes. He was trying to talk in French and he was so out of it.' * Contrary to the expectations of their new-found foes at the French branch of Mercury, The New York Dolls rose early the following morning and arrived on time at the prestigious Olympia Theatre, for a matinée show. Once again, Nick Kent was in attendance:

> The Dolls troop on stage at the Paris Olympia at 3.30 p.m., suitably bedraggled. Johansen decked out in bastardised evening dress with various badges and emblems strategically placed on his costume ('for political purposes, I mean the leftists will get off on my Mao button and …') commandeers proceedings, but the band are immediately dogged by a PA failure which totals the electricity for five minutes. Once underway the sound is distorted and falls like lead inside the hall, pinpointing the already cacophonous sound to a slightly less-than-comfortable degree. And there are other … uh … problems. Johnny Thunders looks about as well as his guitar is in tune. He staggers around the stage in obvious pain, attempting to motivate himself and the band simultaneously and succeeding only in beating his instrument into a ever-more horrendous stage of tunelessness.

Trouble Brewing. (*Bob Gruen*)

The last gig on the Dolls' French itinerary assured Thunders' legend in Paris for years to come. It was without doubt the birth of punk but for Johnny it was a matter of honour and survival. Situated on the Rue Voltaire, the Bataclan was a functional venue which had sold out well in advance. Once the band hit the stage, trouble started brewing in Thunders' corner when a couple of guys in the audience began spitting at him. The guitarist retaliated in kind. A few well aimed kicks followed. The guitarist retaliated in kind. However, when a volley of flying objects was lobbed in his direction, Thunders picked up a microphone stand and sent it spinning like a weighted frisbee at the perpetrators. The gig was aborted after they stormed the stage baying for blood. On 4 December The New York Dolls bade a fond farewell to France before continuing their European tour, returning home in time for Christmas.

Back in New York, Johnny and Sabel cosied up in their new apartment on West 24th Street. Sabel: 'Everything was so good those first few months, like a dream come true. We were going to get married. Johnny was like a child; he'd bring me sweet little gifts, cute little notes and he was so gorgeous. The first

Christmas we had together was so sweet. He bought me an Irish setter puppy and he took me to Central Park for a buggy ride. There was this innocence about Johnny but then he turned so hardcore. There was always speed and tons of marijuana. He'd smoke about twenty joints a day, if there was opium, he'd swallow that. He started getting crazy, any weird thing would trigger him and he'd get in these jealous rages.' Johnny and Sabels' relationship spiralled out of control along with the fortunes of The New York Dolls. 1973 had faded, but there was no real reason for the band to do the same. However, Mercury were agitated. Although The Dolls' debut LP fared well, racking up sales of 110,000, the record company had expected gold and were becoming increasingly less tolerant of the band's transgressions. Redemption lay in their second album.

Producers were now a thorny subject in The Dolls' camp. Todd Rundgren made a reprise as a possible candidate, while Bob Ezrin, who mainly worked with Alice Cooper, was given the once over. Ultimately, the prize went to George 'Shadow' Morton, the mentor and producer of The New York Dolls' soul sisters, The Shangri-Las. The delinquent faction of the girl groups, The Shangri-Las were the most likely to associate with rebel boys or run away from home. Tough yet vulnerable, the girls notched up four top-twenty hit singles between September 1964 and November 1965, including 'Give Him A Great Big Kiss', which The Dolls often covered in their live shows, addressed to the feminine. Shadow Morton also thought he would be addressing the feminine the first time he met The Dolls. In spite of an apparent camaraderie, Morton had no musical empathy with The Dolls' material and succeeded only in dampening their spirit on record. Fortunately, his attempt to tame 'Babylon' fails, but The Dolls' version of The Cadets' 'Stranded In The Jungle', usually a live *tour de force*, has its normal exuberance masked by the studio techniques. With so many rough edges to buff, 'Who Are The Mystery Girls?' makes a stab at brassy liberation but 'Gamble & Huff's (There's Gonna Be A) Showdown', the second of four covers on the album, sounds more like a number from a big budget musical than the rocking rumble it ought to be. 'It's Too Late', one of the finest moments on *Too Much Too Soon*, manages to overcome Shadow's restraining order but the harmonica is overused in places. The album finally transcends the producer's boundaries on Johnny T.'s 'Chatterbox'. Dating back to the earliest inception of the band, the track which evolved from 'The Milk Man' a.k.a. 'Milk Me', marks Thunders' hard-won campaign to sing his own composition and the budding if hesitant desire to take centre stage. As journalist Ron Ross observed in *Phonograph Record*:

> Johnny's double-tracked vocals make him sound like the beehive brunette from Queens we always knew he was.

In the stampede of guitars, Morton loses the reigns and 'Chatterbox' runs wild.

The Beehive Brunette. (*Bob Gruen*)

The same, sadly, could not be said for the rest of the album.

In the run up to the release of *Too Much Too Soon*, The New York Dolls made their last, great extravagant gesture when they staged a St Valentine's Massacre at the Academy of Music. In conjunction with photographer Bob Gruen, the band created a spoof movie in which they starred as The Lipstick Killers – the gang who couldn't do a job without their lipstick on. Bob Gruen: 'We decided we'd make a newsreel of them as thirties-type gangsters as part of the Academy of Music show. The film ends with them riding up 14th Street firing off machine guns, then running into the theatre. Then they would suddenly appear for real, running down the aisles wearing the same gangster costumes, shooting the audience. Now for some people in the audience who were on the right drugs and peaking at the right time, this worked amazingly well. I know some people for whom this was the experience of a lifetime!' *

For the next six months, The Dolls gigged solidly across the States and back again, best that they should keep moving as the critical backlash began. Nick Kent summarised the situation in the *NME*:

> The overall impression though is that this album is messy and shot through with unfulfilled potential. It's exactly the wrong sort of product to launch on a public, liberally weighed out with folk only too ready to pull the whole 'I told you so' number at the Dolls' expense.

Mercury had their hands firmly on their holsters, ready to take aim, while Leber-Krebs began to regard the band as yesterday's wild affair: fun while it lasted but maybe it was time to settle down with the compromise model, Aerosmith. More readily accessible and a great deal less exotic, Aerosmith translated The New York Dolls for the mainstream market. Marty Thau: 'Krebs was very quietly handling their management roster. Later on it seemed to me that he was watching the whole Dolls' thing and when he or Aerosmith saw something they could take from The Dolls, in terms of style, showmanship and musical riffs, they would. I've had my suspicions that Leber and Krebs wanted to keep The Dolls down cos Aerosmith were moving up and CBS was backing them.' *
Of course, The New York Dolls still had an ever-loving bevy of supporters and with proper care and attention they would have survived. Sadly, they didn't get it, although Marty Thau continued to fight valiantly in their corner.

In mid-April, The Dolls began what they described as a miniature world tour, comprising a week's worth of small-club dates in Manhattan, a step backwards disguised as a cute move. Many of the larger promoters had begun to distance themselves from the band, wary of the high spirited crowds they attracted and the Dolls' habitual lateness. The high point of the mini-odyssey was their show at the 82 Club, one of NY's most famous drag venues. Of course they lived up to the occasion, save for Johnny, who steadfastly refused to wear a

The Lipstick Killers; featuring 'Killer'Kane, 'Giovanni' Genzale, 'Rocky' Johansen, 'Legs' Sylvain and 'Scarface' Nolan. (*Bob Gruen*)

dress. Hot on the heels of the 82 gig, The Dolls began a hectic three-month cross country trek to push *Too Much Too Soon*, which had got off to an even more uncertain start than their debut album. The confusion that the band generated was ably illustrated when *Creem* magazine voted them both the best and worst new group in May 1974. On the downside, The Dolls were considered to be even more horrendous than The Osmonds, Grand Funk Railroad, Slade and Dawn. However, they were also deemed to be better than Queen, Aerosmith and Lynyrd Skynrd.

Midway through their touring schedule, Johnny Thunders managed to get his mitts on some uncut methamphetamine when the band arrived in Canada. Never one to moderate his intake, Johnny binged on the pure speed to the point of psychosis, clawing the walls and anyone who came near him. Paranoid and distraught, he refused to go on stage unless Sabel came to Toronto. She finally caught up with the band in Montreal but no amount of gentle persuasion could talk Johnny down from the ledge inside his mind. Eventually he collapsed and had to be taken on to a plane in a wheelchair for the next gig . The episode was a prelude to a string of calamities for the band. A trip to England in July was pulled, and when The Dolls got to New Orleans, they found the venue had burned down. From Fayetteville, the band travelled to Los Angeles, where they had a four-night stand at the Roxy Theater. Owned by the influential music business entrepreneur, Lou Adler, the Roxy was also hosting performances of the *Rocky Horror Show*, a project seemingly dear to his heart

Too Much Too Soon.

for when the musical was made into a movie, Adler was the executive producer. While trying to set up The Dolls' equipment, some of their roadies removed the actors' tape markers. When the cast complained, The Dolls were banished from the theater after only one gig. The incident proved a major irritant to Steve Leber. The band rallied for a great in-concert performance on the *Don Kirshner Show*, a nationally syndicated TV programme, but got a stormy reception when they returned home. Against Marty Thau's wishes, Leber decided to minimise the band's activities, further devaluing their reputation by booking them in to smaller and smaller venues. Johnny, meanwhile, polished off the rest of the methamphetamine, the narcotic equivalent of volunteering to be shark bait, and came out shredded. Sabel: 'He really got crazy and he started hitting me in front of the band, one night when we were in Chinatown. I slit my wrists and Syl had to take me to Bellevue. The doctor said "I won't send you to the psychiatric wing but I want you to get the first plane home." I did.' Left distraught by Miss Starr's departure, Thunders began an ardent campaign to win her back. Done with the brutality of speed, he turned with increasing frequency

Smokin'.
(*Bob Gruen*)

to the soporific embrace of heroin. Nothing was ever half-hearted with Johnny Thunders, from baseball to learning the guitar. So sad, then, that he should apply the same concerted effort to junkiedom. If self-destruction and addiction are different sides of the same theme, they were both playing loud and clear for Johnny.

On 11 October 1974, The Dolls made their way to LA for the last time to take part in the Hollywood Street Revival And Dance. Something has to be over for it to feel like a reunion and a sense of nostalgia permeated the event, which also featured Iggy Pop and a selection of rock 'n' roll riffraff including the remnants of Silverhead and The GTOs. Journalist Richard Cromelin delivered a premature obituary to The New York Dolls:

> More than any of the other acts at the Trash Dance, The Dolls are hooked
> to a time that's inexorably rolling away, and their only redeeming feature is
> the perversely fascinating way they suicidally cling to their path to oblivion.

The Stilletoes, Elda Gentile, Debbie Harry and Rosie Ross, with The Dolls. NYC '74. 'Stick my stilleto in the girls': J.T. (*Bob Gruen*)

At least the gig was a triumph for Johnny, who made up with Sabel Starr. An item once more, they returned to New York together. Sadly, their second honeymoon flickered out with the dying light of The Dolls.

Even though *Too Much Too Soon* had sold marginally less than The Dolls' debut offering, Mercury granted a stay of execution when they opted for a third album. A series of meetings began between the band and their managers, Steve Leber adding the incentive of a trip to Japan, if they cleaned up their act and said goodbye to Marty. The Dolls were in no fit state to negotiate the managerial tug-of-war that had developed between Leber and Thau. Regretfully, Marty walked of his own accord, citing Leber's decision to put the band on the club circuit as one of the main reasons for his departure. Jerry Nolan: 'Marty Thau fought for us against two guys that didn't believe in us, but it was a losing battle.' If The Dolls couldn't look to their managers for stability, they certainly weren't going to be able to find it within themselves. Between the heaviness of alcohol and the anaesthesia of heroin and all the other complications, Johansen and Thunders had drifted apart as a creative team, but The Dolls were not a spent force. Sylvain and David collaborated on 'Red Patent Leather' while Johnny, growing ever more confident as a solo song writer, delivered 'Pirate Love'. They had the material for a third album but the circumstances were tangled. Peter Jordan: 'I would wind up rehearsing all this material with Johnny, some of which would turn up with The Heartbreakers, like 'Pirate Love', but a lot of it disappeared. By then everyone had their own agendas, their own lives. David and Johnny became so fucking alienated they wouldn't work with each other but the real pain in the ass was David wouldn't work with Jerry if you gave him a million dollars. The other thing was Johnny had songs he wanted to do and David said to me one time: "What am I supposed to do while he does his songs, play tambourine? I'm not going to do that."' * Matters were taken out of the group's hands when Irwin Steinberg, the big boss at Mercury retracted the offer of a third album and demanded repayment of losses and loans. The bitter seasoning at the close of business at the end of 1974 came when Leber-Krebs withdrew all financial support from the band. Like Cinderella, the NY Dolls were reduced to standing in line for welfare and playing dingy clubs, as the careers of Aerosmith and Kiss were taking off.

Newly arrived in NY, Malcolm McLaren came to the rescue just as his beloved Dolls were buckling under. He couldn't free them from their ties to Mercury and Leber-Krebs, but he could at least get them functioning again. While McLaren's intentions might have been good, his reasoning wasn't entirely altruistic. Regardless of the band's predicaments, any association with them bestowed a certain tarnished frisson, and McLaren benefited from letting people know he had managed The New York Dolls, especially once he returned to England. Malcolm's official position however, was never clarified. David Johansen: 'I know he says he was our manager but he wasn't really. He was our haberdasher.' * Nonetheless, McLaren was dedicated in his endeavours. Enabling them to continue rehearsing, he rented a loft for the band which they shared with another outfit called The Demons. Malcolm then addressed The Dolls' personal habits: Arthur Kane was packed off to Smithers, a top-of-the-line rehab, and although they took some persuading, Johnny and Jerry saw a doctor. Compounding their problems, The New York Dolls were now in a cultural void. Despite being hailed as royalty on the burgeoning CBGB's scene, and no older than any of the punk bands that played there, The Dolls' music was rooted in a different time; you could jostle to The Ramones or quiver to Television, but you couldn't dance anymore.

Seeking to kill off The Dolls' old image, McLaren took his cue from 'Red Patent Leather' and sent some preliminary ideas to Vivienne Westwood, who produced five varying outfits in the same garish ketchup hue. Of all the associations in the spectrum of red: blood, lipstick, passion, danger, Malcolm chose to politicise the tone. When he relaunched the band like the rent boy regiment of the Red Guard, with a hammer and sickle backdrop, McLaren saw only the artistic aesthetic and not the context. The Vietnam War was still raging. The New York Dolls had already assailed the senses of the moral majority and suffered for it, but taking the Commie route was suicidal. The Dolls became McLaren's crash test dummies, the prototypes for his next project, the Sex Pistols. Jerry Nolan: 'Malcolm's just a parasite. He observed The Dolls and what they were up to and he was smart enough to know what they had, what sold, what kind of potential we had, and he used up everything he learned off us to

Trashed.

put his own group together.' The Dolls unveiled their new look and set list over four shows at the Little Hippodrome in New York, between 28 February and 2 March 1975, with Television and Pure Hell in support. Aside from a dedicated contingent, reactions to the red regime were as critical as Rhett Butler's parting words to Scarlett. Almost immediately afterwards, the band set off on a tour of Florida, accompanied by Malcolm. Wedged in a car, driving through backwater towns that didn't even make it on to the map, en route to the next funky dive, swatting mosquitoes for something to do, Jerry Nolan and Johnny Thunders got restless. Like some B-movie morality tale, the band had drifted from hotels to motels, before they finally ended up in a neglected trailer park owned by Jerry Nolan's step-father. Ensconced in the rusting carcass of yesteryear's mobile dreamhome, Johnny and Jerry started to get sick. Junk sick and heart sick. Thunders: 'We told David we were sick of The Dolls and that we were going back to New York to start again and he said, "Anyone in this band can be replaced." But when we left, that was the end of The Dolls, the *only* Dolls.'

For almost everyone, The New York Dolls finished as a band the minute Johnny Thunders and Jerry Nolan left Florida's sun behind and got on a plane to Manhattan. There was some speculation of reconciliation but it wasn't to be:

- Johnny and Jerry started rehearsing together.
- Arthur went to LA for a year and formed Killer Kane before returning to NY.

- David Johansen, Sylvain Sylvain and Peter Jordan teamed up for The New New York Dolls a.k.a. The Dollettes. Apart from a tour of Japan, they played endlessly around their home town before embarking on different projects.
- Malcolm McLaren combined The New York Dolls attitude with Richard Hell's look and launched The Sex Pistols.

Aside from occasionally crossing paths, the band got back together in their entirety only once, for a photo session organised by Roberta Bayley in conjunction with *Punk* magazine in 1977. Echoing the photograph on the back of their debut album, the former Dolls look as though they have lived a million years, instead of four short ones, since the original was taken. In his lament upon the demise of The Dolls, which appeared in the *Village Voice*, Paul Nelson wrote:

> The Dolls went out with their high-heeled boots on. They did it their way and got carried out dead, but with their pride intact. True, they did not grow old with the country, but that's probably the country's loss, not theirs. Corporation rock 'n' roll, wherein musicians like Bachman-Turner Overdrive, are more gray-flanneled than the businessmen who kow tow to them, is so formularised, homogenised, and impersonal it must surely cause the death of anything that is at all out-of-bounds, mythopoeic, and rebellious. The Dolls were alive. Perhaps it killed them not to become stars, darkened their personalities, drove some of them into private worlds; but at least they had the courage to become figments of their own imaginations.

On The Rocks. CBGB'S.
NYC 1975. (*Bob Gruen*)

On the waterfront, Heartbreakers mk. 1: Jerry Nolan, Johnny Thunders and Richard Hell. (*Bob Gruen*)

3
Malicious Romance

In the same week that the bells tolled for The New York Dolls, bass player Richard Hell left Television. Hell was immediately recruited by Johnny Thunders and Jerry Nolan under the banner of The Heartbreakers. Explaining why he'd called the new band The Heartbreakers, Johnny somewhat prophetically commented: 'It's like the kids that never did anything right, everyone they touch goes out of their minds – like someone who comes along and burns down your house – that's breaking your heart.'

Richard Hell had started (public) life by launching a poetry magazine entitled *Genesis Grasp*. He then collaborated with his high-school friend Tom Verlaine, on a collection of verse called *Wanna Go Out?* which was published under the shared *nom de plume* of Theresa Stern. After the demise of their first band, The Neon Boys, Hell and Verlaine formed Television as an equal artistic partnership. However, when Verlaine started to edit Hell's songs from their set list, he quit. It barely mattered that Richard's bass playing wasn't all that hot, when his ragged street-waif style assured his immortality as the man who inspired the gaunt look of punk. Richard Hell: 'The reason Johnny wanted me in The Heartbreakers was because he liked my songs and he liked the way I looked on stage. We essentially had the same agreement as Television, but I came into The Heartbreakers with many more songs than Johnny, cos I bought with me all the songs I had written in Television.' (Interview with author, which previously appeared in *Record Collector*.)

After a short time playing around Manhattan, the trio enlisted guitarist Walter Lure from The Demons, who had shared The Dolls' rehearsal loft. With his expressionist physique, all odd elongated angles, Lure cast an instant semblance of strangeness over the group as he brooded behind his guitar, blending an almost classic manner of holding the chords with a shrill originality of his own. Jerry Nolan: 'Walter was just a kid from Brooklyn that always wanted to be in The Dolls. I just knew he was the guy for The Heartbreakers.'

In an attempt to break away from the regimes they had all previously played under, The Heartbreakers moved along more shared lines, with each to his own song. The classics started to infuse their sets right from the start, including Thunders' compositions 'Pirate Love' and 'Goin' Steady', which harks back to the tough cuteness of Eddie Cochran, when all you needed was a girl to make it OK. Meanwhile, Richard Hell contributed 'Blank Generation', 'Love Comes In Spurts', and 'You Gotta Lose'. Then of course, there was the highly contested 'Chinese Rocks', which has at different times been attributed to Dee Dee Ramone, Thunders, Nolan and Hell. Ownership details aside, 'Chinese Rocks'

Existential Potential
The Heartbreaker's
first photo session.
(*Bob Gruen*)

concisely defines the gruelling aspects of hardcore junkie life, something that
Johnny Thunders and Jerry Nolan were becoming all too familiar with. Still,
there was always an advance to stave off the sickness. Jerry Nolan: 'When I told
Johnny how to get an advance, boy, that was the fucking biggest gift, that was
like handing over a scroll. I said "Johnny, c'mere, I'll show you how we'll get
high. We got a job at Max's. Right, come with me." He came with me, we went
upstairs to talk to the manager, Tommy. I said: "Listen Tommy, we got a gig,

Shoot first, ask questions later.
The Heartbreakers caught while they were still alive. (*Roberta Bayley*)

you know how much money we make, I want half of it right now." We got that
half and spent it in five minutes, shooting up heroin. Ever since that day,
Johnny knew what it was like to get an advance.'

The local circuit on to which The Heartbreakers emerged was seething with
a new generation's ambitions, home-town contenders like Blondie, The
Ramones, Talking Heads and Television, all fighting for record deals and recognition. In terms of crowd pulling, Johnny and Co. had the lead. Any band featuring two ex-Dolls was always going to generate interest, but Thunders and
Nolan had the reputation as well as the fame. Many unfairly pinned the demise
of The Dolls on them, and the industry steered clear. They also had detractors
within the scene itself. Jerry: 'A lot of bands at the time felt me and Johnny
didn't deserve a second chance, y'know? We fucked up The Dolls so we
shouldn't be around anymore – that dumb number. They really hated us for
getting a band together so quick and making it pretty successful too.'

Johnny and the boys seemed determined to fulfil the expectations of the
legendary caption 'Catch 'em while they're still alive' that advertised their gigs
around New York, accompanied by a photograph of the band with lurid bullet
impacted chest wounds (melted Hershey bars). On stage at CBGB's, The
Heartbreakers looked like B-movie hoods; the kind of guys you shoot on sight
and ask questions about later. With his ratted mane newly tamed into a classic
Wop Crop, the odd curl fell across Johnny Thunders' dark eyes as he twisted his
guitar in a vicious metallic duel with Walter Lure, while Richard Hell gave the
audience a highly wired rendition of his latest song. Stoic as ever, Jerry Nolan
was the only one left in control when the guitars swerved then plummeted into
disarray. Ignoring the shrill whistles that sounded like cracking ice in the black
circle below the stage, Nolan counted into 'Pirate Love', a song that fared better

in the Bowery than the latter days of The Dolls' when the tendency was to aim for a big sound and overplay it. Down at CBGB's, the number blossomed. Shaking the sweat from his hair, Richard Hell muttered: 'This next work was manufactured by our drummer, Jerry Nolan – it's called "Can't Keep My Eyes On You".'

Nick Kent had this to say in the *NME*'s 27 March (1976) issue:

> Right now, The Heartbreakers are ready to break out of their tightly bounded lower West Side pitch and with some decent hard-sell record company back-up, combat the garish synthesised likes of Kiss and Aerosmith with a vengeance. Only thing is, the big uptown wheeler-dealers aren't biting on the bait – yet. Hell, for example is glumly resigned to a further six months in limbo before a half-way decent offer comes the way of his band. Meantimes, they become easy prey for a whole battalion of sycophantic incompetents offering two-bit management deals and the like. It's all very sad and very frustrating.

Aside from recording some demos at SBS Studios in Yonkers, The Heartbreakers made little headway and were in danger of chasing their own tails in ever decreasing circles around the venue circuit. Walter Lure: 'Well ... we played CBGB's and then we played Max's and then we played CBGB's and then we played Max's again ... And it went on and on for fuckin' ages ... once in a while we'd go out of town to Boston ... or a new club would open up and we'd open it ...' Although The Heartbreakers had made a hands-down conquest of their own turf, the record companies were still running scared of signing up the band, fearing a deal in Needle Park. All around them the industry was starting to make overtures but not in their direction; Patti Smith picked up the bouquet from Arista while The Ramones tied the knot with Sire.

Despite the wall of nervous abstinence from the commercial world, Johnny had no desire to play up the past for present recognition. Thunders: 'The Dolls? I never heard about The Dolls ... who were The Dolls? I wanna make a record ... cos I never really made one yet. When we were The Dolls we never made a good record. We always had too many hands in the cookie jar. Now we're gonna produce ourselves – The Heartbreakers, y'know? We're the kinda band that has no fuckin' gimmicks. What we're doing now is more to what Jerry likes. Jerry's my inspiration. Me and Jerry are like Moe, Larry and Curly – in two.'

Meanwhile, a sudden case of mutiny rocked The Heartbreakers when Richard Hell challenged Johnny Thunders' position in the ranks. It was a badly judged move. Jerry Nolan: 'Richard wanted to do all the singing himself, and he figured he'd get rid of Johnny; but little did he know – we got rid of him. He was a little shaken, his ego wasn't sure of that, he thought we'd listen to him

Heartbreakers mk. 2: Rath, Lure, Nolan and Thunders. NYC 1976. (*Bob Gruen*)

and get rid of Johnny, which was a big mistake.' Richard Hell's sudden departure finally pushed Johnny to the centre of the stage. The days of waiting to take
his turn were over. Thunders: 'It was great when it first started [The Heart-
breakers] but, y'know, when Richard was in Television, Tom Verlaine wanted to
sing every song and that's what Richard did to us; I could sing one song out of
ten, and Walter could sing one song a night. Naww, I didn't wanna back up a
lead singer, I'd done that for too long.'

Hell went on to form The Voidoids, and despite his hasty exit from The
Heartbreakers, had the grace to look back with a raw fondness at his time with
Thunders and Co.: 'It was a good experience for me, because without that I
could never have started this band.'

Boston-born Billy Rath was the perfect choice to bring The Heartbreakers
up to fighting strength. Having played bass with various bands in the New
England / Boston area, Billy had just returned from Florida, where he'd been
'working' as a gigolo when Johnny got in touch. Even the outspoken Jerry
Nolan was in full praise of Rath's conscription. Jerry: 'Well, obviously, we didn't
want anyone who was on any sort of trip after Richard, and Billy was just perfect. He's just a bass player who loves playing Rock 'n' Roll. He ain't worried
about bein' a star. No way.'

Nancy Spungen, a Sabel Starr wannabe from Philadelphia who relocated to
NY and developed a massive crush on Jerry Nolan, reviewed the newly revised
Heartbreakers at Max's Kansas City on 23 July 1976, for the *New York Rocker*:

The band were amazingly tight for a first performance. Jerry's already fine

drumming sounded twice as good with a great bass player. Finally Johnny
and Walter were riffing off each other; both taking leads; both providing
interspersing rhythms. All four members together created a perfect chem-
istry, a certain magic, if you will, and the audience sure knew it. They
didn't seem to mind the loss of Richard Hell at all; receiving the familiar
tunes with joyful fervour and accepting the new ones as if they were old
favourites. They went beyond all expectations and certainly erased any
doubts that anyone may have had.

Nancy's review of the gig was made all the more amazing when the problems
the band had to overcome are recalled. With Hell's departure they lost a sub-
stantial chunk of their repertoire, leaving them with a little over a month to
repair the damage. Outpacing any threat by a wide margin, The Heartbreakers
took the boards at Max's armed with an incredible set list, which included the
triumphant battlecry of life on a downward slope that is Thunders' 'Born To
Lose', Lure and Nolan's mischievous 'Get Off The Phone', the moody swagger
of 'It's Not Enough', and 'Baby Talk' which cops its explosive central riff from
The Yardbirds' 'I've Been Wrong'. Plus Nolan's solo stab at romance, 'Take A
Chance With Me' and a cover of The Contours' 'Do You Love Me'.

The Heartbreakers continued to play every corner of Manhattan but the
music industry remained immune for the same tired reasons. Walter Lure: 'We
were drawing a big following, always capacity. New York was such a dead scene
though. Record companies didn't want to know because of our and The Dolls'
reputation. Talk about uncontrollability, drugs, etcetera – much exaggerated.'

The band's newly elected manager, the debonair Leee Black Childers, started
to worry that he'd taken charge of the most talented bunch of pariahs in New
York. Aside from being a dazzling raconteur and photographer, Leee was no
stranger to the rock 'n' roll business world. The former vice-president of David
Bowie's MainMan company, Childers had also looked after Iggy Pop, during a
particularly destructive phase in his career. When Johnny asked Leee to manage
The Heartbreakers, Childers had thought he was finished with the tribulations
of rock life, but agreed anyway. Leee Black Childers: 'I'd sworn I would never
get involved with management again. I didn't wanna die young but I really liked
The Heartbreakers. I loved their songs, I loved the music, I loved the presentation. it was everything I thought rock 'n' roll *should* be and so I realised I had
victimised myself back into it again.'

Childers did his best to get his boys a deal, but the wall of fear still held.

Jerry Nolan sighed at the memory: 'The kids wanted us, but the business
didn't want to have anything to do with us – cos of some so-called "bad reputation", y'knowwhadahmean? We could talk about that all day – our bad reputation, it doesn't matter.'

Maybe not to Nolan, but to everyone else it did.

London '77. (*Erica Echenberg*)

Events took an unexpected turn when Leee received a telephone call from England. Enter, on cue, Malcolm McLaren, whom Johnny once described as 'The greatest con man I've ever met', with a tempting offer for the band. In fact, it was the only serious offer to come their way. Not that they would get paid or anything like that, but with little else on the horizon they accepted his invitation to fly out to England and join the Anarchy tour, alongside The Sex Pistols, Clash and Damned. With only the vaguest idea of what was brewing on the other side of the Atlantic, the 'Breakers got their passports ready. As Childers later quipped 'We would have toured with anybody, even Barry Manilow!' It probably would have been a lot less hassle.

On 1 December 1976, The Heartbreakers touched down at Heathrow airport. The same evening, The Sex Pistols fired their warning shot at Bill Grundy, on Thames Television's *Today* show. Goaded by Grundy, Johnny Rotten and the boys got into a little minor league swearing, the kind of surly comments that can be heard in any pub all over England when last orders are called. It was enough to get the punk bandwagon rolling at full speed.

The Fleet Street rags were hysterical at this unexpected Christmas gift:

'THE FILTH OUR CHILDREN HAVE TO WATCH'

'WHEN WILL IT END?'

'NOT FIT FOR THE EYES AND EARS OF A DOG'

'WASH THEIR MOUTHS OUT WITH SOAP'

'DON'T THEY HAVE PARENTS?'

Malcolm was delighted. The public reaction was a thousand times greater than he could have wished for.

In a blaze of Punk! Rock! Shock! headlines, the Anarchy tour got underway. Sort of. Out of a possible nineteen dates, only three went ahead. Local MPs formed watch-dog committees to vet each band while the powerful Rank Group gave the thumbs down to the possibility of any punk acts playing in their many venues.

Johnny Thunders was amazed: 'They're all fuckin' assholes. They don't know anythin 'They're full of shit. When we went on tour with The Pistols, we had all these people outside singin' Christmas carols. There's more of them outside than at the gigs. In Cardiff they even had these priests with microphones screaming: "The Devil's in there … the Devil's music." Nowhere in America would they do that. Sure, in the Midwest they'd come and break your head but they wouldn't come and pray at you first.'

With cancellations running across England with the speed of the Black Death, it was a surprise in itself that the 'liberal' student body at Leeds Polytechnic got their chance to throw their beer cans at all. Pete Silverton writing for *Sounds* reviewed The Heartbreakers' appearance at Leeds Polytechnic in the 18 December edition of the paper:

> The Heartbreakers have *the* best drummer in former NY Doll Jerry Nolan, and the craziest looking bassist in Billy Rath who could've stepped out of *West Side Story* … they also have a great song about a telephone conversation which ends with one of the parties hanging themselves on the phone flex.

On 22 December the Anarchy tour swerved to a halt. Childers had understandably presumed that cancellations or not, his band would receive some financial compensation. He was mistaken and The Heartbreakers were left to starve in splendour through the Christmas period. Childers: 'We were staying with Sebastian Conran (the ergonomic designer and son of Sir Terence Conran), bless his heart, he took a shine to us and of course he had more money than he could possibly deal with and a fabulous house on Regents Park. So we were staying there. We had a place to live but he didn't feel compelled to feed us, and I was really freaking out cos I had these starving people who were my dependants!'

The band were itching to get back on board a big bird bound for home, where life's necessities, steady drug connections, food and girlfriends, awaited them, but Childers insisted they could make history if they stayed on. It was better than barely making ends meet in NY. Leee: 'The first gig we did in London was at Dingwalls and it was magnificent. You couldn't have got another person in there with a crowbar! It was so packed. I thought … Oh boy … we're

Big Ben joins
The 'Breakers
for a photo
opportunity.

gonna be the next Beatles, we're gonna be sooo rich. Of course the last Beatles
weren't wildly self-destructive junkies, which sort of created a bit of a problem
in terms of our success. Our next gig was at the Roxy.'

Tucked away in Covent Garden, Andrew Czezowski's Roxy Club was at the
forefront of the punk movement. The Heartbreakers became its overseas VIPs
ensuring a sardined safety-pinned crowd at every gig. Johnny and his wise-guys
were not a punk band, in the 1976 application of the term, they were NY street
punks playing rock 'n' roll but the kids still pogoed. Andrew Czezowski: 'Knowing how desperate The Heartbreakers were to do something, we booked them.
They went down a storm and drew more than anyone else.'

Regarded as dangerous aristocracy by the other bands, The Heartbreakers
made quite an impact, as guitarist Marco Pironi recalled: 'I met The Heartbreakers outside The Sex Pistols' rehearsal room on Denmark Street. I only
twigged this was Johnny Thunders when he introduced himself. I was well
impressed. I'd never seen him in the flesh before, all I'd seen was The New

York Dolls on TV and in photos. I didn't realise how little he was without all the high hair and platform boots. I saw every gig that The Heartbreakers did at the Roxy. I loved them. They came across as being incredibly slick compared to the English bands. They could start and finish a song at the same time, which the other bands couldn't do. My theory is that the punks didn't really wear leather motorcycle jackets before The Heartbreakers arrived. They also didn't do heroin.'

For all the glowering amphetamine stares and threatening mannerisms of the punks, the London scene was relatively unsullied in comparison to The Heartbreakers' home turf. Eventually, Johnny and Co. along with Nancy Spungen, who followed them over in hot pursuit of Jerry Nolan, would be held responsible by certain parties for introducing heroin to the English punks. Jerry Nolan told *Village Voice*:

> We hung out a lot with The Sex Pistols. I was the first guy to turn John Rotten on to heroin, the first guy to shoot him up. I'm not proud of that, and I learned a lesson. I didn't like the feeling I got from it, and I changed my mind about turning people on to drugs. I didn't do it anymore after that. Nancy, who I introduced to Sid [Vicious] was the first to turn Sid on.

The Heartbreakers certainly made heroin seem an alluring if risky prospect and were initially cavalier about it. However, in any situation where speed is prevalent, some folks will turn to smack in the comedown, and junk didn't just show up with The Heartbreakers but had been used on the English rock scene for some years.

Before The Heartbreakers' reputation caught up with them, Leee endeavoured to get the band a deal. Always a *tour de force* live, there was no shortage of industry suitors. The French label Skydog were interested, as were EMI, but having been burned in their dealings with The Pistols, they were only prepared to offer a single deal to start with. Arista were enthusiastic and CBS ready to talk, but it was the old team at Track Records, headed by Kit Lambert and Chris Stamp, who were the most persistent. Having lost The Dolls, they weren't about to let The Heartbreakers slip through their fingers. Leaving Leee to sift through the offers, the band split back to Manhattan for ten days. Thunders' return was delayed by a twenty-four-hour stay in a police cell for possession of a small quantity of hashish. He was fined £15.

Back in London, John Genzale a.k.a. Johnny Thunders, Gerard Nolan a.k.a. Jerry Nolan, Walter Luhr a.k.a. Walter Lure and William Wrath a.k.a. Billy Rath gave their legally binding autographs to Track as The Chris Stamp Band Ltd, an indication that all was not what it seemed within the company. The provision was made that if CSB Ltd. were to go bankrupt, all the tapes would revert back to Heartbreakers Inc. which had been set up by Leee Black Childers

Julie, Johnny and Johnny Jnr. (*Bob Gruen*)

and business manager Peter Gerber. The Heartbreakers may have thought they'd hit the big time with the promise of a £50,000 advance, but they'd merely rented a short lease. As they settled into London life, Johnny's bride-to-be Julie Jordan, toddler Johnny Jnr. and baby Vito flew over and moved into The Heartbreakers' communal base. Unlike Walter and Billy, who grudgingly put up with the ensuing domestic chaos, Jerry Nolan relocated:

> I was able to move out of The Heartbreakers' house, which was just mad-
> ness with Johnny's wife and kids. So I moved out to Harrow in the Hills.
> My methadone doctor – he was Keith Richards' doctor too – got me my
> own home, a beautiful apartment. That's how great they treat you over
> there, how good they are. American methadone programs treat you like
> shit.   – *Village Voice*

All the starry trappings that had been withheld from the band in NY start-ed to come their way but, like the deal with Track, the pay-off was always parti-ally obscured for one reason or another. Footage of the Anarchy tour, filmed by Julian Temple, was shelved, although The Heartbreakers did crop up in Don Lett's *Punk Rock Movie*. Meanwhile, the press reported that Johnny T. would be appearing in The Who's movie *Quadrophenia*. However, as The Who were in the process of legally distancing themselves from their management team at Track, it was nothing but a long shot disguised as publicity.

For a while, The 'Breakers became press darlings and all those tales they

West Side Story transported to the UK. (*Chris Walters / Relay*)

drawled about gang warfare, home-made zip guns and scoring smack were
lapped up like tutti frutti until the flavour wore thin. Instead of musical CVs,
the band's history was presented like a trailer for a Martin Scorsese movie. Walter
Lure: 'We all come from New York gangs. Each one is made up of lower-mid-
dle-class kids who think they're in a band or somethin'. Sure, we had street corner fights all the time. Somethin' to do, y'know. Sure we used weapons: zip guns,
car aerials … boy, whip someone in the face with one of those, boy, and he's
scarred for life. Rumbles usta start real easy, but I never broke nobody's neck.'

Gang Tours …

Jerry Nolan: 'Gangs tended to be run on almost military lines. You had
officers, vice presidents, presidents and the like – there was a lot of discipline
involved. A lot of gangs were more powerful because they had better strategy.
But fights between rival gangs were often very heavy – killings sometimes, stab-
bings – a lot of serious injury. It's even more frightening to look back on it now.'

In their press kit, Nolan claimed previous membership in the Ellery Bops,
Master Chaplains and the Young Lords (the junior branch of the Phantom
Lords), while Walter Lure flew the flag for the Green Dogs. Lacking the New
York credentials, Billy Rath upped his status by admitting that he had once
spent an entire weekend with a Girl Guide troop and survived, and Johnny
reckoned he'd run with the 90th Street Fast Boys. Later, Thunders retracted his
involvement, stating that he preferred 'hangin' out in parks'. His baseball bat
really had been for sport, not cracking heads. Continuing with the gang theme,
the band announced that they were going to call their long awaited debut
album *L.A.M.F.*, 'Like A Mother Fucker' being a spray-can warning to keep off

Johnny and the boys consider changing their name to The Junkies. (*Roberta Bayley*)

gang turf. If one mob decided to muscle in on another's territory, they'd prefix the opposing team's Mother Fucking tag with D.T.K. (Down To Kill). Unfortunately, when Tom Petty trod on the toes of their shiny buckled boots and called his band The Heartbreakers, he had corporate protection. Seizing the moment, Johnny and Co. considered a new moniker.

JOHNNY: I think we should change our name to the The Junkies.
JERRY: Yep, he's right.
PRESS: But you'd never get any airplay with a name like that.
JOHNNY: Who fuckin' needs it. The name will provoke a reaction.
JERRY: Walter's seen Tom Petty's Heartbreakers.
WALTER: They're a bunch of pigs.
JERRY: Yeah … but dead.
TOM PETTY: Born to be punched.
JOHNNY: We don't wave flags for or against drugs. Imagine how young kids are gonna get off telling their parents they're going out to see a band called The Junkies.

Aside from some Junkies' badges, the name passed into the annals of rock's 'What Might Have Been'. Commercial suicide, probably.

Preparations for *L.A.M.F.* began when the band booked into Essex Studios on 20–22 February 1977, where they recorded four demo tracks; 'Let Go', Thunders and Nolan's revved-up line to an inhibited chick, the gleeful pessimism of 'Born To Lose', a grinding 'Chinese Rocks' complete with the drooling, junk hungry 'Ooohs and Ahhhs' of the backing vocals, plus Waldo and Jerry's study of introspection, 'All By Myself'. It was all so promising. The following month, Track taped two of their live shows at the Speakeasy, the performances intended as a warm up for the album. Through March, The Heartbreakers set to work on their debut platter, returning to Essex where they laid down – 'All By Myself', 'Let Go', 'Get Off The Phone', 'I Wanna Be Loved', 'Can't Keep My Eyes On You' and 'I Love You' – a perfect rundown of The Heartbreakers' low life cynicism bouncing off Thunders' penchant for rock 'n' roll valentines. Rather than using an outside producer, Track associates Speedy Keen and Danny Secunda sat in behind the mixing desk. The action then switched to The Who's Studio, Ramport in Battersea, where the band recorded eight more tracks: 'Goin' Steady', 'Baby Talk', 'Do You Love Me', 'Born To Lose', 'Chinese Rocks', 'Pirate Love', 'It's Not Enough', and 'One Track Mind'.

However, it was with the release of 'Chinese Rocks' / 'Born To Lose' on 20 May 1977, that the fun began. Somewhere between the studio and the manufacturing plant, the sound got dragged through mud. Walter Lure: 'The record wasn't really up to par production wise. Somebody said the voice is too loud, so Johnny said to have it different. We forgot that when you get it out of a studio and put it on a record the sound changes. No one heard it before it was finally released, and the voice was too low.' Problems also arose with the twelve-inch version of the single, owing to an excess of vinyl on the disc. Despite the setbacks, within a week of its release 'Chinese Rocks' sold 20,000 copies and sailed to the number one spot in the alternative charts, briefly outpacing The Pistols' 'God Save The Queen'.

For a first outing, 'Chinese Rocks' was pretty antagonistic, the lyrics wide open to praise (for its lack of moral posturing) or condemnation. The NME's Charles Shaar Murray knew which side he was on when he commented:

> Anyone who sings 'I'm living on a Chinese Rock' deserves to be marooned
> on one ... you cool fool!

'
Thunders spat back the critical venom when he announced 'They can hate fuckin' heroin and still like 'Chinese Rocks', either they like it or they don't fugginlahkit.' Track's publicity department flooded the market with 'Chinese Rocks' T-shirts and badges, and Johnny explained the dedication to 'the boys on Norfolk St' which appears on the back of the record sleeve, to anyone brave enough to ask. 'It's a street of closed up buildings, boarded up windows and nailed up doorways, basement clubs, Puerto Ricans and black guys, very heavy junkies. It's a very heavy area to be in. Any white boy in the neighbourhood is definitely there for one reason. It's not easy to walk down that street. You've got to know how to take care of yourself if you live in New York.'

Before setting off on the extensive 'Chinese Rocks' tour, the band tried to fix the sound on the rest of the tracks at different studios, but mixed nothing but trouble for themselves. At Olympic, one harassed engineer marked the tape boxes as '2 downers before the overdubs.' Walter Lure: 'It sounded great in the studio, but as soon as it went on record it sounded fucked up. We couldn't get around that, every time we gave them a tape it sounded screwed up.' The Heartbreakers started bickering amongst themselves, growing ever more agitated. Given the way Thunders and Nolan had felt regarding the production of The Dolls' two albums, the possibility of a reprise was almost too much to contemplate, and they sought in vain to rectify the situation before *L.A.M.F.* was unleashed on the public. As tapes later found from the sessions testify, The Heartbreakers played their parts brilliantly, and Keen and Secunda did no wrong. Therefore, the problem was either down to the cutting process or the manufacturing. Although their record company was entering its twilight, Track had a history of quality, from Jimi Hendrix to The Who, yet none of the personnel there seemed to notice the discrepancies between the master tapes and the finished product.

Escaping from the insanity of the studio, The Heartbreakers made ready to go on the road, accompanied by their new tour manager, Leee's friend and Johnny's former room mate, Gail Higgins Smith. Meanwhile, the music papers announced the forthcoming 'Chinese Rocks' dates:

> Johnny Thunders and The Heartbreakers set out next week on a twenty-four venue tour extending until the end of June. The dates are split into two legs to allow for a four week TV and promotional visit to Europe starting in mid May; taking in Holland, Belgium and France.

Petrol fumes, hitchers, a million greasy spoons, and a hostage situation. Who could have asked for more? On 3 June, prior to The Heartbreakers' concert at Leeds Polytechnic, a gun toting stranger prowled the corridors of The Wesley Hotel, where the band were staying. Gail Higgins Smith: 'We were in our hotel room. Johnny and Julie were travelling separately and hadn't got there yet. A guy knocked on our door and said "Could you please keep the noise down?" We weren't making that much noise, but he came back five minutes later with the same request, then pointed a gun at me and said: "Get in the room, I'm from the secret service." Inside there was some of the support band, Slaughter And The Dogs, a roadie and Billy and Jerry. He told us that the hotel was surrounded and there was a man on the roof with a shot-gun trying to kill us, and that he'd been sent to protect us. We didn't know if this was true or if he was just a madman. He kept going out into the hall saying "I'm just checking with the rest of the secret service about the situation, you can't leave yet." We were going, "We have a sound check to do." He was going, "You can't leave, it's

Gail and Johnny.
(*Robert Ellis*)

too dangerous." This went on for about four hours, everyone was getting bored and pissed off. Then the phone rang and it was Walter from downstairs, asking me to come and buy him lunch. I was thinking about how do they do this in the movies, to warn someone that they're in trouble. In the end he came up and the gunman opened the door, pointed the gun at him and said, "Shut up and get inside." Now we're all in this room except Johnny and starting to get convinced that he'd set this up as some sort of joke cos he was the only one not there. Finally, the gunman goes out into the hall and says "My superiors says you can leave now, the coast is clear but because I'm in the secret service, if you call the police, they'll deny I exist." I called the police anyway. They came along and had to fingerprint all of us because they had to take prints from the whole room, to see if there were any of the gunman's. Johnny still hadn't arrived and the fingerprints on the back of *L.A.M.F.* are mine, not Johnny's.'

If nothing else, at least the sleeve artwork for the album was coming together!

DS Lorriman from the Leeds police commented at the time: 'We are treating the matter very seriously and are making further inquiries, including running a check on The Heartbreakers.' Any suspicions the local constabulary may have had

Track Records
Publicity Photo.

about the band were confirmed when certain parties smashed up a payphone trying to get at the change inside. As for the gunman, he was picked up three weeks
later trying to steal a car. A plastic replica of a gun was found on his person.

In between all the dramas the tour continued, the audiences wooed by The
Heartbreakers' brand of malicious romance. Barry Cain reported back for
Record Mirror:

> 'You asked for it,' warns Johnny. 'If you wanna pass the hat around all
> donations will be accepted ...' and cracks into 'Do You Love Me'. Nolan
> is a blur, Rath cruises, Lure sings / plays like there's no next second, let
> alone tomorrow. Second encore: 'Take A Chance' and a stroke of genius –
> 'Chinese Rocks' reprisal. It's so good it hurts. That's no joke.

Noticing Thunders and Nolan's growing status in blighty, Mercury Records
saw a chance to recoup and reissued The Dolls' albums as a single package, piously
trumpeting in their advertising blurb 'Before anyone discovered New Wave
Rock, The Dolls were inventing it.' Still, at least it gave all those who had thought
The Dolls were an offshoot of Max Factor, the opportunity to quickly run out and

Pasta Times: 'Spaghetti by Thunders': J.T.
Heartbreakers at home. London '77. (*Bob Gruen*)

Track Records promo
picture.

'The Al Pacino look': J.T.
(*Bob Gruen*)

paint lipstick logos on the back of their leather jackets to hide The Clash tag.

JOHNNY: They gonna put out the two Dolls' albums in a double package next
           month, even the record companies can see The Dolls' influence now.
JERRY: They should remix the fuckin' albums an' not just re-release them.
           Hey. We gonna get any money outta that deal?

    In his liner notes for the reissue, journalist Tony Parsons wrote.:'They [The
Dolls] were the major influence on such English New Wave Bands as The
Pistols, The Clash and The Damned'.
    Then without warning the Home Office pulled away its eyepatch of finest
bureaucratic silk-lined red tape and cast its freshly released tunnel vision on
documents concerning The Heartbreakers' work visas. An official letter was immediately issued, ordering them out of England within twenty-four hours. An
extreme statement, to say the least, as one is normally given advance warning of
several weeks. The trouble dated back to the band's original entry for the
Anarchy tour, when they had showed up without work permits. Track Records,
however, rectified this once the group signed with them. Spokesman Alan
Edwards: 'As far as we know the band have their work permits in order, and
their exchange permit has been OK'd by both the English and American
Musicians Unions.' In spite of this, their passports were removed by the Home
Office, and the band's gigs became open to speculation. Leee Black Childers
lodged an appeal and was told the decision would be handed down on 4 July –
American Independence Day. The Heartbreakers had been planning to hoist
the star-spangled banner over Hyde Park with a concert and a thousand
pounds-worth of fireworks to celebrate both the date and the success of their
single. The Greater London Council fell over its pin-striped shoe laces in its
haste to turn down the application. The GLC also put the veto on Old Glory
lighting up Hampstead Heath.
    The Heartbreakers' grand plans fizzled out, but they made the most of a
temporary reprieve by the Home Office when they appeared at the Vortex Club
in Wardour street. However, the event was soured by the headlining band.
Walter: 'The Buzzcocks didn't want us to steal their fucking show. They
wouldn't let us have our gear in the place until they had finished. The club
owner told them about it. It was their show and we were going to do a special
set after, but then they wanted us to go on before them at about fuckin' two in
the afternoon. It was a pity all the shit started creeping into the scene.'
    Regardless of the hostility, the night belonged to The Heartbreakers. As this
was to be their last gig for the time being, the audience swelled to include various members of Generation X, The Damned and The Clash.
    Grown desperate for legal grounds to keep the band in England, Track
suggested that they marry the secretarial staff from their Carnaby Street offices.

A spokesman from the company, with all the wit of The Heartbreakers' manager, sneered: 'If it was Peggy Lee, I'm sure they'd find a way round the problem.'

Anxious to keep his charges in the UK, Leee knew that a protracted absence would be a crucial set back, as the release date for the band's forthcoming album loomed. Back home there was little to sustain The Heartbreakers, save for continual gigging in small venues. As Childers snarled: 'Rock 'n' Roll hasn't taken off there yet. You've got CBGB's and Madison Square Gardens and nothing in between.'

An Interview With
Leee Black Childers

NINA: When did you start managing The Heartbreakers?

LEEE: In the Fall of 76. They talked to me then about managing them cos they needed some sort of management and someone to get 'em a record deal. They also talked to Tony Zinetta about managing them at the same time, and then they talked about us doing them together. I begged Ze, Tony Zinetta, to join with me, but at the last minute he backed out, said he couldn't deal with it. While this was going on, Richard Hell decided to quit. I talked to him and I tried to reason with him and get him to stay. Basically, I think it was just a big ego conflict. Half of the audience would be watching Richard Hell and the other half would be watching Johnny Thunders. There were these constant arguments. Richard left and then there was a period of looking for a bass player, and that was when I first started working with them. Once we found Billy, the first gigs we did were two nights at Max's. We placed this full-page ad in the *Village Voice* which was a huge picture, and at the bottom, it said 'plus Friday The Vest, plus Saturday Blondie' in little bitty letters, and Blondie were furious at us. I remember they all went nuts, screaming about how their name was so little, and I had to tell them that it was because it was such a privilege to support The Heart-breakers. Subsequently they all became millionaires, which serves me right! But, the shows went down fabulously, lines around the block. That was the beginning.

NINA: There was a problem, wasn't there, about getting them a record deal?

LEEE: Yeah, well, I'm sure you know the reputation that The Dolls had got-ten? Some of which was deserved. Some of which was hysteria on the part of the record companies. Business men don't wanna have to deal with personalities of any kind, much less strong, heavily destructive personalities. The record companies just didn't wanna know. There was a lot of gossip, it may have been some direct information fed from the previous people that had worked with The Dolls. Partly it was drugs, but mostly the big problem that I ran into when I talked to the record companies, was that they had gained a reputation of not showing up for gigs. Or showing up in the town but not going on for one reason or another. Or doing two songs and storming off the stage and throwing things. Of course this was pre-punk, so it was totally unheard of that anyone could act like that and expect to sell records. I didn't really have much argument for American record companies, because it was before

Leee Black Childers.
(*Linda Clark and John McKay*)

The Sex Pistols. I couldn't very well say 'Oh, but that's good that Johnny calls the audience "MotherFuckers", and that they spit at the audience and walk off stage after two songs and curse', because there was no precedent to prove to anyone that anyone would wanna buy records from someone that horrible. I was just stonewalled. Even companies like Sire, and Terry Ork, who had this little independent label, didn't want to get involved. Particularly with Johnny. He had the real bad-boy reputation. He had taken, I think, not entirely deservedly, most of the bad publicity from The Dolls.

NINA: Was he a real 'bad boy'?

LEEE: Yeah. Oh, he *is* a real bad boy. So is Nolan, and Nolan, after The Dolls, Nolan got away pretty well. Everyone still thought he was such a nice guy, and everyone thought David Johansen was a nice guy, and everyone thought Johnny was the problem. I soon learned who the *real* problem was, but whenever Johnny's name was mentioned, the American record companies didn't wanna know. That call from Malcolm

McLaren was a lifesaver as far as I was concerned, cos I wasn't getting anywhere and they couldn't just sit around in New York playing Max's Kansas City and CBGB's for the rest of their lives – even if no one expected their lives would be that long anyway.

NINA: You shared an office with McLaren, didn't you?

LEEE: Yeah. When he called me in New York and asked me if we wanted to come along on the Anarchy tour, I didn't even know who The Sex Pistols were. I asked Johnny and he thought he'd heard something about them but he wasn't sure. He thought they copied Richard Hell's look, so I called Lisa Robinson and she checked her files and found the Anarchy 'In The UK' single, the EMI one, which had been sent to her. Off we went to England without any promise of any salary. When we got to Heathrow Airport – Malcolm had sent us one-way tickets – we had no work permits, nothing had been arranged of any kind … so you can imagine! They wouldn't let us in. We had to beg and plead. On the other side, Malcolm McLaren was begging for them to let us in. If we'd come *one* day later we'd never have gotten in the country. The next day was when all the newspaper headlines came out about the Bill Grundy thing. Malcolm couldn't have got us in cos he was the biggest villain in the UK then. The next morning we still really didn't know who they were. They took us out to the Great American Disaster, a hamburger restaurant on the Fulham Road, then we went back to this little bed-and-breakfast place Malcolm had put us up in. We said 'What are they? They don't look so weird. They look OK.' Nils Stephenson, who went on to manage Siouxsie and The Banshees, poor little thing, he had spiky hair and one of those big fluffy sweaters, and in America only girls wore big fluffy sweaters. I'd previously been talking to Malcolm's secretary, Sophie, on the phone, so I when I met Nils, I kept calling him Sophie and he kept looking at me real funny.

The next morning, Nolan, who *never* sleeps, and had been wandering the streets of London all night, picked up the morning papers. He came in and woke me and threw 'em down on the bed and said: '*This* is what we're involved in now. What are we gonna do about this?' I said: 'I dunno. I guess you're gonna have to shoot the Queen for you to get in the papers now.'

NINA: When did Track Records first approach you? Jerry Nolan said EMI offered a one-single deal?

LEEE: EMI? Well, Mike Thorn was a producer and he came along. There had been all this publicity because of the Anarchy tour, all the record companies were sending their people up. The Clash got a lot of attention and we got a lot of attention. Mike Thorn really loved the band and he wanted to do a deal but EMI had, of course, just been through the

Pistols thing, and they were very reluctant to get involved with anybody again; and I think that's about as far as he got. He could offer a definite one-single deal – with all those options to blah blah blah – but it would mean they wouldn't give us a huge advance. Arista were very interested and CBS was talking to us, but then I ran into Julian Cracker. His sister used to do make-up for David Bowie. He suggested Track Records because he said they were friends of his, and he took me down there. Track Records were very weird. They had very large offices but they didn't have any acts to speak of. They had Shakin' Stevens but they weren't doing a thing with him. They had The Who and all that, but that was all gone. They were very rich, they had a lot of money. It was very weird, very laid back; Chris Stamp was really crazy and Kit Lambert was kinda wandering blindly in and out in those days. Stamp was nuts and so was Danny Secunda. They became really interested in the music that was happening on the new scene. They didn't like the straight record industry either. They just loved the idea of shocking the pants off it and doing awful things. They'd had Arthur Brown, who used to set his head on fire. And The Who, in their day, had been very shocking. Danny Secunda said, 'Sure. We'll sign The Heartbreakers up.' Without even seeing them!

NINA: Was it true that it was just some sort of weird business set up?

LEEE: Yeah. We weren't really signed to Track Records, although the label on the records said 'Track'. We were on something called 'Chris Stamp Band'. They were going through law suits to try and keep the catalogue they had, and to try to get royalties from 'Tommy'. They had to be a real, functioning record company putting out records but they didn't sign us directly to Track, because if they had then the money they promised us in the contract would be guaranteed by The Who's back catalogue. They signed us to this Chris Stamp Band thing, and promised us what was a huge advance for those days. Then, when they didn't pay it off – which they didn't – they just let the 'Chris Stamp Band' go bankrupt and we couldn't really do anything. Fortunately, we had a genius of a business manager named Peter Gerber, who has since died, who asked Stamp to personally guarantee the money with his own fortune – I mean, his name was on it – and Stamp wouldn't do it. Peter said 'In that case, if you go bankrupt, we want a clause in the contract that we get all of our tapes back.' In other words, the receiver won't get them. Stamp was furious. How dare we insult him. That a company with his name on it would ever be allowed to go bankrupt, blah blah blah. As it turned out, the best we can figure is, that was always his intention. To use us as long as they could.

    The way it worked was, Mathalda Hall, who was the only honest one really, she was a well-respected director who had come from Arista, and she really worked. Chris Stamp said to her: 'Listen, you need a holiday. Go away to Africa for two weeks.' So off she went. During that time, Stamp cut off everyone's funds, no one could get any money, he was insulting to everyone and then he just said: 'The party's over – hit the road.' As far as I know, Mathalda was furious when she got back, but by then there was nothing she could do, he had already closed up shop. Did you hear how we got the tapes? The receivers came and started noting everything down, Jan Stevens the secretary was there, and they told her 'You're being made bankrupt. Get Out.' Jan ran to a telephone and called me. By the time I got down there, everything was closed. The doors were sealed and padlocked, and the tapes were inside. The next day was a Saturday, I was with my friend, Mrs Simpson, who had been my high-school sweetheart, and she was visiting with her teenage son and her teenage boyfriend. We all piled into her little Morris Minor and went down to Carnaby Street. We had the boyfriend and the son climb up the wall and break in through a window. They found a service door that wasn't padlocked and let us in. Then we had to break into the tape vault. The whole time I'm on to my lawyer going, 'Am I doing anything illegal or what?' He was saying, 'Take only what's yours.' There were all The Who tapes, Marc Bolan tapes, Jimi Hendrix tapes and I was thinking, '*Ahhh*, I want those.' But he's saying, 'Take only what's yours and you're fine. You haven't broken any law.' So we did. We found some paint, we wanted to paint 'L.A.M.F.' real big on the walls, and my lawyer said 'No. You can't do that. That would be vandalism.' So we found this huge bit of canvas and painted 'L.A.M.F.' on that and tacked that up on the walls, and that was all right. Then we left. It was weeks before anyone realised all The Heartbreakers tapes had vanished, and they were hidden for years.

NINA: Did Johnny have Julie and the children with him?

LEEE: He had little Johnny and Vito, who we called The Sprog. Poor little thing was always on the floor, kinda crawling around on its back. They lived with us in a house in Islington, but not Jerry. Jerry refused to live with them. We had to get Jerry a separate place in Pinner. Walter and Billy and Julie and Johnny and Sprog all lived together in Chelsea in one of those luxury service flats. It cost a fortune and they all fought constantly, hated each other and threw things and broke things. The phone used to ring continuously in the middle of the night with one of them screaming about another one. It went on and on and on. Of course Walter and Billy weren't allowed to have girlfriends in because it made Julie crazy to have 'groupies' around. They [J and J and Sprog] came to live with me and then I understood everything. I was going crazy. I loved the kids, but they were just … I mean, you don't wanna have little kids around all the time, it drives you nuts.

Then Johnny went to live in Soho and around that time I stopped working for them.

NINA: Do you think there could have been any way to avoid The Heart-breakers' disintegration?

LEEE: No, not at that time. Besides themselves, there was a lot of outside destructive influences. Whispers in the ear, you know? Destructive people. Somebody whispering in Jerry's ear that he wasn't getting fair treatment – that Johnny was being treated as *the* star. Oh, they always, always, complained about it whenever they were billed as Johnny Thunders' Heartbreakers, even though there were other Heartbreakers in America that they could have been confused with. They couldn't stand it! Particularly Jerry Nolan – but they all hated it.

NINA: Jerry said – in the press – that he left because of the bad mix on *L.A.M.F.*

LEEE: Darling, first of all, this was supposed to be raw rock 'n' roll, right? First they went into Essex Studios and recorded 'Chinese Rocks' and 'Born to Lose', and they did a mix with some inexperienced engineer and the whole thing sounded raw … I thought it sounded wonderful … that was what they wanted. But Jerry didn't like it: and in those days what Jerry didn't like, Johnny didn't like, and that was the end of it. So, they had to get a more expensive studio. They were all sort of unsuccessful con artists. I love a *good* con artist who can do a big, million-dollar con. I think that's wonderful, but to do little cons like, 'We can't be at Essex Studios because we've heard about a studio that costs more' and that was really what everything was built upon – what it cost. As if there weren't gonna be any money the next day. As it turned out, they were right, there wasn't gonna be any money the next day. But I just don't think that's the way you can keep on going. We ended up in this studio across the river that was The Who's studio, and it did cost a fortune. The engineers, although undoubtedly very good, were used to all this older type rock 'n' roll stuff. The mixing sessions began, and if you just keep mixing and adding on, and mixing and adding on and getting stoneder and mixing some more, you end up with mud. So we had mud. Jerry Nolan threatened to quit the band unless he alone was al-lowed to remix. This was his big ace in the hole every time he wanted his way: 'I'll quit the band, I'll get a divorce.' So, he was brought ahead, secretly, of the other band members …

NINA: This was when they'd all been deported?

LEEE: Yeah. Everyone was back in America, and Mathalda Hall said, 'Listen, we have those awful mixes.' There's nothing I hate more than sitting

around in a studio while people mix the same song over and over, but
I had to sit there otherwise they wouldn't have mixed at all, they would
have just drunk brandy all night. So I sat there and I saw who was
twiddling the knobs and was screaming and demanding more and
demanding more: and it was the blonde one: not the brunette! I knew
good and well who'd created the mud in the first place. So Mathalda
said: 'Bring him back. It can't get any worse.'

He arrived on his own at Heathrow Airport, eating an apple and
carrying *two* passports. Which is against international law – two
American passports, both valid and he gave 'em both to the Immi-
gration guy. They called me and said that not only were they not gonna
let him in the country, but they were also gonna put him in prison. I
went down to Heathrow and I begged and I cried. Fortunately I can cry
on cue, so I begged and told them how much loss to the British rev-
enue would happen if this album didn't come out, and they relented
and forced him to destroy, or made him promise to destroy, one of the
passports. At great expense, we got him in to the studio. There was just
no point in throwing good money after bad, at that point. The only
thing that could have been done would have been to shoot Jerry Nolan
and put the rest of them back in the studio from scratch – with a drum
machine. Then, maybe they could have gotten something out of it.

NINA: Everything just disintegrated then ?

LEEE: Yeah. Jerry went away waving his arms and screaming that he'd been
screwed! Johnny, at that time was very emotionally dependent on Jerry,
and didn't know what to do, which way to turn. I think the other two
were just tired. It had been a long haul. They had worked very hard
over two years; almost constant touring, recording, doing something.
The whole time just on survival money. I mean, very few luxuries, very
few relaxing moments when they could just let their hair down and
have a party. Clearly, Walter and Billy got back to work with Johnny,
so it wasn't anything personal, everyone had to just stop. I know I did.
I didn't know which other way to go. I had fought and clawed and lied
and cheated and done everything I could do to keep them working as
a band. I couldn't think of what the next move should be. I was
exhausted too.

'Ready in five minutes boys?' Tuning up for the Village Gate gig, '77.
(*Bob Gruen*)

4
So Many Stains And Wishes

NEW YORK ROCKER: How does it feel to be back in New York, Johnny?'

THUNDERS: I hate it … its *sooooo* baw-ring.

The Heartbreakers return to New York must have seemed the perfect mirror for their mood when they stepped off the plane into the total blackness and chaos of a gigantic power failure, the wonderful hieroglyphics of Manhattan's neon vanishing in sequence under the heel of a blackout. Once electricity was restored, the band were surprised to find that essentially, nothing in their city had really changed while they'd been away. The same bands played the same clubs to the same audience. CBGB's was still the centre of NY's punk universe, but overall the scene was more subterranean than in England.

JON SAVAGE: When you walked out on the streets of New York, did you get stared at?

WALTER LURE: They couldn't figure it out. 'Why, they're wearing ties with no collars, clothes that made no sense, weird-looking hair.' Y'see, the punk thing hasn't hit there nationally, just underground.
                    – *Sounds*, October 1977

While the band got their bearings, Johnny met up with his family and told them that he was going to do the decent thing. Anyone who could turn out the sort of love songs that Thunders did, had to be the marrying kind. Mariann Bracken: ' When Johnny originally met Julie, she was about three months pregnant. Johnny knew he wasn't the father. She had the baby and they named him Johnny. When Vito came along they decided to get married in a civil ceremony. We hoped that this was a good move for them. On the way home from the wedding reception, it was announced on the radio that Elvis was dead. It was 16 August 1977.'

Once the confetti and rice had been brushed away, The Heartbreakers tried to make the most of their enforced eviction by rehearsing, and working up some new material. Any plans to play live were initially sketchy, 'Not unless,' quoth Walter Lure, 'we arrange some sort of special gig.' The 'special' gig turned out to be a three-night stand at the Village Gate.

The *New York Rocker*'s Roy Traikin made it backstage for the second show:

The dressing room was a scene of utter chaos, as Leee Black Childers

Johansen and Thunders, NY August '77.
'Hey David, what colour are her eyes?': J.T. (*Bob Gruen*)

would poke his head in every few minutes and inquire ever so demurely, 'Ready in five minutes, boys?' No reaction. He smiled slightly and left. Johnny had strapped on his guitar (he somehow looks as if he is missing an arm when he doesn't have it on) and began lazily strumming. Interviewing became impossible. Childers leaned in again and tried to get someone's, anyone's attention. 'Anarchy In The UK' blared out of the juke box. The boys were oblivious. 'After "Anarchy", OK, boys?' Walter took the initiative. He blinked his eyes nervously and spit it out, 'Let's go, Johnny.' They hit the stage …

Saturday is the last gig in what's been a sell out run, Sylvain Sylvain and Robert Gordon joined the band on stage for an encore of 'Jailhouse Rock'. Richard Hell stood smiling by the bar in certain approval of the events. Thunders got a kiss from Debbie Harry and even David Johansen turned up to pay his respects, causing the *New York Rocker* to ask Johnny if he'd ever play with Johansen again:

THUNDERS: Sure, yeah. I'd fool around with him in a studio – but I'd
never be in the same band as him again.

Walter Lure, while apparently having enjoyed the Village Gate shows, hadn't been blinded to the audience's time-warp: 'Sure, it was good. It was the best

D.T.K. L.A.M.F. (*Roberta Bayley*)

New York audience we'd seen. They must have been educated the six months we went away, but they danced to us. They at least got the energy from somewhere, but they were doing the Hustle. They were *still* doing that, man, jumpin' up and down, the whole number.'

Even if 'Chinese Rocks' had slipped by the tall dame with the torch and was now available in America, the band still had no concrete deal for the US release of their first album. The two main contenders seemed to be Ork Records and Marty Thau, maybe playing on the legendary Thunders' ego, wanted them for his own '*Johnny* Records'.

NEW YORK ROCKER: Would you consider cutting 'Chinese Rocks' or
                   something for Ork?
JOHNNY THUNDERS: Would you cut off your head and eat it?

With the release of *L.A.M.F.* bearing down on them, Johnny and Co. figured they should at least have the front cover ready. With photographer Roberta Bayley in tow, the band set off on a trip down every backstreet the guidebooks tell you to avoid, before finally winding up in SoHo (south of Houston Street). Using some grievously worn brickwork as a backdrop, the band lined up (or rather leaned in line) for Bayley, whose photograph managed to capture the atmosphere of the surroundings as well as The Heartbreakers, who looked every mean inch a part of them.

Walter Lure: 'We went out one night and took some pictures and sent them

David, Johnny and
Debbie Harry at
the Village Gate,
NYC, August '77.
(*Bob Gruen*)

over to England. They liked the one they used, and anyway they were so tired of us fighting [over the sleeve] that they put it out'.

It was then that Jerry Nolan left for England, to try and remix the album.

Billy and Walter had their own suspicions, and returned to London not long after the drummer. Thunders, of course, missed his flight and it wasn't until September that the band got to put the finishing touches to their pre-album EP: 'One Track Mind' / 'Can't Keep My Eyes On You' / 'Do You Love Me'. It seemed the chance to move out of the forever-dimming cult spotlight was within easy grasp at last. A major UK tour was planned to coincide with the release of *L.A.M.F.* on 3 October. Unfortunately, like their record company, The Heartbreakers' days were already numbered. Knowing full well that the tide was about to take everything away, Track threw a pre-release album party in their Carnaby Street office.

Working against the clock and each other, the band tried to salvage *L.A.M.F.* Jerry Nolan claimed he remixed a total of nine tracks, pressurised all the while by the record company's promotion squadron, with their 'fixed schedules to meet', and the ever popular, 'Look, we've booked advertising for certain dates'. Even before the album came out, Nolan knew that principle was going to force him to leave the band. Jerry Nolan: 'Track said, "OK, Jerry, tell you what, let the first five thousand go out and then we'll use your mix." That's when I knew it was over. That first five thousand were gonna go out to the fans and the press, they're gonna judge us by that, right? So I told 'em they could shove the five thousand up their ass, and split.'

If only someone could have pinpointed the source of the problem. Every time the master tapes left the studio, they kept falling into inept hands. Jerry could have done the greatest ever mix, and it wouldn't have made a difference. The sound still would have been muddy, thanks to some engineer working a double shift and guzzling down beer while he cut the record, or a couldn't-care-less worker at the manufacturing plant. Why Track didn't advise the band to attend the cutting process will remain a mystery, like most of their manoeuvres. Maybe they were too besieged by their own problems to take heed.

Johnny's opinion of the situation appeared in the October 1977 issue of *Melody Maker*:

> What happened was we mixed it, right? And everybody liked the mix. Then Jerry Nolan went back to London ahead of us while we were still in NY. We'd heard a test pressing and liked it and then he [Nolan] started remixing the album. I was still in NY and didn't even hear what went down until the album was out. Y'know, he started screwing up all the mixes and so it sounded the way it did. Jerry didn't want the album to come out then cos he knew it was fucked up. Walter and Billy wanted it

Johnny with
Sabel Starr
and Iggy Pop,
CBGB's, '77.
'Three odd
balls': J.T.
(*Bob Gruen*)

out cos it was due three months before and they … ah … forced it out.
Then Jerry quit the band. I didn't know what was happening.

However, Johnny wasn't quite as certain as to who did the damage, when interviewed for this book, years after the episode. 'Jerry Nolan and Walter Lure
didn't get along too well, and, uh, we mixed the album, right … and still liked
it and split back to New York and Walter was still here and he fucked around
and fucked the album up and mixed … then Jerry went in and remixed it again
… and between those two they had it out and then Jerry quit.'

Track Records decided to play down whatever internal problems their main
men might have been having with an off-hand comment from Alan Edwards,
The Heartbreakers' public relations' agent: 'Jerry leaves every two weeks, so why
should this be any different?'

One interviewer asked Johnny if he was happy with *L.A.M.F.*'s production
job:

> THUNDERS: Wellll … lemme put it this way … I wouldn't put it out
>   in the States.
> INTERVIEWER: So you treat us as inferiors?
> THUNDERS: America's a bigger market …

Critics who disliked the band harked on about the murky mix, while those
that liked them blamed the production. All that potential muffled in mud.
Curiously but not unsurprisingly, the cassette of *L.A.M.F.* that came out at the
same time as the record, sounds as though it has had a shower, shave, coffee and
a cigarette in comparison, testifying to either a repeated cutting or mastering
fault in the vinyl version.

With Paul Cook sitting in for the departed Nolan, The Heartbreakers kicked off their autumn tour at Bristol Polytechnic. Steve Jones also climbed on stage for part of the set, picking up a few tips from Johnny.

> Rock 'n' Roll The Heartbreakers are through and through. Punk really isn't it at all – even if they did have half The Sex Pistols playing. It's broader and more mature; doing stuff like The Monkees' 'I'm Not Your Stepping Stone', 'Do You Love Me' and 'Sweet Little Rock 'n' Roller'. They cross barriers that other new wavers wouldn't dare to for fear of losing face. The Heartbreakers are great, hot and anybody's. All you need is a pair of ears and an open mind.   – *Sounds*, 8 October

Just when it seemed the band would be doomed to a series of temporary drummers for the duration of the tour, Track issued a statement to the press:

> Jerry Nolan is no longer a member of The Heartbreakers, but a hired musician. He will be performing with the band for all the British dates through to the Croydon Greyhound on 6 November.

Jerry Nolan: 'That's because Johnny asked me to do it, for old times' sake; so I said sure, I'll do that, I'll even train their new drummer for them.'

To their audience, at least, the band seemed to be the same mean street-roaming boys, but they still had hearts and Johnny and Jerry in particular, were hurting. Not that they showed it. Setting the tone for the evening's entertainment with a few curses, Johnny hung from centre microphone like the blood in his veins was slowly being distilled and Walter turned his cats' eyes upwards, and played with his normal vicious dexterity. Billy patrolled the corner with the usual trademark scarf knotted around one leather-clad leg while Nolan, back in his regular position, pounded the beat. No audience could have asked for more.

The Heartbreakers, however, could.

Jerry Nolan had co-founded The Heartbreakers and whatever casual remarks he issued to the press, the symptoms of suddenly finding himself a hired hand may have eaten into him deeper than even he knew. Away from the stage, Nolan seemed to take his new role to heart, showing little interest in interviews and keeping to himself for most of the tour. Thunders, never one to wallow in tact at the best of times, responded to a journalist who asked him if he was happy: 'Happy? Naw, I ain't all that happy at the moment. Christ, I'm lookin' for a drummer.'

Rumour had it that The Damned's Rat Scabies was up for the post. Thunders: 'It's not gonna be Rat Scabies. We already tried that. He's a great guy, but his style is totally different. Like sixties heavy metal.'

Nolan seemed almost on the verge of paranoia when he decided there were other factors, apart from the infamous mix, behind his reasons for quitting;

as he explained to Barry Cain from the *Record Mirror*, in a particularly cryptic interview:

> There's one guy in this band I don't like. I've discovered he's a coward, and I can't work with cowards. He's done things behind my back, he gave in to allow the album to be released. He's only interested in reading about himself in the papers. I can't live with that. There's also another guy in The Heartbreakers set up who acts more like a middle man in a drugs deal rather concentrating on what he should be doing. The whole thing's a joke and I want out.

Perhaps Thunders sensed the emotion behind the acid and no retaliation was heard. At least not in public.

On Thursday 20 October the tour climaxed with the biggest gig so far, a date at the Rainbow, with Siouxise and The Banshees, plus The Models in support: The lights dim, masking the theatre's decomposing grandeur, then spotlights are turned on an impressive backdrop of a painted street scene with a prominent pawnshop to match a line from a certain song. The band's own tape, consisting of a cut-up asylum of sounds of police sirens, falling bombs, traffic horns gone insane and a Nazi rally comes blasting out full volume as The Heartbreakers stalk onto the stage. According to your line of vision, Johnny Thunders may have thrown a brick at the illustrated pawnshop window. From the opening number it's apparent they're at their very best. It's also apparent that the bouncers are at their muscle-bound worst, taking great delight in clubbing anyone in their way and throwing them out of the hall with a kick for a memory. After Johnny stops the set long enough to comment on the antics of 'the red-shirted fuckers' the bouncers lay off for a while. Their excessive violence leaves a bitter taste with both band and audience alike.

The situation wasn't lightened by the arrest of Siouxsie and The Banshee's drummer, Kenny Morris, after the concert. They were later fined for that trusty legal standby 'obstruction'. Nobody ever said of what.

A depressed Thunders had his own problems: 'I don't have enough money; I don't have a private island and I don't have a jet.' He didn't have a drummer either. By November, Nolan had left with plans to form a band of his own, The Idols.

The Heartbreakers were now a trio looking for a replacement. Walter Lure: 'It's gonna be hard to find someone, but for a lot of the drummers on the punk scene, Jerry's their idol so we should find someone with the right style soon. It's probably better. He's a great drummer and he has a lot of good ideas, but he created a lot of problems. He's the main reason we haven't rehearsed once in the last year.'

The original drummer for The Clash, Terry Chimes, played one out-of-town date with the band, and met with their approval. With Chimes in tow, they began working on a couple of new songs, 'Too Much Junkie Business', and 'Laughing At You', written by Thunders apparently about Nolan's departure, the final line reads: 'There'll never be no one like me and you.'

By playing two nights at the Vortex, The Heartbreakers got the chance to break their new boy in and, as Johnny told the press, the opportunity to 're-move some of the bad feeling caused by over-zealous bouncers at the Rainbow'. The band seemed to have an albatross circling over them. No sooner had they found a replacement drummer, than Track shut up shop. Walter Lure: 'We didn't know at the time there was a whole lot of politics behind the scenes. Track really didn't give a shit about us at all. They were just trying to present us as a Track band because they were trying to get all this money from 'Tommy' from The Who and there was this big law suit going on cos The Who didn't want them to get it, because they said they weren't helpin' them out, weren't managing whatever for them. Track had to show to them and the lawyers that they had a record, and they were working with people: so they just used us as a front.'

At first Track clammed up, then decided that The Heartbreakers owed them £100,000. Before the fight got real dirty, the company was declared bankrupt and the group's last single on the label, 'It's Not Enough' / 'Let Go', was recalled shortly after its release. In some confusion, Thunders related to the press that he didn't anticipate any trouble with Track, as no deal had been signed and negotiations were already under way with CBS. On 13 December 1977, the Mark 3 Heartbreakers entered Riverside Studios with producer Mike Thorne to record a trio of tracks: 'London Boys' – a retort to Johnny Rotten's anti-Dolls diatribe 'New York' – as well as 'Too Much Junkie Business' – a knock-about, slice-of-street farce composed by Lure and Thunders – and a cover of The Shangri-Las' 'Great Big Kiss'. Whether the Riverside demos were intended as an incentive for CBS will never be known, but any further negotiations with the company petered out like the band's career in London. By Christmas it was black curtains in The Heartbreakers' camp. Walter Lure and Billy Rath returned to New York, where Jerry Nolan was busy working with The Idols, while Leee Black Childers issued a terse 'No Comment' to anyone left interested in a four-way divorce and drugs story. Of the band, only Johnny remained in London.

The two shows that The Heartbreakers had played at the Vortex were des-tined to be the last England would see of them as a unit for almost a decade. In the 3 December edition of *Sounds,* arch reviewer Jane Suck, gave them quite a send off:

> Heartbreakers: 'Born To Lose' / 'Baby I Was Born To Lose': but for the fact
> I love Leee Childers, and don't want him to take the first plane back to NY,
> I'd let fly … like, why are The Heartbreakers back in the Vortex? That ain't

cool, that's dumb … and, ah, why is Thunders the most arrogant slob to ever stumble across a stage? Sure, we love The New York Dolls but … '1977' / 'Hope I Go To Heaven': You won't get past the pearly gates, Johnny, not unless you drop the 'Look, Ma, I'm a star' jive. We're all jizbags in London, after all. 'Nice Rock 'n' Roll' / the same old Heartbreakers set: 'Chinese Rocks', 'Get Off The Phone' and, oh dear, 'Too Much Monkey Business' – 'scars, scars / the stars and the bars, my Carmen' – you get what you deserve, Heartbreakers, last week's laundry.

5
Night Of The Living Dead

The slate-grey shroud of winter folded itself around England's capital. 'Punk' hysteria of the Fleet Street brand had been furtively lain to rest in press morgues across the nation.

Billy and Walter flew back to New York in low spirits, Lure returning to his brownstone apartment in Brooklyn Heights and the area's seasonal greetings of frozen winos and junkies trying to sell Colt automatics to pay for their Yuletide fix. Pushing aside any plans concerning The Heartbreakers until after their extended vacation, they played a well received set at Max's Kansas City. Apart from Rath and Lure, the one-off band also boasted Ivan Julian from the Voidoids, Sylvain Sylvain, and Television's Richard Lloyd.

With the ghost of Christmas past, Johnny was left to his own devices and facing a pile of growing debts. The *NME* reported on the wolves at the door:

> The band remains in the same no-record-company limbo caused by the Track break-off, and their former publicist Alan Edwards has been relieved of his duties. More to the point, both bassist Billy Rath and guitarist Walter Lure are still ensconced in their native Manhattan, where they returned for a brief Christmas holiday two months ago. Only the band's communal pad in Chelsea is still operative, though the phone has been disconnected through lack of payment, various other amenities are in jeopardy, and important bills have apparently still not been paid.

Leaving the mail to pile up and the apartment to gather dust, Thunders and family skipped to a new flat in the seedy heart of Soho, in central London. Keeping busy until The Heartbreakers could become a viable proposition once more, Johnny strung together *The Living Dead*, a revue that played a run of gigs at the Speakeasy. A fairly casual concern, the line-up of *The Living Dead* was liable to change from week to week, but the main habitués included Patti Palladin, the feline chanteuse from Snatch; French teenager Henri-Paul, formerly of The Maniacs, the rhythm section of Eddie and The Hot Rods; Paul Gray and Steve Nicol; plus Mike Kellie and Peter Perrett from The Only Ones.

Thunders, who was greatly enamoured by the starry lyric-writing abilities and raffish persona of the Only Ones' frontman, Peter Perrett, at one point suggested that the two of them should form a band, as the reality of The Heartbreakers' getting mended started to look unlikely. Perrett:

Late night of the living dead. (*Marcia Resnick*)

Demonstrating audience
control. (*Marcia Resnick*)

Johnny wanted to form a band with me. I was happy with the way The Only Ones was going, but I liked playing with Johnny, I liked playing his music, it was a diversion and it was fun not being the frontman. †

Saturday night at the Speakeasy:

The Living Dead haunt the shadows around the stage while a twenty-four-year-old Thunders prowls across to the microphone. He looks so anaemic it's impossible. A shark's tooth earring hangs from one lobe and he glares out at the audience with a permanent expression of near-total apathy on his angular face. His eyes bore into the spotlights, hooded, like a set of ruthless wet stones. Beyond the stage, Sid Vicious desperately tries to catch his hero's attention. *

After several weeks of petitioning Thunders to allow him to join The Living Dead, Sid's wish was finally granted. Peter Perrett:

Because Johnny was his hero, he really wanted to play with him. I think Sid used to get stoned with Johnny and he promised Sid that he could play this one gig. We did a sound check and he was meant to be learning the songs – one of which was 'Stepping Stone' which The Pistols sometimes used to do – but he was totally hopeless. Maybe they played it in a different key. I said to Sid, 'Just play E'. He didn't know where E was on the bass guitar. To try and teach him, I put his finger on the fret and moved it about, but it didn't seem to sink in. After the sound check, Johnny said, 'He's too useless, I'm not going to let him play'. †

Johnny relented after Perrett pleaded for clemency on the hapless Pistol's behalf, but when it came to the gig, his amp and bass were discreetly unplugged by a roadie. Less discrete was Sid's other half, Nancy Spungen, who bounced on stage to present the band. Peter Perrett:

For a laugh, Johnny told her it would be really good if she went out top-less and introduced the group. Johnny probably didn't even notice but Sid was really hurt by it, which was ironic because half the world had probably already seen her like that. She went out topless, introduced it, then said all our names. For the first three or four songs, Sid got really into it, he was jumping up and down, posing. Then I think he must have listened out for what sort of noise he was making, cos all of a sudden he realised that noth-ing was coming out of his amp. He thought that somehow it was broken,

---

† Extract taken from *The One And Only* by Nina Antonia, S.A.F. Books

'Great guitar': J.T.

I don't know if he realised it was sabotage. He started calling out for a
roadie to fix it, but Johnny walked up to the mike and said, 'Thanks very
much, Sid, now we've got Henri-Paul coming up to play.' Sid slinked off
the stage, it was like he'd been substituted and thrown off. †

A small contingent of The Living Dead flew over to Paris, at the invitation
of the Gibus club manager, Bernard Torrent, to play three shows in the first
week of March. The dates got a varied response, and Thunders was kicked out
of two hotels for making too much noise.

The Living Dead met their demise when Johnny Thunders was reborn as a
solo artist. The opportunity for a new context arose when Dave Hill set up Real
Records. Hill, who was on his own trajectory to fame – looking after The
Pretenders – signed the guitarist for a one-off album deal. The contractual details and the pledge of a healthy advance had been mapped out by Zena Perrett,

Sex Pistols Steve
Jones and Paul
Cook at the
Speakeasy with
Johnny
Thunders.
(*Paul Slattery*)

Peter's wife and the manager of The Only Ones. However, in a moment's desperate need, Thunders traded his forthcoming advance for some ready cash. Peter Perrett:

> Zena was furious and I was really pissed off with him. He'd gone out and
> bought either a quarter ounce or a half ounce of coke or smack but he
> hadn't even got a good deal. Whenever he gave you drugs, he was really
> pleased because normally he was broke and on the scrounge, so when he
> was the person to give it to you, it made him feel good. He asked me and
> [Mike] Kellie to record the album with him but we were only available for
> a week. †

Before work began on the album which was tentatively entitled *So Alone*, Thunders first product on Real, the single, 'Dead Or Alive' / 'Downtown' was released on 26 May 1978. Joined by The Rod's Paul Gray and Steve Nicol, the 45 was an invigorating taster, Thunders flirting with his own fatalistic reputation on 'Dead Or Alive', while the flipside is an offcut from the later days of The Dolls. In co-producer Steve Lilleywhite, who worked with Thunders on all his output for Real, the guitarist had finally found a sympathetic ear.

Back in London, waiting for the *So Alone* sessions to start, Billy Rath and Walter Lure recruited Steve Nicol and Henri-Paul, and recorded a single under the name of The Heroes: 'Seven Day Weekend' / 'Too Much Junkie Business', with the intention of having it released on Speedball Records, a subsidiary of Island. Unfortunately, Speedball collapsed, and the tapes languished in no man's land for some years, until it was released on SkyDog in 1983.

With the fade-out of The Sex Pistols, Sid Vicious had gone to Thunders with the idea of forming a band around a 'Living Dead' format as a regular thing, with his beloved Nancy at the managerial reins.

> VICIOUS: Nancy's managing me at the moment, but I don't know if
>   Johnny will have enough faith in her.
> JON TOBLER: So when will we see the results of Nancy's business acumen
>   as The Living Dead get on the road?
> VICIOUS: I can't answer that. I'd like it to be today … tomorrow …
>   but there's legal hassles … and Thunders' general unrelia-
>   bility.   – *Record Mirror*

Johnny though, didn't seem to be over-confident in the idea: 'We got it to-gether a few times, but it wouldn't have worked out.'

At a reception held for Patti Smith, Thunders encountered the well-known PR man, B. P. Fallon who had made his reputation with acts like T. Rex and The Boomtown Rats. Fallon became his latest manager, and any thoughts regarding The Living Dead became purely reminiscent. Johnny:

> It was a good period. I like playing with different musicians. Actually I got
> in a rut playing with The Heartbreakers for so long.
>
>   – *Zig-Zag*

As if to prove the point, the guitarist assembled 'Johnny Thunders' Rebels' with Steve Jones, Paul Cook and Henri-Paul. Work began on putting together a new set with a different edge that featured, amongst others, a cover of the Chantay's echoing instrumental 'Pipeline', Nancy Sinatra's classic 'These Boots Are Made For Walking', and a collection of songs from Thunders in a slower, more interior mood than ever before: 'I always had a lotta slow songs, but they didn't wanna do 'em in The Heartbreakers. I always wanted to do 'em but we never did "It's Not Enough" on stage. Jerry didn't like playing slow songs … I got my chance to do it now.' (*Zig-Zag*).

The old love and drugs, and love of drugs, Thunders / Heartbreakers numbers now found themselves side by side with more introspective material. From a past that most people didn't know existed, Thunders retrieved 'You Can't Put Your Arms Around A Memory', and reanimated 'I Am Confronted', circa the Actress period, as 'So Alone'. Other numbers followed, including 'She's So Untouchable', but just to show the poison sacs were still as full as ever, Thunders also introduced 'London Boys', from the tail-end of the 'Breakers'. What sweet irony to rebuke Rotten while playing with two members of his old band.

Dave Hill: 'They had such empathy, Steve [Jones] and John together. It would've been a great band, it really would, but John just screwed it up and Steve and Paul couldn't take any more and they left. So that was another chance down the drain. It was really great, even when they were only rehearsing, but they did play together a few times down at the Speakeasy.'

Nick Kent offered his opinions in the *NME*'s 29 April issue:

> Immediate plans call for the band to record 'Pipeline' at the very least, and they will probably work as a unit for the whole of Thunders' up-coming album. As far as Thunders is concerned, though, it is his last shot. If he blows this one, it really is all over. Brooklyn sass meets Shepherds Bush rock action – an intoxicating mixture, no doubt about it.

The Rebels didn't last, but Thunders carried most of his material from their set on to the album, and continued to work with Jones and Cook in the studio, alongside Chrissie Hynde, Phil Lynott, Patti Palladin, John Irish Earle, Walter Lure, Billy Rath, Steve Marriot, and, from The Only Ones, drummer Mike Kellie, guitarist John Perry, and Peter Perrett, who joined the ensemble between touring commitments, plus Steve Nicol, Paul Gray, Henri-Paul and Zena Perrett's sister, Koulla Kakoulli. The sessions were split between Island Records' Studios in Hammersmith and Basing Street. Peter Perrett:

> Me and Kellie ended up doing the first half of the album. I played guitar and sang backing vocals. The session was as together as anything Johnny was involved in, like during the 'So Alone' track itself, in the middle of the lead break, he fell over. He just fell backwards into Kellie's drums. The lead guitar stops and there's a great big crash. I thought they should have put it on the record because it summed up how things could get with Johnny. †

Unfortunately, the title track was left off the album, as was a version of Marc Bolan's 'The Wizard'. Both would be unearthed when the album came out on CD, after Thunders' death.

In August 1978, Real Records began the album's promotional thrust with a suitably glowing press handout:

> A peerless collection of musicians held together by the dominant person-ality of Johnny Thunders. In fact *So Alone* is the first solo album in many a moon to really reflect the personality of its creator. A complete album, it has plenty of balls, quirky humour and, perhaps most impressively, plenty of tender moments on emotive ballads such as 'Memory' and 'Untouch-able'. *So Alone* is a rare treat of an album.

But Johnny's luck was running true to form, and not long after finishing the album there came yet another Home Office order to leave the country. Thunders:

They escorted me on the plane and made me go back. I had a manager who never took care of all my business – my passport extensions and stuff. It got worse and worse and they threw me out.... New York's really a drag. It's nothing like it used to be. All the kids I used to hang out with are either dead or in jail.   – *Zig-Zag*

On Johnny's return, The Heartbreakers made it up long enough to play a series of shows at Max's. The *NME*'s Tony Parsons accosted the jet-lagged duo, Rath and Lure, at CBGB's.

> WALTER: We're just playing together until Johnny goes back to England
>   for that one-off date at the Lyceum next month to promote his
>   album, *So Alone.*
>
> PARSONS: So it's just money for sweets, eh? Who you using for a drum-
>   mer now?
>
> BILLY: Anyone we can, man ...
>
> PARSONS: But John's coming back to NY after that show, ain't he?
>
> BILLY: Yeah. He wants The Heartbreakers to reform when he gets
>   back ... but we don't wanna.
>
> WALTER: He's too unreliable.

The Heartbreakers with their usual patent for paradox set off on a mini-tour that took them as far afield as Los Angeles and San Francisco. Fresh from the coast, Thunders then joined up with local boys, The Senders, a rhythm 'n' blues combo whom he considered at that time to be 'the only good band in NY', to help them out on a short-term basis while they hunted for a guitarist to replace their own who had split in the middle of a series of dates.

In mid September Nancy Spungen made the arrangements for Sid to play Max's. Peter Crowley, manager of the club, seemed concerned about Vicious' health – a fact that *Rolling Stone* Magazine would play up in its 30 November copy:

> His four shows at the club, with former members of The NY Dolls and
> The Heartbreakers [Jerry Nolan's mob, The Idols – Arthur Kane, Steve
> Dior and Barry Jones] received a mixed reaction. Friends said the idea of
> forming a new band appealed to Sid but represented a terrible labour. 'Sid
> was extremely weak,' said Peter Crowley. 'He was not well physically and
> he was getting beaten up regularly at the methadone clinic. He was very
> depressed.'

Beside backing Vicious at his run of gigs, Jerry Nolan kept an eye out for Sid and Nancy, and after they got attacked while trying to score, the drummer introduced them to his methadone programme. A small mercy in a tough town.

The 'Johnny Thunders' Allstars' concert, London Lyceum, 12 October 1978. The Only Ones' Mike Kellie keeps the beat. (*Chris Horler*)

Meanwhile back in London, Real Records released the 'Memory' / 'Hurtin'' (B-side co-written with Henri-Paul) single in both the standard seven-inch size and a limited edition twelve inch, in a variety of coloured vinyl including blue, pink and ordinary black. Despite the push behind it, the record company was still taken by surprise at the amount it sold, and had failed to press up enough copies, thus blowing it for Thunders, who could well have found himself with a hit record on his hands. On Monday 9 October the guitarist took flight number Air India 116 into Heathrow in preparation for the prestigious Lyceum gig. Billed as *Johnny Thunders' Allstars* the show was intended to coincide with the release of the album, and to feature most of the players involved. However, certain members of the team dropped out of sight including, on a more peripheral front, B. P. Fallon.

Although touted as joining the line-up at the Lyceum, Steve Jones and Paul

Cook made a last minute exit. Thunders: 'Malcolm wouldn't let them do it, said I might be a bad influence on 'em. Nuthin' was said, but Malcolm didn't want them involved. Paul, I get on with alright, Steve … he's an egomaniac, I think, nothin' specific just his general behaviour. He thinks he's a guitar hero. A pity he learned all his riffs from me, which is quite evident on the Pistols' album. I'm not losin' any sleep over them not playing.'

Any of Thunders' detractors had to take a back seat to the wave of enthusiasm the release of *So Alone* generated.

> The first surprising thing to a lot of people will I'm sure, be the overall excellence of this here recording. Mr Thunders is, of course, one of Rock 'n' Roll's more erratic luminaries – one night's Jet Boy, the next night's snailman. It's a part of his magic to be sure – like The Stones, his mistakes make him more loveably human, that much more believably real than those flawless characters who make up the Bruce Forsyth contingent which dominate rock as it does all other entertainment forms.
>
> – GIOVANNI DADOMO, *Sounds*, 14 October 1978

> THUNDERS: I'm pretty happy with the album, well, ninety-nine per cent of it anyway.
> ZIG-ZAG: What's the one per cent?
> THUNDERS: I don't wanna get into that. Might offend some people.
> ZIG-ZAG: How long did the album take to do?
> THUNDERS: About three weeks. Much easier than before. I was in complete control and had nobody to argue with.
>
> – *Zig-Zag*, November 1978

'Say, Mama, will ya come out tonite?' 12 October, the anniversary of the death of black leather's first champion, the great Gene Vincent; also the night of the *Allstars*' concert. Johnny sways out first, a bleached figure in bandanna and gypsy velvets, and kicks off the set with 'Pipeline' – which instantly blows out his amp. Thunders looks through glazed eyes, mutters 'aw … fuck …' and shakes his head. The rest of the gig is beset by various electrical problems – angry punters get tired of sonic whistles doing damage to their ear drums and start to heckle, some of the crowd are angry at the non-showing of the two ex-Pistols, others at the quality of the sound. Johnny sneers out the introduction to 'London Boys' with: 'It's great to be back in London … I shoulda stayed in Queens.' Next up is 'Great Big Kiss', Patti Palladin trading verses with Thunders, the teenage ghosts of Mary, Marge, Betty and Mary Ann Shangri-La aching to join in. Somewhere between songs someone bellows out a question concerning Johnny's religion. Thunders: 'Naw … I ain't fuckin' Jewish. Do I look Jewish? It must be the nose.' 'These Boots Are Made For Walking' runs into The Senders' 'Living End', 'Born to Lose' and 'Japanese Socks'. The encore, 'Be Bop A Lula', was for the spirit of Vincent, not the audience, and Thunders walked off stage without even a backward glance.

Friday the 13th is spent giving interviews and eating grapes for his sore throat, and contemplating the fate of Sid Vicious who had been arrested in New York for the murder of Nancy Spungen.

THUNDERS: Sid? uh … it's horrible. Well, he beat out Keith Richard for the story of the year ‡ … that's heavy. Poor Sid. (Thunders is dissecting cigarette papers on the table, which he has laid out in the shape of a crucifix.) Wow. The poor guy, man. I feel worse for him than her. It's the worst thing that could ever happen to him anyway.

SOUNDS: What will you be doing when you get back to the States?

THUNDERS: My dream come true. I've got someone to finance me to go to New Orleans and I'm gonna try and find a bunch of old black musicians and start a band with them … rhythm and blues, rock 'n' roll, New Orleans is full of the greatest music you ever heard in your life.

SOUNDS: What if the proposed band concept falls through?

THUNDERS: I'll find somebody else; a sax player … three chick singers.

SOUNDS: How is life for you at the moment – how do you feel about things?

THUNDERS: It's progressing.

SOUNDS: It's looking up?

THUNDERS: Huhhh … couldn't get no worse.

– ANDY COURTNEY, *Sounds*

With 'Memory' and 'So Alone' at numbers seventeen and seven respectively in the alternative charts, Johnny got ready to leave the UK for that capital of gamblers and vampires, New Orleans. Prior to his departure, he was spotted by *Zig-Zag's* 'family tree' man, Pete Frame, selling off complementary copies of his album to a second-hand record shop. He would have got more if he'd autographed them first.

---

‡ Following a drugs bust in Canada, Richards was fined and ordered to play two shows for the blind.

An Interview With
Dave Hill

NINA: Why, out of all the people you could have signed up, did you choose Johnny Thunders?

DAVE: Why did I pick on Johnny? Because he was basically a hero, in a sense. I saw The Heartbreakers play in very early 77 at Dingwalls and they were just one of the most exciting things I've ever seen. When the opportunity came that John wanted to do some of the other side of his stuff, less rock 'n' roll, more of his personal songs – I'd heard some of the demos of those songs and I was really impressed with them, I thought it was a viable project. I mean, you had the rock 'n' roll side *and* these really great songs. I thought we could make a great record and show people that John had a lot more to offer than just this image of a loser, a rock 'n' roll loser. I still think he has a lot more than that, but that's why I wanted to get involved in it, really. I liked the guy, I thought it was incredibly exciting, plus I thought it would make a good record which would have a very wide appeal.

NINA: What was he like to work with?

DAVE: Disastrous, really, that's the one word I can say, it was just totally un-together. It could have been so much better, if John had been in a better state, but he wasn't. Any money we had, he would just go and spend on drugs. It was all done very slap-shod, we'd waste a lot of money in the studio, we'd waste a lot of time in the studio. Considering how it was done, I'm amazed how well it turned out, but like I said before, I think it could have been a perfect record but unfortunately it isn't.

NINA: Oh, I still think it was a great record.

DAVE: Yeah, it's a really good record but I don't think it's perfect and I think John would agree, but also I think John was the reason why it wasn't a perfect record.

NINA: Why didn't 'The Wizard' or 'So Alone' tracks appear on the album?

DAVE: 'The Wizard' never got finished, that was the thing; they just did that and sort of fooled around and it was never finished enough to put on the B-side. The title track of the album, 'So Alone', was never finished and it was supposed to be. It was a great song and it was to have been a real focal part of the album and it was never finished because John was too untogether to finish it – it was one of those days. Some of the days he'd go into the studio and everything would be just great and they'd get stuff done really quickly, and the next time it would just take hours for him to tune up a guitar.

NINA: How well did it sell? It seemed to do pretty well in the alternative charts.

DAVE: It did really well. The single was almost a hit but for various sort of record-company reasons it wasn't; they didn't press enough twelve inches. I think it could've been a hit. It caught them by surprise; it sold very well and I was really pleased with it. I think people consider it John's best work, I certainly do, I wish it could've been how we really wanted it to be. There's a lot of different producers involved in that, different people trying to produce it, one minute Steve Jones, the next minute would be Peter Perrett, the next it would be Johnny, the next would be B.P Fallon, so it was all chaotic.

NINA: How long did B. P. Fallon manage Johnny? It seemed to be about a month, not a very lengthy partnership at all.

DAVE: No, I don't think he could handle it. John would let anybody work with him, he was a very soft guy in the sense of, if somebody came along and thought they were trying to help him John would encourage them, so at the end there'd be all these people involved in it, just to add to the chaos. We had a week's rehearsals booked for the *Allstars* gig, and I think John probably rehearsed one day over that week – I made sure he got there the week before; but he just didn't do any work, didn't turn up for rehearsals, or turned up stoned.

NINA: Apparently some people were disappointed at the *Allstars* gig because not everyone who worked on the album showed up.

DAVE: The only people that were supposed to turn up who didn't, were Steve Jones and Paul Cook. They were advertised to play and they were going to play but Steve Jones was in America and couldn't get back and Paul didn't want to do it without Steve, so that's why it didn't happen, which was a shame. But I mean that concert was untogether in the sense that it hadn't been rehearsed properly, we'd planned for it all to be rehearsed and to be a really good concert, but it wasn't as good as it could have been, yet again.

NINA: Did Chrissie Hynde enjoy working with Johnny?

DAVE: Oh yes, she had a laugh. At one stage The Pretenders were talking about recording one of John's songs – 'Memory' or 'Untouchable', something like that. A lot of people really thought they were good songs and John has a lot of other good songs as well. I just wish he could get it together to do those songs properly. Maybe it will happen but I doubt it somehow, but she [Chrissie Hynde] really respects his work a lot, really does.

NINA: Where was Johnny and his family living at the time of *So Alone*?

DAVE: He was living in Soho with his wife, Julie, and his two kids, about two blocks away from my office. He was living above a brothel or underneath a brothel [in D'Arblay Street, over a 'sauna'] and there'd always

Scars and Stripes. (*Marcia Resnick*)

be problems going on. I'd come to work about ten o'clock in the morning and invariably John would be sitting outside my office, on the floor, waiting for me to get in, demanding money or there'd be some problem or other to sort out.

6
Too Fast To Live

In February's first cold week in New York, Sid Vicious, a tragic young man without the talent to strengthen his dreams, died of an 'accidental overdose' while on bail for the fatal stabbing of Nancy Spungen. One of the first people to have seen Vicious after his release from prison on Riker's Island, where he had undergone heroin detoxification, was Jerry Nolan: 'Me and Sid were very close. The day he got out of jail, he was looking great, very clean, he had brand new clothes on. Malcolm [McLaren] happened to have bought him new jeans, new boots and a new sweater, and I gave him my black and white motorcycle jacket. We got to talking, the conversation started getting a little serious – he brought up Nancy – he said, "I'm kind of feeling low", though he wasn't into no suicidal talking – he says, "You know, Jerry, I'm going to fight this thing." When Sid got arrested, the police made some not very clear comments about something that gave them some information, by what he said, that led them to believe that he did stab her. I knew Sid, he was pretty egotistical, but he wasn't the sort of guy who'd put himself on edge, just for the attention. He looked me dead in the eye, cos he knew that Nancy had been in love with me at one time. I never had a relationship with her, we were friends. I respected her and liked her because she was one of the few people that understood where The Heartbreakers were coming from musically. Sid knew this and he said, "Jerry, I didn't touch her. I didn't stab Nancy." I believe that.'

It was left to Thunders, at a later date, to record an effective goodbye in 'Sad Vacation'. Often introduced live as being to 'My man, Sid …' the lyrics say it all: 'I'm sorry I didn't have more to say, maybe I could have changed your fate.' Even that's doubtful, but it was a well-meant premise. Talking of destiny, Johnny still hadn't made it to New Orleans. With his career seemingly running in a circle and his heroin problem now out of hand, the music papers, never his most loyal supporters after The Dolls, began branding him a loser and printing snide asides about his longevity – or lack of it. The Heartbreakers reformed for a series of ongoing 'Farewell' gigs, Jerry Nolan occasionally making it back to the drum seat. As journalist Richard Gabriel put it: 'They still choose to play the parts of decadent bad-boy rockers living dangerously close to the edge. It's really a sad and shallow image, but after all this time they wouldn't know what to do without it. It remains an article of faith that the entire band could be found slumped over dead in some closet at any time.'

If only the band had been play-acting, it might have made it a little easier. Jerry Nolan: 'We were very selfish. We wouldn't go on stage until somebody delivered our drugs, and the kids were waiting two hours for us. The gigs come

Johnny keeping bass company, with Richard and Sid. (*Eileen Polk*)

first. The gigs come before drugs, and that's were we made our mistakes. We put our drugs before the kids that came to see us play. That's why we got hurt, why we got punished, because we fucked them over many times. Sure, face to face, we signed autographs, listened to their stories, it'd be in one ear and out the other. We just couldn't wait to get into the bathroom and shoot up again. That's why we suffered and we got our punishment. The kids had saved their money to see what was the greatest band in the world, to them, and they didn't want to be teased. You know, me and Johnny, in a way we would say it was just like going to a drug dealer's house. All drug dealers got something in common, they're on a power trip. They know you're strung out and sick, they'll open the dope real slowly, take their time while you're sweating. They're teasing you, because they know you need them. They're being a musician, being on stage, getting all the glory and we're suffering. We got the money, we got everything – give us the fucking drugs – but if you say that to them, it's "Listen man, you don't like my drugs, go somewhere else." What the fuck are we going to do? You can't play a gig sick, all the time, although we did it. But you know something funny? No matter how sick we were, when we counted off "1 2 3 4" and started playing, you couldn't tell we were sick. Our music was so powerful, we were just as good as if we had shot ten bags of dope. The power of the music covered our sickness. Between songs, Johnny would walk up to me, "Oh God, Jerry, how many songs did we do?" "Johnny, we only did three." "Oh my God, it sounded like eight." "Look John, play and you'll get through it, play ten songs, don't get sick.' Somehow we'd do it.'

On 6 July Beggars Banquet released *Live At Max's Kansas City* and a single,

Wayne Kramer: 'A
pretty benevolent cat.'
(*Marcia Resnick*)

'Get Off The Phone' / 'I Wanna Be Loved'. The set, which was recorded in late
1978, is a fine example of live Heartbreakers, short of actually seeing them, the
only downside being Nolan's absence from the ranks. The band, with Ty Styx
on drums, come across as much a part of NY (musical) mythology as the Alamo
is to Texan (violent) legend. Peter Crowley co-produced the album: 'These guys
are assholes. Nobody will put up with them but me. They're the greatest band
in the world – but what a bunch of assholes.' Lure and Thunders constantly try
and talk each other down at the microphone, taking turns to insult the audience or demand that all the club's tables are overturned before they continue.
The stigma of having once been thought of as London's own elite is sliced to
ribbons, these guys are as American as a gunned down President or eggs on rye.
Live At Max's isn't intended to convert or convince – though it might – it's
simply The Heartbreakers on home ground airing their limited vocabulary.
Most of the songs, as always, deal with subjects often found sprayed on sub-
ways, while the rest revolve around narcotic abuse and various vendettas. An
ill-tempered gem of an album. Walter Lure: 'It captures us as we really are, a
great live band that's eating, living and breathing Rock 'n' Roll.'

Sounds' Pete Makowski gave the live album a four-star credit:

> As people these guys are odious creeps (too real for their own good) but
> plugged in they are *magic*. This features all the greatest 'hits' – 'Milk Me',
> 'Chinese Rocks', 'Get Off The Phone' (or getoffadafuckinphone) – the
> projected single, 'London' – dedicated to Joe Bummer, 'All By Myself' (à
> la cocked-up intro) and Berry Gordy's 'Do You Love Me' as encore … 'Beg
> for it,' snarls Thunders.

Nick Kent had his own opinion, writing for the *NME*:

The whole enterprise stinks and there is absolutely no reason for even the most rabid Heartbreakers fan to purchase this piece of shit.

On one of their odd sojourns out of NY, The Heartbreakers played Detroit, where they were joined on stage at Bookie's club, by The MC5's former guitarist, Wayne Kramer. Thunders: 'I had always wanted to meet Wayne Kramer: he's one of my teenage idols. He jammed with us on "Do You Love Me", and we got to be friends after that.'

Johnny, who had seen The MC5 play in NY as a teenager, jumped at the chance to forge an alliance with Kramer. Although the high voltage kings of the late sixties were to have a profound influence on the sound of American hard rock, The MC5 never got their just rewards during the course of their short career. After the demise of the band in the early seventies, Wayne filled the void with drugs and crime and dreamt of getting a new group together. Kramer: 'On paper, the plan was to finance the new band by dealing drugs. As an organised criminal, I was a complete and total failure. I'm not a killer. I'm a pretty benevolent cat! I'm sensitive, an artist, I care.' (Interview with author, which previously appeared in *Record Collector*.)

After a three-year stay in Lexington, Kentucky, where he played in a prison combo, Kramer returned home in 1978: 'I put a band together and worked around Detroit and met Johnny. Johnny came to Detroit and wanted to break up The Heartbreakers yet again. He invited me to the gig, said he had some bookings and would I consider using my rhythm section and we could do something?' (interview as above). That 'something' was christened 'Gang War', with drummer John Morgan and bass player Ron Cooke, who was later replaced by Bobby Thomas.

Thunders and family moved to Detroit, setting up base in Dexter, Michigan for some eight months. It was, according to the guitarist's agent, a 'healthier' place to be, but not a good one to set up home in, Julie unexpectedly taking off with Johnny Jnr, Vito and new-born baby, Dino. Forever. Unsurprisingly, Johnny, became none too fond of Detroit but, as a self-confessed 'Kramer groupie', stuck it out anyway.

For quite a while, love songs were most definitely off JT's agenda and he pitched straight back into dirty rock 'n' roll. Although Gang War's repertoire mainly consisted of Thunders numbers, Kramer contributed 'Hey Thanks' and 'I Still Hate' (co-written with Mick Farren) plus 'Ramblin' Rose'. The majority however, was J.T.'s own work. For someone who was not usually the fastest of songwriters, he turned in 'M.I.A.', 'Alone In A Crowd', 'King Of The Gypsies', the obnoxious 'Just Because I'm White (Why Do You Treat Me Like A Nigger)' and 'There's A Little Bit Of Whore In Every Girl'. From the remnants of The Dolls, he also brought in the instrumental 'Courageous Cat', based on the theme music of a kid's cartoon show, and 'Endless Party'. Various covers were also given

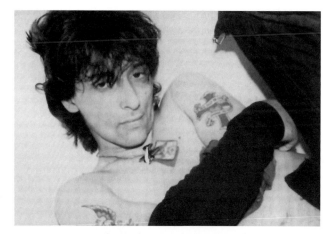

Gramercy Park
Hotel ...
(*Marcia Resnick*)

... the Italian
Stallion.
(*Marcia Resnick*)

the Gang War treatment as well, including The Stones' 'I'd Much Rather Be With The Boys', Jimmy Cliff's superb 'The Harder They Come', Fats Domino's 'I'm Gonna Be A Wheel Someday' and Chuck Berry's 'Round And Round'.

With Thunders keeping only occasional company with his old band as Gang War shaped up and started playing live, the rest of The Heartbreakers began solo ventures. Nolan, of course, still had The Idols. Walter Lure was considering doing some stuff for NY boys The Blessed. Billy Rath gigged with Iggy Pop on the Soldier tour from late 1979 to early 1980 and did some studio work with Ronnie Spector. Rath and Lure re-formed The Heroes, with Walter's kid brother Ritchie, and Nolan's some-time replacement in The Heartbreakers, Billy Rodgers. The Heroes were short lived, cutting exponents of choice rock 'n' roll, but after Rath fell sick and was forced to leave, Lure seemingly lost heart in the project and eventually, much to Thunders' amusement, got a job on Wall Street and became a stockbroker in iron, leaving any musical activities till after dark. The *NME* reported that:

After five years, two albums, and a lot of screwing around abetted by Thunders' decline into pathetic drug passivity, Lure and Rath formed The Heroes around 1980. An ace pop 'n' rock band somewhere between The Byrds and The Dolls, The Heroes (in their time one of the best bands New York had) met with almost no critical or public response, and petered out by the end of 1981, having recorded one 45 ('Crazy Kids') with producer Jimmy Miller that remains unreleased.

Heralded as a charismatic vehicle for both Thunders and Kramer, Gang War headed for New York, where they hoped to make an album. The offer of a deal came as something of a balm for Johnny, who was still smarting over Sire Records' decision not to release *So Alone* in the States. Sylvain Sylvain was approached by Thunders to produce. Sylvain in *New York Rocker* (1980):

> I'd like to know what kinda budget he has, first, I mean, I can work pretty cheap but I don't know if I can work on his budget.

Events turned out as they so often had before, and the task of recording the band wound up with the bootleggers. After a year, Thunders' teenage loyalties started to dim along with his enthusiasm for Gang War. They played 'The Boy's Night Out', at the New York Ritz, on the same bill as The Lenny Kaye Band and The Senders, and a gig at 'Heat' which was covered by Andy Schwartz for the *New York Rocker* (February 1980):

> While critics carped, the crowd gave Gang War one of those obligatory 'It's 3 a.m. and we paid $6' ovations. The band returned for an encore of (get this) 'My Sharona / Ayatollah' (Johnny ranting unintelligibly about Iran, hostages, and Marines), followed by Chuck Berry's 'Around and Around'. Suddenly, Iggy Pop leaned out of the audience to sing and dance along, and the place went wild in a way that Gang War alone could never have inspired.

Gang War travelled on through Canada, Boston and New England – stopping off long enough to talk Billy Rath into, briefly, joining them – before returning to the concrete heartland of New York, where it got pretty messy.

Johnny Thunders in *Zig-Zag*:

> We did two shows over two nights and Wayne Kramer didn't wanna play cos I wasn't paying him enough money. So it ended up with me and Peter Perrett ... and he only knew a limited number of songs that we both could do: so David and Sylvain came up and help't me – the real friends ... *the real* boys came through.

Wayne Kramer: 'The reason why we stopped playing together, was Tommy Dean from Max's had booked Gang War. The way that Johnny and I worked the band was as partners. As Johnny's habit got more and more out of control, he phoned me and said "Look, Tommy Dean doesn't want it to be Gang War, he wants it be Johnny Thunders, but if you come and play, I'll give you $100." Of course, I said: "I'm not going to come over there and play for a $100. I'd stay at home and watch television for a $100." Every time we'd try to set something up, he'd fuck it up.' (Interview with author, which previously appeared in *Record Collector*.)

Gang War bit the dust and Johnny, rather alarmingly, ended up face down in his own legend.

No apartment. No manager. No record deals. No motivation. Nothing but breath.
(*Marcia Resnick*)

7
Something's Got To Give

Caught between a black cross and a white banner, printed on his skin with a telegram clarity, are the words 'Too Fast To Live – Too Young To Die'. An over-dramatic, self-perpetuating mythology that fits neatly on his arm along with a death's head and the large unlucky thirteen. Thunders is living out the dime-novel legend with the whole city as blind audience. No apartment. No manager. No record deals. No motivation. Nothing but breath.

Marcia Resnick is one of New York City's better photographers. Because of her talents with a camera, she had been commissioned to help put together a movie on night life and personalities, and chose Johnny as her main subject. In part payment for his name and involvement, Thunders moved in to her place. Some short time later the movie's producer, Christopher Giercke, received a phone call from Ms Resnick who insisted that he help her 'get this guy out of my flat'. The resulting meeting between the German film-maker and Johnny proved to be an unexpected second chance for the guitarist. Christopher Giercke recalls how the photographer had arrived at his house with Thunders, looking wasted and worn, every inch a man taking the count. Almost a carica-ture of his own reputation.

Giercke shrugs and touches a match to the end of a thin cigar: 'You know, I may perhaps consider it … but I don't give too much importance on some-body's reputation. I make up my own mind. See what I see, you know? When a person is called a 'junky' it is a projection: you are supposed to react in cer-tain ways like … say … junkies are supposed to steal. So don't leave your purse out. If you tell a person that – OK, you're a junky, but I still expect you to be responsible in other areas – very often that approach will work. When I decid-ed to work with Johnny, to manage him, I rented him an apartment below mine. I gave him keys to my apartment and to the safe too. I told him: "Look. If you need money, there is money; but be reasonable and tell me if you need to take some when I'm out." Trust. Try and build up the details of the day on that basis. I hope, over the past two years, it has been of some help to Johnny. If only to make him see that you don't have to steal, to take anything. He's never really been what I think of as the stereotype junky. The people who have brand-ed him in that mould, the press, they don't have the human experience to dis-tinguish between different characters of people, they fail to look for the strength or the problem. They do their job to make their weekly wages, their payment for the story. They have short cuts to fill up their stories, and they don't con-cern themselves about what they write may do to the subject of their articles.'

Giercke has worked in film – including documentaries – alongside such

Real Gone.
(*Michael Beal*)

well-known American luminaries as Jack Palance, Nelson Algren and Andy Warhol. His background is as a creator rather than a manager of another's form of expression. 'I look for a certain intensity in anything. For example, I don't have one particular form or style of music that I enjoy above others. I try to feel something that is behind the music, something inside the people who play the instruments, this may be classical or rock 'n' roll. With Johnny, I thought he was trying to start a new life, and I thought I could help him. At least part of the way. I can try and help him be what he wants to be, but he must have his own self-definition. Nobody can give him that.'

Christopher Giercke has the ability to weigh a situation and its effect with the eye of an artist, a darkly abstract, almost secretive mind that fuses itself with a practical edge worthy of an assassin. An important combination when dealing with Thunders, as he was to find out.

Heroin is perhaps the physical extension of an Escher print: the pattern repeats and repeats until its final fade into an irrelevant darkness. No social reason exists for an excuse. The Chinese called it 'The Time Of Delight'. If it ends in the death of either the body or the individual, then it seems to be a price

Steve Mass pushes Johnny out
on stage at the Mudd Club,
NYC. 'Roll'em, wheel'em
out, Rawhide!': J.T.
(*Marcia Resnick*)

most users of the narcotic are more than willing to pay. A needle in the arm
can't erase surroundings for anyone except the person involved.

Johnny Thunders comes on stage with his eyes closed and starts the opening run into 'Pipeline'. His guitar isn't plugged in and he hasn't noticed. The
audience are ecstatic. He starts to sing one of The Heartbreakers' songs: his
voice sounds like a half-insane alto sax trying to get a point across in a crowded
bar. He stops and goes into a story about faggots. He's almost incoherent and
whatever Johnny is trying to say gets lost in the three-watt wasteland between
his brain, mouth and microphone. It doesn't matter: the audience are delighted.

Heroin the anti-hero.

Johnny's skin is a sickly, transparent blue under the fluorescent strip lights above the amps. His hair is tangled around his face like day-old spaghetti and he's obviously having trouble remembering why he's at the club at all. Thunders is the danger line (most of) his audience wouldn't cross for a mention in Howard Hughes' will; but he stands as the fantasy symbol for a whole army of Walter Mittys who have grown up on William Burroughs instead of Edgar Rice. They flock to cheer every time he seems considerably unsteady on his feet: each slurred word and missed chord. Fuck the music. Look at the condition of this guy. Johnny Thunders: 'Hey, I'm not a professional drug-taker. I just wanna make 'em dance.'

J.T., the sordid, back-street adventurer in the grimy white shirt and Mexican hat; the lowlife loser with the perverse winning streak, coming back against the odds and giving a one-finger salute to everyone who bets on his staying down. Thunders does things that certain portions of his audience admire: hangs out in mean areas to pick up heroin on corners, or in bars decorated with eighty per cent urban poverty. Stories arrive before him at every concert about how he might not show tonight because: the Mafia want him, he's overdosed on the Lower Eastside, he killed someone on the way to the date, the cops are looking for him.

Thunders is the angry Christ figure casually carrying out the dark rituals of a teenage society that Ivy Leaguers only dream about in bed or at the movies.

The music press on both sides of the Atlantic need to add to their sales. Thunders makes good copy. He also provides a way in which liberal journalists with limited backbone can attack the drug problem in such a way that avoids the need to go into print against more popular public figures who might just use their record company muscle to take legal action. On Thunders, however, it's a long open season. Roy Traikin, in January 1981, used his space in the *New York Rocker* to turn in one of the most sensitive articles ever written about the guitarist:

> He has at once profited, and been made victim to, the rock dream as nightmare. He teeters on a tight-rope between life and death, living out our vicarious dreams of self destruction and rocking Thanatos. Isn't it about time we all grew up and accepted the responsibilities of our actions before it's too late?
>
> There's no reason Johnny Thunders has to prove he's an artist by dropping dead for our amusement: all he really ever had to do was give us the guitar break in 'Vietnamese Baby' or the aching refrain from 'You Can't Put Your Arms Around A Memory', the kamikaze attack of 'Bad Girl' or the poignant, often self mocking rant of 'Born To Lose'. Hey, Johnny, you ain't no loser to me. At least not yet.

Heroin was responsible for more than just the damage done to Thunders' health and career. Everybody gets hurt who risks a close proximity with such an obviously dangerous chemical – those on the sidelines and the participants.

Christopher Giercke, as astute as any business manager, and probably more shrewd than most, managed at least to anaesthetise, if not to exorcise, the various demons that lurked in Thunders. Christopher's actual presence, as well as his advice and guidance, seemed to be needed, and when Thunders left to play Sweden, the German director was not on hand to watch the house of cards start to slide.

When people go to see Johnny Thunders play, they expect the atmosphere around him to be volatile; his image and his lifestyle is such that he comes on as a catalyst for obsessive extremes. In England and America, his reputation is known, accepted, even applauded by certain scumbags who see him as their private martyr, but he *is* known. In Sweden however, he was to provoke responses that ranged from the hysterical to the homicidal. The band, comprising Jerry Nolan, Luigi Sciorrci and Thunders, were delayed by twenty-four hours because of an extended recording session with The Rolling Stones' old producer, Jimmy Miller. Matters weren't helped in the studio by the guitarist's tendency to go AWOL, as Miller explained: 'Any excuse and he'd disappear. I mean if the headphones went and we'd have to change them, I'd ask Johnny to give us a minute and he'd be gone. It was very difficult. I feel like I never really caught him at his best time.' (Interview with author, which previously appeared in *Record Collector.*)

Booked to play Sweden's *Mandagsborsen*, a prime-time TV music programme which went out live, the band's late arrival at the studio upset the camera crew. Before Thunders and Co. even got to the point of a sound check, Nolan, who had been ill on the plane, had to have a doctor called out, who confirmed he needed 'a good rest'. The technicians were again angry when the drummer didn't show up with the others for the sound check. Exactly why it mattered to them is anybody's guess. An agreement was reached: Thunders would perform his four-number set and it would be transmitted in the next edition of the programme.

Three hours late …
Johnny staggers on stage looking the worse for wear and then some. The set starts with 'Green Onions'. By 'Just Another Girl', Thunders is holding his guitar at arms length, and kicking it. He slides (literally) off the stage into the restaurant area, climbing to his feet long enough to bum a cigarette from a girl standing mesmerised by an amp.

Thunders had fucked up badly, and the watching journalists lost no time in telling the rest of the country about it:

BURNT OUT, WASTED: *MANDAGSBORSEN* MAIN ATTRAC-
TION STOPPED   – *Exspressen*, headline

A DRUGGED HUMAN WRECK: THIS IS JOHNNY THUNDERS,
THE ROCK SINGER THAT *MANDAGSBORSEN* DIDN'T DARE
SHOW   – *Afton Bladet*, headline

The tapes of the performance were destroyed.

To put it as mildly as possible, the Swedish majority over-reacted to an
incredible degree. OK, under the circumstances it would be difficult, if not
impossible, to defend Thunders, but to have him as the front-page shock story
with a half-page photo as accompaniment in a city with a drug problem the size
of Stockholm's, is as hypocritical as it is over sensational. Thunders was the
strung-out apotheosis of a lot of parental fears, a syringe-waving scapegoat; and

he was, of course, selling papers. His every move found its way into printing ink; his crying after the TV show, or his shivering in tour manager Sukhedo Doobay's hotel room, as reported in the 23 March edition of *Exspressen*:

I DON'T HAVE THE STRENGTH TO PLAY TONIGHT

He looks wasted after a sleepless night. He looks terribly wasted as he walks over to his guitar. He sat shivering in a black dressing gown. No photos are allowed. When we are about to leave, he mentions tonight's show in Sundersvall: 'I can't do it. I can't do it,' says Johnny.' 'Oh yes, you'll be fine soon enough,' says Doobay.

What followed was even more incredible. Aside from the widely circulated story that the Swedish Salvation Army wanted to kidnap Johnny in order to 'save his soul', circumstances turned the situation into one where it became more a question of saving his jeopardised sanity for the duration of the dates. The next gig, with the black, macabre planning of some Ortonesque spirit, is in Sundersvall – for an anti-heroin cause. Despite the police's efforts in stopping and searching the band every time they moved, Thunders had enough chemicals on hand to ensure his new anti-Christ reputation wouldn't be damaged by uniformed authority. Shortly after taking the stage at the anti-drugs show, Johnny collapsed and pitched headlong into the audience. Thunders again makes front-page headlines: 'POLICE ARREST POP STAR'.

On arrival at Bromma Airport, the band made life easy for any in-transit terrorists by having the airport security, the local police and a dog, surround them when paranoid air hostess, Monika Emblard, instantly put the finger on Thunders and Sciorrci, having found her plane's medical box abandoned in a toilet, with its supply of Valium missing.

Johnny Thunders found himself placed on a mile-high rebellious pedestal by local kids, and about as popular as leprosy with their parents. Sometime later, when the Terror of Sweden was back doing a couple of gigs there, Johnny remarked to his enthusiastic and happy audience: 'You kids are OK ... it's hard to believe your parents are so retarded. Is it the water they drink or somethin'?'

By now, reports on Thunders in Sweden were reaching England, coinciding with the news that he is due to arrive in London, any day ...

At a time when visiting rock 'n' roll 'stars' had reached a limited impasse concerning credibility and stance: when only large concert halls and football stadiums had the capacity and financial ability to act as an entrepreneur's magnet, the return of the original bad boy generated, at least amongst his followers, a level of excitement and anticipation that would have been worthy of the return of Jesse James.

A prevalent question, unasked and unspoken, in connection with Johnny Thunders, is do you listen to him or do you live him?

With a lifestyle like a warning television documentary, his fans have always tended to revel in every slip, every public outburst of narcissistic indulgence. Every time Thunders rolls his tongue, gathers saliva and spits full into the face of the parental system, the judicial system and the social order, his standing grows among the make-believe outlaws, the suburban outcasts and the after-school desperadoes. And with the fools come the real shadows, the genuine dregs of Parisian nightmare not out of place in an abstract thesis on surrealist crime. As nor would Thunders be.

With the same cast as Sweden, Jerry Nolan and Luigi Sciorrci, Thunders returned to England for a proposed two month tour, the emphasis on the capital with the occasional out of town gig. A handful of dates in, Sciorrci is replaced by Steve New, and the line-up finalised by bass player Tony James (ex-Generation X and founder of Sigue Sigue Sputnik). As for their frontman, Thunders is holding himself together against the rumours and the reputation.

On stage he scowls and smiles, whines and curses, and, above all, demonstrates why he's one of the best and most original guitarists alive. He sways around the footlights, legs like gelatine scissors shrouded in leather, eyes glowing with poison while he swears like an expert in colloquial abuse at audience and musicians alike.

Hope and Anchor – 20 April
THUNDERS (TO SOUNDMAN): Hey ... Yo. Yo ... can you give me some more reverberation on my damaged voice? Yeah ... yeah ... that sounds more like me ...
MEMBER OF AUDIENCE: Just play some fucking music.
THUNDERS: Hey, Scumbag, shove it up your mother's left nut.

Kensington – April 30
THUNDERS (UNHAPPY WITH THE SOUND): Hey. What is this shit?
MEMBER OF AUDIENCE: Oh ... fuck off, Johnny.
THUNDERS (REFLECTIVELY): Naw ... as a matter of fact, I don't fuck at all.

Rock Garden – 1 May
THUNDERS (SCORNFULLY): You kids have some sense of humour, huh? What you kids do? Watch English TV? You laugh when the microphone's fallin' ... Awrite ... listen: a funny thing happened to me on the way to the show tonight. I took a taxi cab – har har har. Funny, huh?
MEMBER OF AUDIENCE: Get on with it.
THUNDERS: Hey. You don't like it? You paid your money – go home.
MEMBER OF AUDIENCE: We paid our money.
THUNDERS: Big deal. Go peek at your mother's pussy. Fuck you.

Even Jerry Nolan is treated to a brief sample of the guitarist's wit – during the band introductions:
THUNDERS: He's been with me just about as long as my mother ... naww ... Jerry's my father actually.

An Interview With
Tony James

NINA: Did you know Johnny prior to the 1982 tour?

TONY: Maybe around The Heartbreakers period. I know I met Walter and Jerry so I'd probably spoken to him. Thunders was always one of my heroes so it was great meeting him and brilliant to actually play with him: I mean, I could play 'Jet Boy' legit with the man that wrote it.

NINA: I believe you put Johnny up during the tour?

TONY: He only stayed here for two weeks but it felt like three years. Things kind of fall apart all around Johnny, it's like having ET in your house. I'd just be lying in bed and I'd hear him running around disconnecting everything. He always had this big fear of leaving things plugged in. I might be pissed off and I'd come home in the morning to find he'd unplugged everything in sight – pulled all the wires out of everywhere, records all over the place … God. It was like the chaos in that scene from *ET*, when he's pissed. It's just Extraterrestrial Thunders.

NINA: I heard that you were going to maybe produce Johnny.

TONY (LAUGHING): Johnny? Produce him? Fuckin' hell. I wouldn't walk him across the road, let alone produce him. He'd probably want to stay here again. Never, never again. Johnny's got quite a clear idea of his own – and I don't think I could add anything because I have a very similar approach.

NINA: What's he like to work with?

TONY: A nightmare – but it's good fun. I found it more fun playing with him than I did playing with Generation X because he plays the sort of music that I *really* like. It has this great unpredictability about it – a great attitude – just going out and playing. Never rehearsed once. They taught me the numbers in about half an hour before we did the Venue. Just taught me them here on an acoustic guitar, then he handed me a list of about thirty songs that I was supposed to have learnt, and we went and played the Venue. He was carried unconscious into the sound check, but he went out and played. Absolutely no bullshit involved. I think he has a heart full of soul – I mean, there are *no* groups that have got that soul – that real rock and rollness in them. They play from the head, from what they read in books. I think Thunders is a living legend. The only thing I don't like is, obviously, him being so fucked-up on heroin. I don't think it's cool to be a junky, it's fuckin' stupid to be a junky. That was the only problem I had – being the only non-junky in the band. I mean, people think that I do junk, but I don't. I'm totally against all that shit. It's such a waste of talent and a waste of human life.

22 April.

Clad in uncharacteristic denim, Thunders lurches through the still-drawn Venue curtains and tears into a set of Heartbreakers' standard classics, cut with the mandatory Dolls' infusion, and includes some of his more recent writings.

A rough-looking chick stirs up her own trouble when she makes a pathetic grab for Johnny's balls. She's rewarded by being dragged on stage and expected to perform an impromptu strip, bump and grind routine. A sudden burst of public modesty, probably brought on by the barrage of crude comments screamed from the audience, causes the girl to hide in an attack on the smirking guitarist. Johnny nimbly avoids the fist and pushes her towards a couple of bouncers who drag her backstage by the hair. Sylvain Sylvain, also on tour with his band, The Roman Sandals, climbs on stage to Thunders' obvious pleasure, and together they go into 'Chinese Rocks', which Sylvain changes to '... he's living on Chinese Rocks'.

Sylvain later told the *NME* that there was 'a certain charisma about a guy that everybody thinks is about to drop dead. It's like when Daffy Duck blows up on stage and then you see him in heaven as an angel saying "Yeah, folks, it's a great show: but you can only do it once."'

Thunders and band played their last UK date on 3 June before flying to Sweden, minus Steve New who was fired on the eve of their departure. It was hoped, God and Johnny willing, to be the beginning of a major tour, starting with their first night at the Facade in Gothenburg.

Thunders sets the tone for the evening by collapsing a few seconds after walking out on stage. He pulls himself slowly up the microphone stand, brushes his fingers across the guitar strings once, and begins the show. Thunders: 'Hey. Turn th' fuckin' monitors up. Hey ... hey! Is there a bartender down there? Huh? Listen, bring me a bottle of fuckin' brandy if you wanna hear more than three fuckin' songs ... yeah, an' a pitcher of ginger ale.'

The audience are getting more than restless. Jerry Nolan starts up his beat and Tony James pushes a vicious bass line into the middle of it, both hoping that Johnny will decide to start playing the guitar and / or sing. Instead he walks slowly to the front of the stage and orders the house lights up. He notices the girls clustered around the toes of his boots and goes into a hardly audible insult tirade against Swedish girls: Thunders: 'Have ya ever seen such a motley crew? They don't know if it's the sixth month of their period ... Maybe ... maybe ... their boyfriend's left 'em an' they stuck somethin' frozen up their pussies cos they were so horny ... an' it got stuck, huh? Awwrite, darlings?'

The concert collapses in a near riot and Nolan and James drag Thunders back to the hotel which they now have no money to pay for.

Nolan,
Thunders,
Tony James
and Steve
New.
(*Michael
Beal*)

Tony James: 'Three of us went, me, Jerry, Thunders. We just managed to make
the plane, but that was in typical Thunders' style. We're both on the plane waiting, and he ain't there. In the distance we can see Thunders zig-zagging towards
us, totally not rushed at all … couldn't give a shit. On the way over we fell out
cos I didn't bring my other guitar. Johnny didn't have a guitar – he'd flogged it
– and I didn't realise he'd wanted me to bring it, so Thunders and me weren't
talking. When we got to the gig, I don't know, someone gave him something,
and he wasn't very lucid; in fact he was totally out of his brain. It was such a
big deal, because the first gig was the one they were saying, "If you get through
this, we'll let you play the rest of the country." All the Swedish papers were
there to see if he'd fuck up again. He just walked on stage, and fell straight off.
Then he started insulting the Swedish girls. Someone managed to hold a guitar
round his neck, and he started playing – I don't know what he was playing –
he started this number, then he ran off. Me and Nolan started a twenty-minute
version of "Waiting For My Man", but the man never came, so we abandoned
it. The audience were rioting, and wanting their money back. We didn't have
any money to pay the hotel, and they threw us out, but Johnny would not get
out of bed. Then, the next day, he wouldn't get in the van. I mean, he refused
because we were both "scumbags". For some reason, it was *our* fault. We were
like, driving to the airport, and he's walking behind the van because he wouldn't
sit in it. Eventually, we had to get the boat back. We were gonna do some more
stuff, but then he got busted at the airport, and all that shit, and he flew back
to New York.'

Johnny Thunders found it surprising that the tour had whipped such a
semi-hysterical reaction in Sweden, and commented along those lines to
journalist Kris Needs (April 1983):

Too buckled
to swash.
(*Michael
Beal*)

I was there for ten days and they put me on the front page of the daily
paper eight days in a row. I did nothing. I actually did nothing. I never
warranted the attention they gave me. It was ridiculous. I mean, what
started it off was I played a television show and I played live – and I was
too fucked-up so they wouldn't show it. That started the ball rolling with
the press, and then they started following me to gigs.

Jerry Nolan decided to remain in Sweden for a time, forming his own band
The Teneriffa Cowboys. They released a single, 'Take A Chance' / 'Pretty Baby',
on the Tandan record label in 1983, toured for most of the year and then
recorded another one, 'Havana Moon' / 'Countdown Love'.

Johnny was probably wishing he'd followed Nolan's example in terms of
location. Twin stories exist as to what prompted the guitarist's stay in prison in
London, both erratic and both with typical discrepancies. All that seems certain
is that Thunders was stopped at Heathrow – either because he was drawing
attention to himself or because he's always stopped anyway – searched and
arrested once they found his works and a small amount of heroin. He was detained at Pentonville Prison before being taken to court and fined fifty pounds
for possession. Rescheduling his flight home, the guitarist went into Croydon's
Wickham Studios and laid down some backing tracks, including 'Ten Com-
mandments Of Love', 'Sad Vacation', and 'Give Me More', with drummer
Mike Hellier and Malcolm Hart on bass.

Once home in New York, Thunders spent some time trying to secure a deal
for the Jimmy Miller produced tracks. In early July, he teamed up with Walter
Lure for a gig at the Peppermint Lounge, and later that month celebrated his
birthday by playing the Irving Plaza, forging the final links with his enigmatic
manager, Christopher Giercke.

'Crucified at last': J.T.
(*Marcia Resnick*)

Meanwhile, film-maker Lech Kowalski was waiting for summer to turn into winter before shooting *Gringo*, a cinematic take on the viciously claustrophobic world of heroin addiction. At one point, Johnny was to have featured as its central inhabitant. I asked him how he saw the film: Thunders: 'It's a film about copping drugs on the Lower East Side of Manhattan and all the evil parts about it. It's just what the lifestyle's like: dangerous and dirty.' *Gringo* should have been released in the summer of 1984, but various artistic disputes held it back. By early 1985, the sequences involving Thunders in an assortment of scenarios, including onstage at the Mudd club, were cut out of the film. Kowalski subsequently decided to use the footage for a movie entitled *Stations Of The Cross*. Although Roir Records released a soundtrack in conjunction with Kowalski, the film footage wouldn't see the light of day until Thunders' demise, when the director grafted the sequences on to a documentary about the guitarist, called *Born To Lose*. At the time, neither Johnny or

You lookin'
at me?
(*Marcia Resnick*)

Giercke raised any objections when the director cut the sequences involving the guitarist from *Gringo*, as it was Thunders' addiction that led him to the project in the first place.

Realising the potential of an interview with Johnny Thunders, a reporter from a Swedish current affairs show called *Studio S* flew to NY to interview the guitarist. The programme also included a more in-depth session with Jerry Nolan.

Thunders is gazing into the depths of the camera without seeing it. He lights cigarette after cigarette and the only movement he makes is to run his tongue along his dry lips, in between giving stock answers to dull questions:

> THUNDERS: I hope this isn't going to be another boring interview about drugs.
> STUDIO S: Don't you like talking about them?

Another interview about drugs. Johnny on Swedish television.

THUNDERS: I'm not a professional drug taker – I don't think.
STUDIO S: Do you remember when you started with drugs?
THUNDERS: Yeah.
STUDIO S: Tell me about it. How did you start?
THUNDERS: I started smoking pot, the way the other kids do ... got into
            heavier things and I guess it's a hard thing to get out of once
            you've started.
STUDIO S: Do you remember when you started shooting?
THUNDERS: No.
STUDIO S: Do you remember why you started?
THUNDERS: Just to have a good time. There was no ... nothing to escape
            from or nothing like that: no problems ... Like, a lot of kids
            start because they're bored or lonely, y'know. It makes them
            feel like they're alive, I guess. I would *never* turn anyone on
            to drugs. It's a hard thing to handle and once you get into
            it, its *really* hard to get out of.

Jerry Nolan is both communicative and sick. Despite being under the effects
of chemical stimulation (or relaxation, depending on your politics) he is polite
and informative, even when pressed by the most banal questioning. Jerry leads
off with a conflicting account of their early heroin days:

NOLAN: That whole drug era in the late sixties, for some reason, even
         though most kids my age were getting into drugs then, I
         never got into it really. Not even smoking pot, not drinking
         ... but then, when it was all over, even after The Dolls were
         over, I started experimenting with drugs and, unfortunately,

with the wrong kind of drugs: hard – real hard-core, addict-
ing drugs like heroin … and … well … me and Johnny sort
of got into that at first for a while …

STUDIO S: At the same time, or had he [Johnny] been on it a longer
            time?

NOLAN: No. Not really … it's like I say, very late in life: but heroin is
            such an addictive drug it was a little too late before we found
            out enough information about it, before we realised what we
            were getting into. It was much too late. Much too late …

STUDIO S: Is it the average person on the street's business if a musician
            or a teenage idol wants to take heavy drugs?

NOLAN: I don't think it's his business unless he wants to make it his
            business. It's up to him, if he wants … but …I will always try
            and talk to any young person I know is using hard drugs; and
            maybe if they respect me … or even just respect my music …
            they'll listen … but I can't talk to everybody because I don't
            know everybody …

In closing Thunders mentioned that one of his final ambitions was for people
to remember that 'I have a heart, y'now, I'm still a human being.'
   It was the most honest statement in the whole programme.

(*Jungle archive*)

An Interview With
Patti Palladin

NINA: You and Johnny have similar backgrounds, what was it like growing up in New York?

PATTI: To survive in that sort of environment, it's essential to develop your 'attitude' at a very early age. Although I grew up in Brooklyn and Johnny grew up in Queens, the similarity of our backgrounds is strong – the basic 'neighbourhood mentality'. The neighbourhood was sliced into gang-governed territories; my neighbourhood was more or less shared by the Phantom Lords and the Hell Burners; Jerry was a Young Lord. The letters D.L.A.M.F. (Down Like A Mother Fucker) and D.T.K. (Down To Kill) were as common as one-way signs. Yet, *style*, not violence was the main motive – your main concern was really your profile. Mind you, there was a fair amount of bloodshed over who had more style – violence was merely the result of too much style and too much attitude. I can't erase all that, and I'm sure Johnny and Jerry can't either, but I also can't erase the fact that I've lived in London for the past ten years.

NINA: What made you decide to live in London?

PATTI: It was more a conclusion, I just didn't want to be in America anymore. There are things that are not specifically New York that are decidedly America, that make me ill; certain views inherent in the American mentality that are fundamentally lame. Mind you, at that time, it was nowhere near the ridiculous levels it has now reached ... actually, my decision to leave America was probably more intuitive than anything else, I don't regret it.

NINA: And why England? Do you really prefer it here?

PATTI: At the time, it was a pretty obvious move ... I was much more interested in what was happening here – creatively, socially – generally. London is metropolitan, and of course the fact that there was no language barrier made it all the more attractive. New York had had it's heyday. You could no longer stroll into Max's and find Truman Capote sharing a table with Lee Radizwell, Brian Jones and a local wino. It seemed to be slipping into a state of animated suspension. Don't get me wrong, there was lots of activity, but at that time it seemed to lack direction, and somehow it just became rampant energy.

NINA: You've known Johnny from way back, what do you make of his self-destructive edge and the kind of folklore that surrounds him?

PATTI: There are moments when Johnny is absolutely definitive, and every

Patti and
Johnny.
(*Alan Horne*)

damaged cell is a legend in its own right, but, sometimes he is just sooo
jive. He respects so little, he's a cunt really – well, he always tries it on.
You gotta love him – you gotta hate him. He's got a lot to live up to,
y'know, he always will. The Dolls were so fucking brilliant, it must
create a constant pressure – plus, the obsession with his death plays
such a major role in his career now, it seems his success is gauged by it.
I suppose the value of his catalogue would soar. This could explain why
so many major names appear to be brain dead!

Johnny is the ultimate self-destruct hero, the sheer essence of what
rock 'n' roll is said to be. He always seems to be within arm's distance
of an axe, even if he has to crawl to it, regardless of what state he's in,
you can throw him a guitar and yell 'Jet Boy' and he'll play it … well,
he'll certainly have a go. If it's totally unrecognisable, he'll probably tell
you: 'Something's wrong with your hearin' – I played fuckin' great
tonight!'

He's had so many line-ups, some have been flawless, some have been absolute shit. Yet to some degree the band is irrelevant, cos Johnny usually gives his audience what they came to get. For them, that's great but for him, well, I don't know – it does get pretty brutal sometimes.

NINA: Somebody told me something really bad – I hope it's not true – that Johnny is very sick in hospital with pneumonia.

PATTI: Yeah, someone told me something really awful, I didn't say anything to you because I don't like hearsay on Johnny at all. I get really annoyed when people come up to me and ask: 'Is Johnny really dead?' In fact someone did tell me quite recently that he was in hospital in Paris and that he was paralysed on one side or something, but as I said, it's grapevine bullshit. I never really listen to it. I usually wind up calling his sister to find out if anything really bad has happened to him … he's died hundreds of times but he just keeps coming back (laughs), let's face it, it gets pretty tedious really.

NINA: Johnny is in a strange situation, really. I mean, he's made brilliant records that should have kept him at the top, but he's still in an unstable position.

PATTI: He's made some superb records. If he was receiving royalties for inspiration – for the influence he has had on so many other musicians, he'd probably have to seriously dodge the taxman. The Dolls' albums, even with all the bad production shit, are brilliant. *L.A.M.F.* was great, too. Once again, the content was so strong, bad production couldn't totally destroy it. *So Alone* was a real gem – 'You Can't Put Your Arms Around A Memory' is classic. It's a real shame, lack of know-how and commitment really anchored that record. Basically, bad deals, business or otherwise – blew it! His reputation, that's his main problem, his bad reputation. It keeps him in demand; it keeps him at the bottom – ridiculous, eh? It's really just all the social taboo about junk, it lingers, the big boys don't want to know, it's much too intense. It's illogical and irresponsible, they can't control it, they just don't need the aggro, I can understand that. Basically it's just too risky to command serious financial commitment. Johnny's reputation is so lousy – he'd probably have to stay spotlessly clean for a decade before anyone in charge of the purse-strings would believe him; it's unjust really, he has calmed down considerably. I think with a bit of serious interest, he'd probably deliver, I'd love to see him get the recognition he deserves.

NINA: What do you think about Christopher Giercke and his relationship with Johnny?

PATTI: Ah yes, 'darling Christopher' – a most peculiar creature. It's a bit incongruous really – he's articulate, well read, well dressed, etc., so why manage Johnny? Curious fascination? For art's sake? … maybe a deep-rooted Marty Thau fixation – why manage anyone? Perhaps it's a need to control – I don't know.

Christopher is quite an intricate character, he's got a great sense of drama – he loves a good crisis, he really is quite amusing. It may seem strange, but I do think that respect is a very important issue to Johnny, he has little regard for most things beyond his own existence. Yet if he respects something, he protects it, it's typically Italian, really. Christopher is German – fire and ice; I think they both enjoy the game, they both enjoy the power struggle.

NINA: You've collaborated on a lot of stuff, what's he like to work with?

PATTI: Working with Johnny seems such a natural thing to do – besides, it's the only real chance I ever get to play 'the cocky dumb bitch from Brooklyn', I suppose it's obvious, really. I couldn't think of playing that role for anyone else: Johnny genuinely does in many ways see women as dumb bitches. He's playing that Stanley Kowalski role and he needs someone to play it against. Can't think of anyone else in London who could do it better, can you?

'Jailhouse Rock': J.T. (*Angie/Mama Prod.*)

8
The Art Of Cosa Nostra

With the familiar confusion that always surrounded the guitarist's private and public life, 1982 ground to a vinyl encrusted finish that spilled over into the New Year. With the participation of New Rose Records of Paris and, to a lesser extent, Jungle Records in London, Thunders' aficionados suddenly found themselves with a flood of imports to choose from, along with a surge of bootlegs of Swedish origin.

New Rose started the disc spinning by releasing the excellent 'In Cold Blood' single, a live and studio version of the one song. A live album and twelve-inch record also appeared as a package under the same title as the single, with the well-respected Jimmy Miller producing the EP. The studio cuts have Thunders playing both lead and bass guitars, debuting new songs from sessions at Downtown (October 1982) and Euphoria Sound (March 1982). Under the circumstances, Thunders was angry:

> It was a double album; but it was only meant to be an EP. It was only demos that were put out, they weren't finished works and I'm not really pleased with it.   – *17* magazine

Although Thunders disowned the release, the press still reviewed it in much the same way as any of his official output. Coolly. *In Cold Blood* was later withdrawn, then put back on the market without the live album, in a new sleeve. PVC Records put out a remixed version of the same tracks with the inclusion of 'Endless Party' under the title of *Diary Of A Lover*. Meanwhile, Jungle Records began their involvement when they issued a live single, captured in 1977, of 'Chinese Rocks' / 'All By Myself', which they followed up with *D.T.K.– Live At the Speakeasy*. The release of the single and album created new problems from old ties, of both a contractual and personal nature. Before Thunders and his manager reached an understanding with Jungle, Johnny was adamant about the album's position: '*D.T.K.* is illegal. I'm involved in a law suit with them.'

The second week in April saw the guitarist and Christopher Giercke in London to negotiate with Jungle Records, who had now released a three-track EP *Vintage 77*.

Down in Wardour Street, Thunders, together with Christopher and Tony James, bided their time in that haunt of posers, pushers and rejects, the Ship pub, before going to see the inimitable Dr John play a set at the Marquee, located only a block or two down the street. Johnny is looking quite healthy:

Zippered up
Heart.
(*J.B. Mondino*)

considering he'd died four or five times that week. He smirks and rests his glass
on the overcrowded table: 'In Paris, I died three times. It was in the papers. Jerry
Nolan phoned up from Sweden and friends phoned up from London. Your
guess is as good as mine who starts 'em, probably someone at New Rose or
Jungle or someone records, I guess.'

Alan Hauser, the man at Jungle Records who virtually instigated the company's decision to re-issue as much of the Johnny Thunders / Heartbreakers
catalogue as possible, sits in his office surrounded by pyramids of Thunders
promo badges and related material.

Why Thunders?

Hauser: 'Leee Black Childers mentioned that he had these tapes and he
didn't think anyone would be interested in them except maybe in France. He
went off, didn't get a deal, came back and I said that we'd be interested. At that
time, Johnny hadn't been heard of for a couple of years since he'd vanished from
the scene, he wasn't sort of a name on everyone's lips. I'd had his singles from
the early days of punk, loved them and was sure lots of other people did, so …
we knew we had a live album, and we got the *L.A.M.F.* tapes back from where
Leee had left them in France. Just as we were ready to release them, I saw in the
papers that Johnny was playing Sweden: and that was the first that had been
heard of him for ages. He'd got all this press there so, consequently, *D.T.K.* sold
four or five thousand copies on export to Sweden, and it got into the national
charts at number thirty-three, I think.'

But what did Thunders himself think about old tapes being pressed into albums and sold when, at the time, he and his manager knew nothing about it, did they?

Hauser: 'No. Well, Leee hadn't been in touch with Johnny, and Johnny hadn't been in touch with *anybody* – no one knew where he was when we did the original deal. Leee was in the right, he was the management company and when Track Records liquidated, the rights to all the tapes reverted back to him. Johnny didn't realise this ... and also, Leee had lost a lot of money in his management of The Heartbreakers and I think he was justified in getting some of it back. Eventually, both parties came to me to try and sort it out. Leee spent three months in London just looking through papers. At this time, Christopher was in Katmandu or wherever. We sorted it out.'

Johnny sits curled in a corner of Tony James' sofa, eyes narrowed against the smoke that curls from his cigarette as he mumbles his set of stock answers to the person attempting an interview from *Flexi Pop*. *Performance* is playing on the video and Thunders finds it a lot more interesting than answering the same questions over and over. At last the man from the paper realises he's lost to Fox and Jagger, hands down, and leaves. *Performance* over, Johnny puts on a fresh video, while Christopher alternates on the telephone between arranging European dates, arguing legal matters and putting the last details into place for their move to live in Paris. Thunders drags most of Tony James' furniture across to the window and erects an unsteady barricade against the sunlight. Christopher puts his palm over the telephone mouthpiece and nods toward the video screen where a cannibal is dining on human flesh. 'Finger lickin' good,' he smiles and returns to a serious conversation across the wires.

Johnny ejects the cannibals and starts watching *Christiane F.*

Slowly, Friday turns into evening and the room is suddenly very quiet. Johnny is gently playing a match along some tin foil, smiling whilst Christiane gets her first taste of heroin and throws up.

'Cosa Nostra' resists any direct translation into English. For a generation or two of cinematic hoodlums, it evoked images of Al Pacino or, depending on the chronological scale involved, George Raft. Well aware of the mythology associated with the name, Thunders christened his latest outfit Cosa Nostra. With Billy Rath on bass, Jerry Nolan on drums and Henri-Paul on guitar, the band played a three-night stint in Paris at the Gibus Club. Any further activity was put on hold when Johnny succumbed to a severe bout of pneumonia, which gave rise to a particularly unpleasant series of rumours, including death, overdose and paralysis.

ROIR Records in New York released an album-length tape *Too Much Junkie Business* which, despite his later disowning of it, Thunders had agreed on to the extent of providing a narration between songs. Christopher, for no obvious

Milk, the healthy alternative. A scene from *Personality Crisis*.

reason, described the cassette as being 'a positive point against drugs'. Even in
Sweden, where Thunders was seen as the very incarnation of penny-dreadful
villainy, his commercial potential had begun to outweigh other considerations.
The decent quality bootleg, *Cosa Nostra Never Sleeps*, reveals Thunders breaking the Swedish hex in Sodertalje Park, before a massive audience of adoring
kids. After one of the shows, Johnny met an attractive hairdresser named
Susanne who was to join him in France and become an almost-constant
companion.

Following a well-received (and well-bootlegged) tour around Europe,
Thunders returned to Paris where he began working on a movie with the award
winning director, Patrick Grandperret. The film, which was originally called *Go
Back To Go*, later evolved, along with the story line, into *Personality Crisis;* and
features the guitarist playing a character with a past not a million miles away
from his own. Thunders, in the precision-made shoes of Johnny Valentine, described the plot as being about 'a guy on heroin who knows he's got to get his
life back together. He's walkin' out on stage and collapsing. I guess it's about
different relationships I have with different people, like my manager, who plays
the lawyer in the movie.'

By October Thunders has returned to England. The ground is an icy mirror and the sky a dull grey over London. Giercke's wise manipulations have
taken the band away from the dismal surrounds of their last visit. Billed as
Johnny Thunders' Cosa Nostra, their one and only concert at the Lyceum is a

An American in Paris. (*Francors Etienne*)

sell out, surprising everyone except Thunders. His new-found confidence was largely due to his trust in Christopher Giercke, in whom he had not only a manager, but also a friend and guide. One on whom he was to rely perhaps a little too much. Thunders' increasing popularity in Europe, especially France and Sweden, coupled with his self-proclaimed efforts to cut down on his chemical intake, appeared to give him a drive that the years had slowly chipped away.

I asked Johnny if he regretted the past.

He grinned, pausing slowly as he lit the latest in a seemingly endless line of cigarettes: 'Well, I'm glad its over. See, now is a new start. I finally ended my career as a drug addict …' He smiles again, contemplating keeping his last line reserved for future press interviews.

It's a freezing cold afternoon when Cosa Nostra arrive for the sound check. Burly roadies strain under electrical equipment, while poker-faced bouncers check that the locks are still secured on the outer doors of the venue's baroque entrance. Today, it's hard to imagine that the Lyceum once had a natural dignity beneath its gaudy façade, and was managed by Bram Stoker. Things have got a lot less genteel. After a brief inspection of the dressing rooms, the band return to the ballroom. Johnny positions himself next to Susanne on a roll of carpet, and insists the bar staff ignore licensing hours, while Jerry Nolan turns jet lag into an art form. Having just moved from Sweden back to New York, he'd barely had the time to catch up with himself, before flying to London.

Subversion and
Style.
(*Ian Dickson*)

In transit, part of his drum kit has been lost. After telling the road crew, 'Wake
me up when you find it,' he pulls the brim of his hat down over his eyes and
goes to sleep. Billy Rath fluctuates between his normal surly impatience, pacing
around and checking his reflection from various angles, while carrying on an
affable conversation about some recent production work he's been doing in
New England.

    Two hours later. Nolan's cymbals have been found and the band, including
Michael Thimren who has taken over from Henri-Paul, do the sound check for
the evening's show. Johnny leads into the Pink Panther theme, which turns into
'Jet Boy' into 'Subway Train'. While Thunders is explaining to the soundman,
as always, that he needs 'Reverb – turn up th' fuckin' reverb', Jayne County
(tonight's support act) slips quietly into the hall carrying an armful of shopping

bags, hat pulled down as low as Harry Lime on a wet night, and collar turned up to add to either the incognito effect or the eccentric normality.

By the evening, Jayne has metamorphosed. Wearing a silver lurex ensemble, she sits on her knees under the spotlight, washing in the blood of rock 'n' roll.

Upstairs, the dressing room is full of smoke and tight nerves. A large table has been filled with fruit and drink, the fruit is ignored for now. Jerry Nolan is sprawled out on a sofa, making it clear he is not in a mood for conversation by letting his silence build an effective wall around him. Johnny is putting the final touches to his appearance before a full-length mirror. He catches the reflection of Patti Palladin as she slips into the room, late. Johnny half turns towards her to ask where she's been. Patti shrugs: 'My clutch went.'

Thunders returns to his minute inspection with a faint grin around his lips: 'Yeah? Sounds like one of them female things.'

One of Peter Perrett's children is running around with a banana. Satisfied with himself, Johnny surrenders the mirror to Patti and strolls across to talk with Perrett senior. Billy Rath sprays his hair and pats it into place. Anita Pallenberg, clad in traditional spy uniform of trenchcoat and black glasses, goes over and greets him warmly.

Downstairs in the ballroom, the capacity crowd starts stamping their feet when the house lights abruptly dim. Thunders picks up his guitar and leads Cosa Nostra along the backstage walkway which is now filled with well-wishers, Tony James, Stiv Bators, Siouxsie Sue, Dave and Laurie Vanian, amongst them.

A syringe is thrown to land at Billy Rath's feet as he walks on stage. He checks the needle has been devenomised for the event, and throws it back. Flowers would have been nicer. Half an hour before, a couple of pushers, one dressed in black PVC with face powder thicker than a Japanese hooker, have argued with Christopher about his policy of keeping trash away from the band. When attempts at a cold politeness fail, he gestures at the nearby bouncers who roughly escort them from the area.

The set lasts over two hours. Thunders paces himself like an expert. Obviously happy with the night's strength, he plays and sings, jokes and curses with a calm crowd control that works better than his normal indifference. The absence of a guitarist of the calibre of Walter Lure is noticed when Johnny goes off stage at one point to talk with Susanne and Christopher in the wings. Michael Thimren, the second guitarist recruited from Jerry's Swedish band, cannot hope to cover for him. Thunders returns alone for an acoustic set that includes 'Memory'. Even he looks mildly surprised as the audience starts singing with him. Not one for sentimentality, Johnny lets the guitar hang around his neck while he tries to buy a joint: 'Hey. Nobody got a joint tonight? I don't need batteries for my fuckin' brain, somebody gotta have a joint: I got a quid if you got a joint.'

Lyceum, London '83.
(*Ian Dickson*)

Thunders ends negotiations by burping loudly into the microphone:
'Awright ... awright. I'd like to bring up my friend, Peter Perrett ...'

The rest of the introduction to the former leader of The Only Ones is lost
in a burst of applause.

'... I'd like to bring up little Patti Muppet from Snatch ... you know that
old whore ... I'd also like to bring back Jerry Nolan and Billy Rath ...'

The audience pounds its collective feet loud enough to be heard above the
trademark roar of Thunders' guitar. Johnny interrupts the final chords of
'Pipeline' with a nonchalant wave. He's very obviously aware that, if he ever lost
London, he's just won it back.

(*Marcia Resnick*)

After returning to France, Thunders set out on a short tour that mainly concentrated on the south. When the dates were done, he started working on *Hurt Me*, an acoustic album scheduled for a November release on New Rose.

The Lyceum concert, meanwhile, brought him some of the most favourable reviews that he'd received in England for a long while, marking a slight thaw in journalistic attitude. Like anything given grudgingly it was to be taken back. Even the *NME*, who almost seemed to have an editorial policy against anything Thunders did, let their man on the spot, David Quantick, muse over why:

> It's a paradox the way Thunders goes from suicidal gloom to defiant euphoria in the space of two songs.

Sounds let Robin Gibson wheel out the soapbox to report that:

> He didn't fall over and he wasn't so noticeably arrogant. Thunders thankfully concentrated simply on playing with his – slightly shaky – panache, and with a surprising coherence. The legend, the lifestyle and the cringe– inducing tribute to Sid Vicious, all of those stink: the rock 'n' roll

though – highly predictable, yet immensely pleasing – does not stink. That
understood, all that can be expected is that Thunders will keep on playing
it, and on this evidence he's still very capable of doing so.

Towards the end of November there is a small, low-key announcement that
Thunders is going to reform The Heartbreakers, and play a short tour. These
plans, however, are shelved for financial reasons. Instead, to coincide with the
release of *Hurt Me*, Thunders returns to England for two small dates at the
Brighton Escape on 5 December and Dingwalls on the 6th.

In Camden, the manager of Dingwalls is starting to panic. For Thunders, a
two-hour lateness shouldn't raise an eyebrow. The staff at the club search for
Johnny's hotel phone number, to confirm whether he has left for the gig. He
has. The venue is so packed one can barely see the small figure wandering on to
the stage – or the raised platform that serves as a stage at Dingwalls.

Just Thunders and guitar. The pub/club is too hot for any uncycled breath
to reach the lungs and the crowd surrounding the front make Johnny invisible
apart from the occasional glimpse of his black hat. Even the spaces around the
various video screens that are transmitting the show, are filled. Like a voice in
the wilderness, Johnny plugs a gig later that evening, before withdrawing to the
dressing room. He's been paid, and from his unfocused eyes and slurred speech,
so has his medicine man. His companions, Peter Perrett and his wife and
Johnny's girlfriend, are not exempt from the chemical alterations.

At the Pipeline, Thunders passes a test pressing of *Hurt Me* to the DJ to play
while he gets himself ready. By word of mouth alone, the tiny club is packed to
and well beyond it's capacity and a percentage of the audience have left, thinking the album was the man. Thunders walks slowly on stage in the early hours
of the morning and busks his way through a collection of his own songs,
reinforced here and there with a couple of Bob Dylans and one or two Rolling
Stones. Towards the end, he is joined by Peter Perrett:

> There was a gig when he made me play acoustically with him. I must have
> realised it was going to be bad cos I turned up late. I was meant to be play-
> ing with him at Dingwalls. The only reason he was doing it acoustically
> was to have more money to spend on drugs, he didn't have to hire equip-
> ment or pay musicians. Later that same evening he was supposed to play
> a set at *Gossips* [the Pipeline] and as I was there, I had to go on with him.
> I agreed to do it even though everything told me not to, but he had this
> way of acting so hurt. I was given an acoustic guitar, it didn't even have a
> strap on it. There was one mike between us and the audience were two feet
> away. I don't mind the audience being close while I'm confident and

Just Thunders and guitar. (*Marcia Resnick*)

enjoying it, but when you're feeling like that, 'What am I doing here?' It
was the only time I've been embarrassed on stage. †

Retiring to spend Christmas in Sweden with Susanne, Johnny watched as
Hurt Me reaches number twenty-two in the charts. The album's liner notes have
been written by the guitarist. Next to the Cosa Nostra track, in his inimitable
scrawl, it says 'Kiss me in Italian', a reference to the fatal endearment used by
hitmen familiar with their target. Although missing the essence of what
Thunders can present live, *Hurt Me* is still more than just an experimental
acoustic record by someone whom electricity was invented for. With a gentle
clarity on his production, J.T. manages to act as both addict and iconoclast to
the effects of popular romance, in his interpretation of (mostly) his own songs.

Returning to London in February, Johnny again puts a new slant on some
established material, this time aided by Tony James. The pair are ensconced in
Greenhouse Studios, hunched alternatively across the mixing desk or around
the gas heater, trying to restore *L.A.M.F.* to what it should have always sounded
like. Thunders sits immobile by the tapes, ignoring the early dawn chill that has
everybody else present huddled into coats and blankets. Susanne is somehow
attempting to catch a brief nap on the sofa underneath one of the huge
speakers. The latest in a seemingly endless line of untipped cigarettes hanging
from his lips, Thunders pounds his fists on his knees, miming the drum intro
to 'Born To Lose': 'Do it harder, harder. The first crash has gotta be harder –
really bangy.'

Christopher arrives, pleased at the productivity around him. The present situation, for perhaps the first time in almost a decade, allows for a (very) careful optimism. During 1983, Thunders played forty-five sell-out concerts, established himself with production work and now, less than a month hence, a Heartbreakers reunion concert is planned, with a live album and video.

Patti Palladin makes a grand entrance; tonight its her birthday: Christopher opens a bottle of champagne and raises a plastic beaker in toast to the Brooklyn singer: 'May all those things you dream of come true.' Thunders wishes her a 'Happy Birthday, scumbag' before jumping up and chasing her round the mixing desk.

Johnny takes a deep drag on a joint before offering it to Tony, who waves it away in favour of another bite of cold pizza. Thunders holds up a hand and then intones slowly: 'I don't need society to open up my pride for me ...' before pressing a button that releases the remixed 'All By Myself' into the room. Tony James decides that 'a miracle has been performed'. Johnny just nods. 'Yeah, the tape sounds better.'

Christopher lights another cigar and does a headstand worthy of Gomez Addams. 'I can drink on my head too.'

Johnny looks at him in some amazement: 'Four in the mornin' too.'

The Heartbreakers pull off an unexpected coup on the ears of England when, on 24 March, Radio One's Richard Skinner put the censored and remixed 'Get Off The Phone' on the deck as a preface to interviewing Thunders on his early evening, nationwide show. Johnny, despite sounding like Dustin Hoffman doing his 'Ratso' voice, is very much on the ball. Even his one liners are well thought out and sarcastically witty. The DJ leads him through a string of obvious questions about The Dolls until he generates the guitarist's interest by asking him if it was in 1975 he first met with Malcolm McLaren:

THUNDERS: Yeah – and that was a large part why everything went the way it did.

SKINNER: Why?

THUNDERS: Why?!?

SKINNER: What was the influence of Malcolm McLaren on The New York Dolls in the end?

THUNDERS: Malcolm had this thing that he thought we only hadda dress good, and he didn't really care about the music much. I mean we played good, we just ... we never hit it off together. He was English and we were American. A sea apart.

SKINNER: Was he practising, in a way, for what he did later?

THUNDERS: Well, if you're asking me – there's your own answer.

SKINNER: You're not going to say any more than that?

THUNDERS: Do I have to?

The interview continues with Richard Skinner's surprise that Walter Lure, one of New York's most respected and better-known guitarists, was working on Wall Street as a commodity broker.

THUNDERS: Believe it or not, yeah.

SKINNER: That's great. He's having a quick vacation with The Heart-breakers?

THUNDERS: He goes back to work on Wednesday.

SKINNER: If people want to see you in London tomorrow, where will they see you?

THUNDERS: The Lyceum.

SKINNER: All right. Have a good gig.

THUNDERS: OK. See ya. *Be there or be square.*

'Chinese Rocks' marks the end of Thunders' stay at Radio One. Richard Skinner comes back on the air laughing:

SKINNER: That's a terrific record ... 'Chinese Rocks' from Johnny Thunders and The Heartbreakers. I saw them live – round about 1977/8 – terrific night. The sight of Johnny Thunders dodging glasses will stay with me for a while to come.

The Lyceum: a red mini bus containing the band pulls around the back entrance. Billy shakes his head. 'Do you see that crowd? We've sold fuckin' out.'

Jerry, ever dour with a manic, humorous edge, fixes the bass player with a poker face and half a smile: 'What did you expect – only our moms would check us out?'

The addition of a film and recording crew has typically unnerved Johnny, and before going on he downs eight double vodkas in record time. The gig is heralded by the blasting instrumental of 'The Man With The Golden Arm'. Following a split-second lull, The Heartbreakers take their places on stage, Johnny stumbling theatrically before they launch into 'Pipeline'. The unspoken aggravation between Lure and Thunders' guitars produces a mesmerising tension. Both take turns on lead with equal ease and urgency. At one point during the set, Johnny tries to attract Billy's attention by walking over and kicking out at the bass player's legs. Rath's stony glare is enough to instantly send Thunders pirouetting back to the stage front like a demented prima donna. Jerry Nolan, as always, ignores the antics of his colleagues and continues to pummel the drums into submission.

There is something hilariously sinister about watching this rabid pack of debauchees singing 'Seven Day Weekend', twisting the innocent lyrics into something much darker.

Thunders cuts short his acoustic spot: 'Awrite ... that's enough of this shit ... I'll get th' boys back on...'

The Heartbreakers are back, gunning from the lower levels; time has made them harder.

Thunders is drunk ...

Rath looks annoyed ...

Lure looks nonchalantly bored ...

Nolan looks unmoved ...

During a guitar pause in 'So Alone', Johnny decides to add a touch of blasphemy to his public sins. After a story-telling tangent that sees him tarry rather too long on the subject of a kid on the lower East side, who loses his virginity to a 'big black guy in leathers' he piously makes the sign of the cross before intoning slowly: 'Our Father Who Art In Heaven, Hallowed Be Thy Name ... Fuck You.'

In early April, the guitarist featured in the Swedish press again. Only this time the tone was a great deal calmer. Under the simple headline 'I WILL BE BACK', a reporter noted that 'Last night Johnny Thunders left Sweden and took the ferry to Abo, from Stockholm. When the boat left Swedish waters he picked up his guitar and played a free gig in the restaurant. It was, said Johnny, "a private protest against the Swedish bureaucrats."'

Thunders had been in Sweden for a week, unable to play his advertised concerts due to claims made by one Gunner Oldenir (63) that the guitarist would be taking employment from Swedish musicians. Oldenir's obscure and stupid reasoning won Thunders a certain level of sympathy from within the Swedish music business. Johnny told the press that Oldenir's statement was 'dead silly to stop me for that reason. Besides, I'm free from my drug problems; I've been on methadone for the past two years, and I've quit that too. It happens that I drink quite a lot, but which rock star doesn't?'

Describing how his only controversial gig during the last Swedish tour had been an 'accident', he explained to a party of journalists that he had been so drunk he couldn't keep on his feet. The guitarist's attitude combined with a rare display of public diplomacy won over the press, who started describing him as looking 'healthier' and 'alert' every time they mentioned him. Johnny pressed his media victory by telling them: 'In a week I'll try and get a new work permit. I won't judge Sweden by one bureaucrat. I like being here. My girlfriend, Susanne, is from Stockholm and the audience has always been one of the best.'

Leaving Thunders to sweet talk the papers, various music and promotion companies went to the government's Minister of Culture to complain about Gunner Oldenir's obstructive behaviour, and to try to effect a change in the law concerning foreign performers who cannot get work permits. Thunders' Swedish promoter, Lasse Lindros, insisted that: 'We have to stop this nonsense.

As a protest against Swedish bureaucrats who had refused him a work permit, Johnny played a free gig on a boat as it left Swedish waters. (*Bertil Wölner*)

Every musician is unique. You can't replace Johnny Thunders with someone else. The Home Office's motivation is stupid.'

In Finland, where the tour had started up again, Johnny requested written reports of the four gigs he played there from both the local police and the Home Office, in an effort to make the Swedish authorities retract their decision. He was adamant: 'I'm not gonna give up until I can play to my Swedish fans again.'

By June the Swedish government had backed down and Thunders returned with what he called 'The Revenge 84 Tour', consisting of Jerry Nolan, Billy Rath and Sylvain Sylvain.

As well as covering some of Sylvain's material, including 'Teenage News', which dated back to The Dolls, Thunders sang a couple of new songs, namely 'Size Ten Shoes' and 'Have Faith', which featured on a range of Thunders' T-shirts. Back in England, the release of *Live At The Lyceum*, drew the sarcasm of the English press. Content to praise The Heartbreaks the band while they remain a memory and a safe distance away, able to make slightly censorious comments with a good natured liberality on the band's stance, the reality of a new album and a special reformation was simply too potent to handle. Both the major music papers reissued all their old one liners and trite puns about needles and nastiness, for a new generation to see.

Pirate Love

9
Ask Me No Questions

Johnny Thunders likes publicity and hates giving interviews. He has a utility belt of stock answers to certain questions that are slurred into every tape recorder placed before him; either that, or chanted in a *Midnight Cowboy* monotone that makes it clear he'd rather have stayed in bed or whatever. His manner during interviews is frequently enough to give all but the extra thick skinned a bad self-confidence crisis: his fingers play with whatever's around at the time; a book of matches, a lighter, a television set – anything to distract him from the boring question-and-answer routine. Certain aspects of his private life are taboo – which is, of course, Johnny's right. The most frustrating thing about him is his left-field sense of humour and bleak, almost Runyonesque one-liners that almost always surface after the interview time is over. The adoption of some strange tactics have been necessary to get a word or thirty with the real man behind the public front. Even, at one point, going so far as planning, with the help of Susanne, to kidnap him in their hotel room, keeping him away from drugs, friends, videos and television, in an effort to get him to talk. As the book developed, along with a sense of familiarity, Johnny opened up as far as possible. Could you speak up a little, Johnny?

JOHNNY: I hated school. I always did terrible anyway, couldn't wait to leave. I quit when I was about fourteen. See, school in America is very social, I guess. And I never really joined a gang, I used to have more fun just hangin' out in the neighbourhood parks. Kids get involved with the street gang scene for lots of reasons ... for protection ... 'cos their friends are in one, y'know. Background has lot to do with it too. Certain areas, stuff like that. I was brought up in Queens, which is sort of a middle-class area of Manhattan. I used to play baseball all the time, ever since I can remember. I grew up with just my mother and my sister. We lived in a one-and-half room apartment till I was about twelve or thirteen. Then we moved into a big house with my grandmother; her husband died, so we moved into the house with her. I guess I stayed there right up until I was fifteen. My mother got married so I moved out and found my own apartment.

I still see them or talk to them on the phone or whatever. It was good living with a sister who was older than me. I got to listen to all of Mariann's records, lots of the sixties' girl bands like The Shangri-Las, The Ronettes, The Crystals, The Angels. I liked music ever

Beyond the fringe.

since I was a little kid … Eddie Cochran and Gene Vincent. Yeah, music's always been important.

NINA: You must have been very young when you came to London the first time?

JOHNNY: Yeah. I was really young then. It was 69, something like that. A friend of mine in New York was workin' for a magazine so I got to borrow their press pass and when me and a girlfriend came to England we just kinda went around checkin' out all these bands for free, y'know. I saw, must have been fifty or sixty bands. I saw Tyrannosaurus Rex. It wasn't long after I went home that I got into music myself.

NINA: So The New York Dolls would have been your first band?

JOHNNY: Yeah, more or less. We were called 'Actress' for a time.

NINA: Does it bore you answering questions about The Dolls period in your life?

JOHNNY: Sort of … not bore me … but, y'know, you kinda run out of ways of answering the same questions after a million times or so. And nobody was that interested at the time The Dolls existed, but, I guess that's often the way, huh? I mean, I still play with Jerry sometimes, and I had Sylvain in my band a couple of times. I've run into David. I never see Arthur but nobody sees Arthur. I did hear he got married and lives somewhere in Brooklyn. Who knows? To have been a part of it was great, in the beginning we had a lot of fun. The Dolls

A wink and
a prayer.
(*Alison Gordy*)

played some great gigs, we played the Waldorf Astoria, one of the
biggest hotels in New York, on Hallowe'en. We had all these crazy
people coming to see us in all kinds of weird make-up and stuff. The
Dolls set a lot of styles. We got ripped off then and we got ripped off
now. I thought the band had gone as far as it could. Towards the end
we had Malcolm McLaren managing us, and he wanted us dressing
in red leather and stuff. Me and Jerry thought it was more important to get a new set together. We had five or six new songs and we
wanted to get back to New York – we were in Florida – and work on
them, but David thought we should stay with Malcolm … and he
liked calling the shots, so me and Jerry just split back to the city and
started up The Heartbreakers. I don't gotta name names to tell you
how much The Dolls' influence is still around. The Dolls had a
couple of managers, Leber and Krebs, who didn't give a fuck about
us at all. They just wanted to make lots of money for themselves. I've
always had problems with managers though.

NINA: Tell me a little about The Heartbreakers.

JOHNNY: What's to tell? Me n' Jerry, we got back to New York and we got hold of Richard Hell, who'd just left his own band, Television. We thought it'd make a great combination; and it did for a while. Then we found Walter Lure and we stole Waldo away from The Demons, his band. Richard had this thing, kinda an ego thing, I guess, he wanted to sing all the songs himself. It wound up with me getting one song a night to sing, and Walter getting one song a night, and Richard doing all the rest. I'd had it with that number. I'd backed up a frontman long enough. Anyway, I was gonna quit, but Richard saved me the trouble. See, he got Jerry and Walter together and tried to suggest they get rid of me, but he didn't know Jerry. So we just kinda threw Richard out and got Billy Rath in on bass. It was a lot better with Billy. So that was The Heartbreakers. We got Leee Black Childers in as manager. We played Max's, CBGB's , we musta played every fuckin' club for miles and we had this really big hard-core following. Every place we played was sold out.

NINA: But you had some trouble with record companies, didn't you? Some trouble getting an actual recording deal?

JOHNNY: *Some* trouble? We invented the word. See, the companies was after kinda safe products, and The Heartbreakers had the worst reputation. Lots of people put the finger on me and Jerry for splitting The Dolls, and the press liked to write stories 'bout all The Heartbreakers wanted was drugs and sex and stuff ... and I guess the big companies thought we only wanted a deal so we could get an advance and go blow it on drugs and die ... naww ... we wanted to make records as well. The bottom line was, they were afraid of us. They wanted a band they could control and we obviously didn't fit that description. Then Malcolm invited us to England to do the Anarchy tour so, of course, we went and played it. We enjoyed it a lot, it was fresh or something.

NINA: And you got an album deal too?

JOHNNY: Yeah, we did *L.A.M.F.* for Track Records. They treated us OK at first, but they had lot of underhand things going on, that we didn't find out about for a while. Tax business or some shit. Typical fucking music business men.

NINA: Was that one of the reasons behind The Heartbreakers splitting up?

JOHNNY: I guess it had something to do with it, but there were other reasons apart from Track pretendin' to go bust. See, none of us was happy with the album mix. It sounded OK when we played the songs in the studio but when we got the tapes back it was fucked up. We mixed the album, right, and I went back to New York. Then Walter, who was still in England then, came in and mixed it again and fucked around with it, and then Jerry, who didn't get along too well with Walter, came in and remixed it again. I mean, fuck, nobody knew who did what in the end. Anyway between them it came out, and it hadda wait years before I got the chance to get back into a studio and fix it up the way it always should of sounded so Jungle Records could reissue it . Anyway, like I was saying, then Jerry quit the band. Walter 'n' Billy did a couple of singles together, I think, and I stayed on in England to do a solo album with Real Records.

NINA: That was the *So Alone* album …

JOHNNY: Right. I got the chance to do a couple of slower songs on that for the first time, things I'd written up but would've sounded kinda out of place on an LP by The Heartbreakers.

NINA: What did you do after *So Alone*?

JOHNNY: Vanished. Naww, I went back to America and tried the family life for a bit. I got three kids; Vito, Dino and little Johnny. I did other things too. Moved to Detroit and met up with Wayne Kramer and started Gang War. That coulda been a good band, but it just didn't work out. See, me and Wayne were different generations, right, and we didn't understand each other. It was a great idea, but that's not enough.

NINA: Do you think your career, your life, would have run a bit smoother without heroin?

JOHNNY: Of course. In certain ways. I mean, obviously it bothers me when I got busted for drugs or something. Nobody likes that shit, I mean, I would never advise anyone to start using heroin. All it does is fuck you up. But, at the same time, I ain't no fucking preacher either. I ain't gonna lecture people on how they live their lives. See, I was very young when I started using heroin. Young and innocent and I thought I knew it all, right? But I didn't know it all, and I'd never have conformed to it even if I did. I had nobody to warn me off, to tell me it wasn't right. I guess I was about eighteen when I started using heroin. I tried it and I liked it, and in some ways I don't regret ever having used it. I … I loved taking drugs, right? I thought I was having a real good time, taking drugs and playing rock 'n' roll, but I wasn't. I only realised that when I started playing without drugs. See, for me, it's much the same at the end point anyway, I can play great without drugs, but I can play great with drugs, as well. It's real easy to start, right? It's when you come to stop you find out you got problems. Like, I've had to go on all sorts of methadone pro-grammes and it's … well, it's horrible. You find that you get to kind of depend on drugs in certain situations, and it's much harder

King of the Gypsies. 'Nijinski': J.T. (*Marcia Resnick*)

          having to deal with them straight. But really, drugs just cocoon you,
          cut you off from the real world, alienate you from the entire fuckin'
          world. But the problems are still around, y'know? After the drugs,
          you always still got the same problems.

NINA: Does it make you angry when people want to see the legend rather
          than the man?

JOHNNY: I don't feel nothing about it. I get up on stage to make a little money,
          make the kids dance. I play for the kids who come to hear me play

Johnny
Thunders and
Nina Antonia
(*John Tiberi*)

guitar. Maybe some of my audience come to see me because of
something they heard or something they've read, but not too many.
Writers write whatever they want; people think what they want to
think. I don't live up to anything except myself. I don't usually read
anything anybody writes about me ... it might distort my mind!

NINA: Do you feel you've changed much over the years?

JOHNNY: I still feel the same way about music. I still won't compromise it and
I still ain't rich. I've maybe changed more in certain smaller ways,
like, the way I write songs or something. I usta write a lot of songs
about objects rather than people. Like, when I was young I used to
pick all my girlfriends by their shoes. If they had nice shoes I'd be
interested in them. Other things too, my tattoos for instance. I was
crazy. That was something I always wanted when I was a kid, so I

just did it. I wish I never did ... but... I like staying home more now, watching videos or something.

NINA: Are you content with the way your career is going now?

JOHNNY: I don't think it's too smart to ever be content. So much can happen so quickly. Since *So Alone* I've done so much. I've played all over the world and made records. I've started to make a couple of movies. That's a good example, see, when I was in Paris I started this movie about an American rock star getting off heroin and all that shit, right? I was also doing one which was, like, a gang movie, real violent, I get to kill about twenty-five people and I was really looking forward to doing them, and what happens? One runs out of money and the other movie, the guy behind it gets busted for a kilo of cocaine and he'll be in prison for ten years or something. You never know in this business. I like living in Paris and London but New York is always home. I'm dying to go back there and get those motherfuckers with my new band, y'know, cos they're used to seeing me with Nolan. We gonna do all new songs. I'm gonna start the show with me in a tuxedo singing 'New York, New York' – that's gonna be the intro of the show. You always gotta move. That's why I produced the *Hurt Me* album, and I've produced other bands too. I've produced Justin Trouble and I'm gonna produce this band in France called The Untouchables. I'm gonna do a single with Patti, we're gonna do a song called 'Crawfish', it was on Elvis Presley's *King Creole* album. Things look OK, but you never know. You can trust yourself ... some of the time anyway ... but it's everyone else you gotta watch for. I started The Dolls with managers who didn't give a fuck about us or our interests, they were just out for money. They showed me how cold and nasty people can be, and I just couldn't see what that had to do with rock 'n' roll. It's really hard to trust anyone in this business, and we were all so young in The Dolls, we didn't know what we were doing. The way we were treated was really, really rotten. Then, when I started The Heartbreakers, it was the same shit ... and I was just amazed to see how people just blatantly rip you off, you know? Then when I made *So Alone* with Dave Hill, and I thought he was a nice guy, but it was just another story of somebody else ripping me off in another way. It's just sad, the way they used us, all the different people. It's a real bad business if you don't understand it. It's a real bad business even if you do. It's ... it's just a rotten business. It's worse than being a whore.

NINA: And now?

JOHNNY: Now I try to be more positive. I have Christopher managing me, it's really good. I look on him as a friend; I never really had anybody before, a manager that I was a friend with. If you play Rock 'n' Roll tho', you always got problems. If I can have the same amps and the same PA every night on tour, then I'm happy. It's so defeating when you play with different equipment every night .... and it's different every night.

From the Spanish TV show *La Edad D'Oro*: a 1½ hour feature of concert and interviews. June '84.

10
Christopher And His Kind

The small Chinese restaurant in Soho is hot and without ventilation. Christopher Giercke obviously has more on his mind than dehydration as he toys, with great dexterity, with chopsticks and sweet-and-sour spinach.

Looking in from outside it might almost seem that with every live concert and record release, Thunders' public stature continues to grow. From the manager's point of view, things are far from black and white, and it's his job to hold them together with a mixture of tact and (subtle) tyranny.

Christopher waves a black-draped arm in the general direction of the Marquee Club that is playing host to Thunders and two Heartbreakers for the entire week.

'Of course it's good that things are going well,' he explains, 'but things can complicate each other so quickly. At the moment I have enough business problems without having to also worry about the personal lives of the people whose careers should be my fundamental responsibility. I mean, right now I am re-structuring deals for Johnny with Italy, Japan and Spain. Also an English tour with Hanoi Rocks is being set up.'

Christopher Giercke is a strange mixture of manager, artist and philosopher. While more than able to keep pace with the various sharks that infest his financial waters, he still has the nature of the individualist and looks on his charges with a humane, coupled with the abstract, gaze.

'So,' he continues, 'that is more than enough for one man. Johnny and The Heartbreakers still have to be considered a problem. Not one that cannot be surmounted, but … Johnny thinks everything is fine. He's 'A Big Star' … but they have a tendency when everything is good to get greedy. Today; they didn't want to pay for batteries for a tuner, yet they get $150 a day. They sent the soundman out to buy strings for them.

'Now, Johnny decides he doesn't want to play Dingwalls, thinks it will spoil his reputation. OK. It's not a great place, but it'll pay a couple of bills perhaps. They don't appreciate money. It may be their ruin. I try to present things to them in a diplomatic way to make them understand they have to be able and quick like everyone else living on this planet. Yesterday they are supposed to go to Foubert's Valley Of The Dolls. They are given taxi fares and people are waiting to see Johnny – a different Johnny – journalists, press agents and lots of fans waiting and what happens? Johnny doesn't want to go.'

Most problems, for The Heartbreakers, it is generally assumed, result from having more faith in plastic bags of white powder than in themselves. Giercke nods.

Ice and fire:
Christopher
Gierche and
Johnny T.
(*Marcia Resnick*)

'Drugs are always such a danger. Three years of hard work to make sure everything goes smoothly. Then, one single shot, and *out*! Tours broken up, health broken up, thrown out of the country maybe for just £50-worth of smack: but that's it! *Are they out of their minds?!?* Johnny's real problem is lack of responsibility, that's why they never got anywhere. When there is no leadership, then that's where the problem is. I suppose that's what I'm trying to teach him: leadership, standards and certain rules.'

The Marquee is overflowing with punters. Out front the cardboard sign 'House Full' is already up but people are still pushing to get in. It's the hottest August on record for years, and the overpowering stench of sweat and beer in the club isn't helping. The dressing room offers no respite, Neon Leon and The Bondage Babies sprawl around pondering the wisdom of playing saunas. By the end of their five-night stint as support, the entire band are stir crazy enough to spend much of their last set throwing cornflakes to the audience.

It's 20.45 and the otherwise tranquil Christopher Giercke is taking frequent glances at his wristwatch. The Heartbreakers, of course, are late when the door swings and Johnny, clad in an undertaker's frock coat, strolls in and politely requests the dressing room liggers to be cleared out. Jerry Nolan follows dressed like a priest who decided to become a pimp on a whim. He sticks to his customary pre-show regime, finding a quiet corner and staying in it. A few minutes pass and then Billy Rath wanders in, seeming to be unaware of his surroundings until someone hands him his bass and his eyes suddenly snap into focus.

Nobody talks very much. It's hard to say if the silence is brought on by nerves, drugs or surly dispositions; or all three. Walter Lure and Sylvain Sylvain were supposed to be playing tonight, but both are still in America, held back by Wall Street and a family illness respectively. Jerry comes out of his corner to ask how the book is coming along. He also confides he's thinking of writing one himself but has a 'real terrible memory', a distinct problem.

'Well, there are lots of people around I can ask, y'know … see if they remember what I was doing on such or such a date.'

With the band all present, Christopher visibly relaxes and circulates from band to road crew, reminiscing about the days he spent in the Amazon.

Hanoi Rocks are crowding the bar, waiting for their main inspiration to take it. They and the audience don't have long to endure as backstage things are at the casual phase when there's nothing left to do except plug in the guitars. Jerry is devastating an apple with real hatred, while leafing through a French magazine called *Losers* which has a large article about Johnny and The Heartbreakers in it. Thunders passes him a copy of *Red Patent Leather*, The New York Dolls' live album which Sylvain mixed, that has a sleeve shot of the band in their ketchup-hued phase. It used to be a bootleg and now it's official. Like most 'under the counter' items, it had a certain charm but, as a legit release, it's unlikely to help The Dolls already (in retrospect) legendary reputation. Thunders slings it into his now empty guitar case.

The lights out front have dimmed to a dull red glow around the equipment and the baying has begun in earnest. Untroubled, Johnny goes through his pockets slowly and comes up with a cigarette which he ignites, and then straightens his shirt inside his black and purple spangled trousers and, just like every night, pauses to give Susanne a kiss before preceding Billy and Jerry on stage.

Make 'em wait. Thunders stands with his back to the crowd for a long minute with crushing, unfamiliar notes shaking from the speakers. He turns, his frock coat curling around his ankles, and prowls quickly to the centre microphone:

'Well if you lookin' for trouble, you come to th' right place … I'm tellin' you, baby, don't waste my time …'

Johnny surges through 'Countdown Love', 'Who Do Voodoo', a couple of

bars of 'Alone In A Crowd' and a wall-shaking 'Personality Crisis' before pausing long enough to tug loose his tie and toss his coat to the side stage. 'Man,'
he gasps, 'it's *so* fuckin' hot. Holy shit.' Thick clouds of cigarette smoke filter
sluggishly through the stage lights giving his skin a moist translucency. While
Thunders grabs a few seconds to breathe, a guttural chant for 'Jet Boy' starts up.
Johnny teases his guitar into the opening notes and then drops it.

'Uh … this is about a guy I usta know. S'called "Too Much Junkie
Business"…'

These words, together with the chords that accompany them, produce an
acrobatic psychosis in the audience. Burly blokes spray sweat in every direction
as they hurl themselves forward in a convivial attempt to drag underfoot as
many as possible. One of the athletic lemmings actually makes it to the stage,
where he goes into a frenzied spin until a large roadie sends him somersaulting
back into space. Thunders turns a wary backward glance to the side of the stage
where Susanne stands, to check on her safety and, once satisfied, finishes the
number.

The Italian restaurant, while still within the clichéd corners of Soho, is a lot
more up-market. At least its bill was. Christopher muses over it briefly, before
returning to more pressing matters. He is still worried about drugs: temptation
and effect. Thunders is almost, for the first time in many years, free of his addiction to heroin. His methadone intake is also decreasing. Christopher wants
to keep it that way.

'Some equations are obvious and must be made. If you drink ice water you
get a stomach ache and if you shoot up with dirty needles you get an infection.
Johnny is very talented and that gift takes away the right to indulge in self-pity.
Once you have a talent you also have an obligation to express it. You can't go
out on stage and not know where you are. You can't. You can maybe get away
with it for a short time but, in the long run, there may be a time to bring all
that beauty together, and if you can't do it, then the gift might be taken away.'

He pauses for a moment, his thoughts obviously on Billy and Jerry.

'Of course, it's also possible to make great music and in reality be a scumbag. Billy and Jerry are sick in medical terms. If you have to take sixty mil. of
methadone then you are sick. But they are closet queens about junk, they want
to be applauded and yet make problems in not being healthy.'

Don't you think it's possible for them to clean up their acts?

'They've broken promises hundreds of times … But I don't write anyone off.
We all have to make decisions. We all have to try and survive, don't we? They
have to be clean from their dominating obsession with self-pity. I mean, they
are not leprous outcasts with some fatal disease. They are very privileged and
talented and fortunate. If only they could see those privileges and talents. There
are so many junkies living without talent, without hope or attention.'

Was Johnny very ill when you met him?

'Well, a while back I took Johnny to a Corrida … a bull fight, you know … and it sickened him so much he almost passed out. Every thrust from the matador's sword was more wounding, more terrible to the animal. It was in great pain, but would not fall. Does that answer your question?'

What made you decide to take Johnny on in the first place?

'It was his birthday and I thought I could help him.' He smiles and lights a cigar. 'Johnny is much more critical now, and that is good. As an example, when we filmed the Lyceum show … 25 March 84 … we had a 24-track unit so they can see and hear what they do. On the Saturday everybody is using junk, right? On the Sunday, the night of the concert, the dealer does not show. So Johnny drinks eight large vodkas and goes on. When he watches a video of it now he is embarrassed and critical. You have to learn to know your weakness and to project. The process of changing is slow. Inside, perhaps, the first step is to be aware and curious. With heroin you can't do that, and I think Johnny knows that now.'

Outside the restaurant it's almost cool for the first time in days, and the air smells of rain. Christopher decides we've spent too long over the meal and is forced to hurry the half block back to the Marquee, dodging traffic and tourists, only slowing down when he sees Johnny and Susanne sitting quietly on a car outside the club.

'Sad Vacation', as always, is dedicated to Sid Vicious. Dozens of Instamatics take advantage of the night's traditional gentle moment, and Johnny is illuminated by dozens of flash cubes exploding in sequence. That bit of the repertoire over, he gives Patti Palladin another affectionately licentious introduction as she joins them on stage for three numbers.

Alone again, The Heartbreakers tear through various of their classics until, during 'I Wanna Be Loved', Johnny lets the bass carry the tune as he mops his face and starts to say goodbye:

'Thanks a lot, kids, it's been wonderful but it's hot … we had a really good time … I'm hot, you're hot … everybody is hot. We … we need a little fire to cook up some 'Chinese Rocks' for you now and we … we'll see ya …'

Everybody has been screaming for this song from the minute they took the stage and nobody is disappointed. If anything, it's even better than when they first released it. 'Can't Keep My Eyes On You' and 'Pipeline' serve as encores and then it really is over.

The taxi driver sticks his head out of the window to hurl a stream of curses after the lady in the grey Jaguar, that had cut out in front of us. He continues scratching at a heat lump growing from the middle of a blue ink tattoo until he draws blood. After what seems like forever spent driving around the

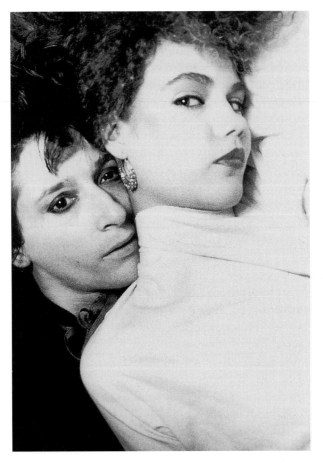

Sweethearts.
(*Marcia Reanick*)

clogged rush-hour arteries of Kensington, he stops outside a block of apartments that could have been designed for a Chandler film script. Susanne opens the door and Jerry sticks his head out of the bathroom in greeting before vanishing for the rest of the afternoon. Johnny is relaxing before another round of interviews. Just before coming over to play the 'Thunders Week' at the Marquee, he had once again been involved with the filming of *Personality Crisis*, as well as gigging in Sweden and Finland. On 18 August he played in Amsterdam, then headed off to Rotterdam for Pandora's Music Box, a mini-festival which also included John Cale and The Gun Club on the bill.

Susanne likes the apartment they're renting for the duration of the Marquee stint. It's more like a flat than the normal faceless hotels they usually wind up in. She's carefully unpacked: neat lines of guitar cases surround the bed, and scarves and belts tilt over the room's single chair. On a table beneath the window sits the latest of Thunders' hats, this one boasting a stuffed cobra coiled around the brim.

Susanne Blomqvist first met Johnny when he played her native Sweden over a year ago, and has been with him ever since. She remembers her parents' fears when she told them she was going away with the guitarist, and how those fears had been, slightly, quieted once she'd brought Johnny home to meet Mom. Since then she's been living his nomadic life, and longing for a settled base in either New York or London.

But not Manchester, where the next gig is. Even the horrific summer here is submitting to autumn in premature apathy. The pristine modern technology of an empty Hacienda gives an unreal element of sci-fi to the city that time ignored.

The atmosphere is tense and ready for an argument nobody wants.

Johnny slowly breaks the tip off his cigarette and considers my question: if he's been enjoying this stage of the tour. In Nottingham someone had thrown a bleach missile which had left Jerry Nolan temporarily blinded for part of the set.

'Not especially, no.'

Billy is standing by the table testing a selection of relish laid out in a large tray in the small cafeteria at the side of the club. Jerry hasn't said a word all through the sound check and continues to sit apart from the others, managing to dominate by his silence. Christopher mentions that a Swedish record company have been wondering what condition the band are in. Conversation turns to their last tour of Finland, which had come to an abrupt conclusion after the band hightailed it out of the country five hours in advance of their scheduled flight, upsetting the Finnish promoters.

'Everyone', remarks Christopher, 'lost 1000 marks [about £125]. Sylvain felt great about it.'

Johnny matches the irony: 'That's too bad for Sylvain.'

Jerry looks up abruptly: 'I live my life for Sylvain.'

The manager turns more fully towards Billy and Jerry before continuing:

'Look, I'm going further in the red and I see that drugs are bought. I can't pull a gun on you; it's your own life, your own choice: but you deprive yourself. I can't go to a record company and say, "They're in great shape". I have to admit I'm helpless. It's not good.'

Billy: 'C'mon ... you've been saying that for a year now.'

Christopher: 'I'm worried you could get busted ... anything could go wrong.'

Jerry suddenly stands up. 'Just pay my salary and air fares and I'll do my job to the best of my abilities,' and walks out of the room.

Evening.

Going into the club everyone pauses to look over the audience. Johnny smiles faintly at the dozens of black hats swaying around the dance floor that mimic his own. By day, the Hacienda dressing rooms double as a hairdressers and, as

Go Johnny Go!
(*Henry McGeough*)

we enter it, Susanne sniffs knowingly, 'Hairdye'. The small fridge in the corner has been filled to their specifications with the normal champagne, orange juice, Perrier and beer. Christopher opens a bottle and falls into conversation with Johnny and Susanne. Jerry is asleep. Billy is explaining how, by positioning yourself in just the right spot in the middle of an open road, you can avoid being swept up by a tornado.

They clatter up the designer interior fire escape and under the house lights. The audience is clustered tight in front of the stage and the band is as good as ever, but something is missing, Johnny obviously isn't having as much fun as he does in London. He is doing the encore when he finds himself alone on stage. Billy and Jerry have already made it halfway back to the dressing room when they hear him singing and pivot back up the stairway to finish the short set.

Everyone seems pretty emotionless on the drive back to the hotel.

With only days to go before the co-headlining Thunders / Hanoi Rocks concerts begin, Billy Rath and Jerry Nolan have left and are back in Sweden. Their replacements are comparatively adequate but no more, and the entire weight of the upcoming shows will be on Johnny's shoulders alone. With a bad cold, Johnny and his band join up with Hanoi Rocks and play a series of dates with them, including an unadvertised twenty-minute guest-starring bit at the London Lyceum.

By any standards, the Savoy Ballroom is the absolute pits.

Just like in the song, the plaster's falling off the walls. Outside the toilet someone has artistically placed two bottles of champagne, a heap of plastic cups and a crate of beer. If the toilet light is used, a roadie for the ballroom warns, it will fuse the hallway and the entrance to the stage.

The show is OK but with nowhere near the edge of the Marquee week gigs. The best moments come with the encore when Thunders parodies Thunders and Mike Monroe does a David Johansen. The audience, perhaps caught up in the spirit of their surroundings, remain lacklustre throughout.

The bar is no less depressing.

A fifty-year old woman holds court to a circle of liggers. She is clad in a tiny mini skirt and has a fine set of varicose veins running up each leg. Mike Monroe lies dramatically across the length of the bar like he's posing for a calendar photograph.

Johnny is remembering the recent date he played in war-torn Belfast: 'Those kids are starved for music ... I really felt something for them.'

He recalls the tanks in the streets, going back and playing 'Chinese Rocks' over and over for them.

Johnny socialises for a while and then decides it's time to call it a night. Jungle Record's Alan Hauser offers a lift back to the hotel. When the car pulls up in the Maida Vale courtyard not a light is left on. A tired Johnny waves goodnight as the elevator door closes.

Alone in a crowd. Gibus Club, Paris, France, 11 May '84. (*Wayne O'Farrell*)

11
Private World

In 1984, Johnny Thunders played ninety-five concerts world-wide, spanning continents in an almost endless agenda of sound checks, hotels and suitcases. Russia, Italy, Sweden, England, Spain, Holland, Berlin, Japan. The dates spill over into 1985, the backing bands change from city to city. For the last few months however, Thunders has acquired a more stable outfit. Out of the group that toured the UK with Hanoi Rocks, only bass guitarist Keith Yon remains. Experienced in the sudden call to arms, Henri-Paul has once again been drafted: how long he will remain is uncertain. His position, according to Christopher, is 'more then than now'. Only the new drummer, T (Tony St Helene), is an unknown quantity to Thunders' English audience. Having previously played with Keith Yon in the reggae / jazz outfit, The Tribesmen, T had come to Thunders', as a replacement for Terry Chimes who, in turn, had joined Hanoi Rocks after their drummer Razzle was tragically killed in an automobile accident in December 1984.

Mid-February. Thunders and Giercke are back in London for casual negotiations with the Beggars Banquet record company. A futile meeting takes up most of the first day. By early evening Giercke is drowning his sorrows in a bar before leaving the next morning for the Berlin Film Festival. Thunders has to stay in London a little longer to pick up some money he's owed, before returning to Paris, where he will hopefully add to the footage of his own movie.

In a small Italian restaurant just off Regent Street, Thunders is practising his celluloid alter ego, Johnny Valentine, a mixture in equal doses containing brief hints of De Niro tangled up with Pacino's hood from Havana.

Thunders as himself is an almost intangible presence. Polite and insulting. Charismatic and insular. He ignores social norms like flies on the wall. He sits at centre table; black hat tilted to the nape of his neck. A white dressing gown hangs around his shoulders while he breaks bread in an absurd reflection on the last supper.

J.T. holding court is an experience for the others in the restaurant, shyly peering around menu cards to catch a better look at the Lewis Caroll table behind them. Mike Monroe is presented with a small box wrapped in a print of Mount Fuji that Johnny has brought with him back from Japan. Waiters hurry backwards and forwards to keep pace with the conflicting orders. Pall bearers in sunglasses dining with an S and M flamenco troupe.

Johnny has returned from Japan with a good impression of both people and place. Each concert had sold out well in advance of his arrival. Even the journalists had liked him and treated him with a respect rare in that profession.

Johnny, Tony St. Helene, Henri-Paul and Keith Yon in Japan, January '85.
(*SMS Records*)

A miracle not unnoticed by Christopher Giercke: 'They didn't ask stupid ques-tions about drugs. Johnny was just perfect … he fits in there.'

Thunders rises from the table, taking Susanne's arm, and wishes everybody a casual goodnight before leaving. Stiv Bators leaves soon after with Mike Monroe and Terry Chimes following. Christopher lights another cigar, wipes the smoke from his eye and orders coffee. A question about the immediate future for Johnny brings a tired smile: 'Well, you know, we have to keep our fingers crossed for the unseen … but if all goes well, we play some dates in Norway before a return to Spain to finish off a television special and then, on April the first … a date which is unfortunate … we start three nights at New York's Irving Plaza.'

Christopher pauses while the coffee arrives, pulling on his cigar and warm-ing to his theme: 'New York should be quite something. Lots of Johnny's friends will be turning up to maybe do a guest spot with him: Walter Lure, Jerry Nolan, Sylvain Sylvain, it should be good. Johnny Thunders comes riding home. I think if he is clean when we get to New York, free of all medication, then he would be a real hero. There is nothing in his way then to stop him. He could be another Lou Reed or John Cale.'

Christopher Giercke, while still remaining very careful, is hoping that Thunders can at last shake off the 'junk-sick rock star' tag: 'I mean, three years ago, out of twenty-four hours, he would sleep twenty-two. All that has changed now. His level of methadone is down now to fifteen milligrams. It's all up to Johnny.'

Spotted in Japan
(*Mike Ariga*)

For lots of people, the Marquee week was a turning point for Thunders. Not for far too many years had the guitarist been so confident, so in control. Night after night he had stalked onto the small, overheated stage, flanked by Rath and Nolan, and turned in a set of raw perfection: one of rock 'n' roll's last surviving icons, a man without dreams or peers. The best.

A common idea is that Thunders needs The Heartbreakers before he attempts another leap at the stars; the grainy romanticism of The Heartbreakers is a tempting one. Even the journalists that came to hate their innards never denied the band's power or style. In retrospect, The Heartbreakers have left a mythology that's almost impossible to follow or imitate and the band themselves know it. Walter Lure said, with just a trace of bitterness, that nowadays he would 'just shut up and play for the money. It isn't really as exciting as being part of a group ... so I guess I don't do it for the pleasure of it now.'

Billy Rath has exiled himself to Sweden: 'I love to produce bands. That's what I'm actually working myself into now. In lots of ways, I think I prefer it to playing.'

And Jerry Nolan?

His relationship with Thunders spans some thirteen years. A friendship that has often touched on blood and a subversive loyalty to one another. Nolan is someone on whom Thunders was once dependent. Giercke described them as 'animals who went hunting together'.

Thunders' warped humour and his on-stage lectures and tirades that might've made Lenny Bruce blush, come as no surprise to his regular audience, but his new band consisting of two black musicians does.

Tony St Helene: 'I know Johnny gets his kicks from playing with us. We have a lot of fun seeing people go "What??? Black men playing with Johnny Thunders?" But, the same way we have to adjust our perspectives is good for them too.'

Christopher is amused by the radical swing in the Thunders' image and sums up with perplexing abruptness: 'They say: "We are Rastaman." OK ... it would be as easy to say as "I am superman" ... it all turns to cultural fascism.'

Jungle Records enter the video sales business with a forty-five-minute account of The Heartbreakers at the Lyceum Ballroom. With import orders being received from America and Japan, Jungle, headed by their Thunders' expert-in-waiting, Alan Hauser, attempt to make the product as alluring as possible within the realms of their limited resources by incorporating clips from *Personality Crisis*, which includes, along with a brief sequence featuring an attractive actress in gratuitous nude cameo, Thunders singing 'Hurt Me' in a seemingly deserted recording studio.

Jungle also stepped in to rescue the collaboration between Patti Palladin and Thunders; a cover of 'Crawfish' teamed up with their self-penned 'Tie Me Up', as the flip side. Originally it was to have been on the Swampland record label but arguments over the cost of the final mix caused friction and delays. Jungle's intervention let the record be released as a seven- and twelve-inch issue, together with a limited edition picture disc.

David Johansen, meanwhile, was on one of his periodical visits to England, playing two nights at Dingwalls to promote his latest album, optimistically entitled *Sweet Revenge*.

The onus of the show rests on the past. At least a quarter of the set is taken up with a New York Dolls novelty pastiche; a medley featuring Johansen dressed in a Florida bowling shirt, set off by an outsize pith helmet. He waves an umbrella with a toy ostrich hanging from it, trying desperately hard to convince the audience he doesn't care about fame and fortune, only having a good time. When the gig is over, Johansen and band set about getting drunk around a chicken dinner at a large table at the back of the club.

The singer had changed from his jungle garb into a flying helmet with goggles swinging from the long ear flaps. It's something past three in the morning and David is now tired and drunk. He manages to keep the smile on his face and when he hears Thunders' name mentioned, passes Johnny off as: 'I ... ahhh ... a guy I used to know who plays guitar an' used to play baseball.'

Ex-baseball starlet, Johnny Thunders reaches across Susanne and shakes a

Johnny and
Susanne,
London '84.
'True Love': J.T.
(*Marcia Resnick*)

cigarette out of the pack from the bedside table. Keith Yon and Tony St Helene
are crowded into the hotel room to watch some television. On the small screen,
like some pompous psychedelic Buddah in shades, Todd Rundgren is talking
about his astral artistic abilities. Thunders nods at the flickering image with
calm distance: 'He produced one of my albums once ... what an asshole.'

T and Keith leave and Johnny starts looking through various photographs
for possible use in this book: 'Naaah ... I don't really like these, y'know. It's
really important to have some good pictures too. I mean, my idea of a good
rock book is, like, eighty per cent photos and twenty per cent text, that's what
I like anyway. I tell ya, I got some good photographs back in New York. I'll
bring you some.'

I ask Johnny if he's pleased with the video.

'Jesus. Ain't it borin?'

Susanne protests that it isn't, and also points out that the guitarist's fans will
like being able to buy an official, good-quality video tape and not have to pay
exorbitant prices for a hardly watchable print, bootlegged from the States or
Europe. Thunders, who had to redub some of his guitar and vocals for the
video, is adamant: 'Nawwww. Its borin'.'

He sprawls out on the bed and asks Susanne: 'Hey, we going to go round
an' see Jerry tonight?'

Jerry Nolan is due to fly into London to headline a concert at the Fulham
Greyhound the following week with The London Cowboys. The one-off con-
cert has been advertised in the capital as: B.A.M.F. [Bad Assed Mother Fuckers]
Clean Bill Of Health Gig. But the drummer's luck is almost the equal of
Thunders: mostly B-A-D, and, on the night of the concert, it was left to one of

At a press conference in Japan.

The Cowboys, at the beginning of the set, to announce that Jerry had been arrested. Nolan had returned to Sweden on a brief visit and been stopped by the
police at the airport. With his passport held over, the drummer had been unable to return to the UK in time for the concert.

Johnny finishes off a second packet of crisps and groans loudly: 'God. I'm
so fuckin' hungry. You girls wanna go out an' get some Chinese food? I'm

starvin' to death. Get me some shrimps in hot sauce ... and some sweets, huh?'

On our return, Thunders gets into bed with his shrimp dinner and starts talking about his favourite audiences: 'The best audiences are in Sweden. I go down real big in Sweden, these days ... Japan was great, I really enjoyed it. The first gig was on this little Island called Kochi, off the mainland. I had such jet-lag, I went right to bed. I woke up and the clock says it's twelve, y'know, so I phone room service to order breakfast and they say 'What????' It's midnight.' Great place, the kids really liked it. Even the press were OK. I can't wait to play there again.'

Susanne remembers how they had returned home with about thirty kimonos as gifts for family and friends at Christmas. Johnny is watching a news programme on television, intensely. The reporter is talking about a Brazilian agency that sells babies to foreigners wealthy enough to afford them. He flicks the set off – 'fuckin' disgusting' – and falls almost instantly into a deep sleep. Susanne shrugs: 'I doubt we'll make it over to Jerry's tonight.'

Later that evening, as I'm just about to leave, Johnny wakes up and walks me to the door, offering some final advice on the book: 'Listen, make the end the beginning, something new. Whatever that is. I don't know.'

(*Kazuhiro Kobayashi*)

12
Hurt Me More

In Paris the sun still slants between the spires of the old church atop the Rue Lepic, turning the long stairs an orange dream of romance, worthy of a travel magazine. The fresh smell of detergents still haunts the carved balustrades, and the woodland sheen brings on a genteel nostalgia.

The tourist-motivated Parisiennes have delared war with junkies. Henri-Paul goes out to buy cigarettes and is detained for looking the part of the enemy.

Johnny himself is sick. He's flown to London and the process of trying to come clean, to detoxify himself after some thirteen years of heroin addiction' has left him weak and badly disorientated. Some days before his arrival in England, and in a completely separate incident from Henri-Paul's arrest, Johnny is also picked up by the police in Montmartre, who then worked him over. This example of police public relations has left Thunders shaken and paranoid. Christopher Giercke has located a young doctor he hopes Johnny will respond to. It's not going to be easy ; the terrible mood swings are the desperate actions of a young man who knows, if he can't kick the poison, then this time it may well kick him. To death.

Johnny Nine-Lives on the eighth.

Several weeks later, Christopher, still disgusted by the needless setback, is hoping that perhaps the situation can be restored: 'Without the intervention … it might have worked out but what has happened, has happened. Even though the detoxification failed for now, at least Johnny attempted it. Maybe he will have learnt something else about himself again. Bit by bit he's gaining some inside information about himself and that might just turn out to be the most important factor of all. I hope so.'

Christopher is much more of a friend to Thunders than a manager. They don't even have a contract. Trust. If Thunders understands that, then the battle's half over. If he doesn't, then that sword of Damocles may well be on a very thin thread: getting weaker by the moment.

March is coming to an end with Magnum grey skies making a last try to keep April in its summer confines. Thunders and band are in Tin Pan Alley Studios, to work on a demo tape. I ask the engineer how it's going. His only answer is a good-natured grin and a roll of his eyes as if hoping for help from that great technocrat in the sky. The studio is a sixteen track operation, now mostly used by pre-contract bands. After a quick checking out of his new surroundings, Johnny positions the band in their places and the soundman, Hessu, behind the mixing desk. He begins the warm-up by picking out some morbid

Sword play –
Johnny tests his
new James
Trussart guitar
in Paris.
(*Angie / Mama
Prod.*)

blues that sounded like it could have been the Howlin' Wolf classic musical essay in depression, 'Silver Spoon'.

Tony is just picking up on the beat when Johnny slaps a hand to his head and makes with a string of curses. Keith Yon looks up from his bass to ask 'What's up, man?'

A suddenly animated Thunders spits out his cigarette and opts for sarcasm: 'Wrong? Oh, nothin' much. I just forgot the fuckin' song books with the lyrics in. Shit …'

Johnny pushes some money in my hand: 'That should cover the cab.' Five minutes later I'm heading back to the hotel to collect his lyric books from a forewarned Susanne. The object of the journey is a small unlined notepad with a Japanese print cover. 'New Songs' is scrawled in large letters on the front page of the interior. Thunders' odd jottings turn up throughout, often with large blank spaces between pages, a few one-liners on a single leaf, a title here and there. Sometimes the odd familiar phrase like 'King Of The Gypsies', all carved in his strange, almost occult handwriting with its phonetic spelling.

Back at the studio, Johnny and Mike Monroe are on their knees searching for a block of dope they'd dropped. Monroe at last locates it and Johnny produces a pack of rolling papers.

'I'm gonna dedicate this joint to you.'

The engineer's voice comes over the studio intercom: 'Are we ready to roll yet?'

The band attempt Jerry Nolan's 'Countdown Love', but the song doesn't quite come off with the power it should and Thunders decides to take a break.

Back in the studio, after a stale cheeseburger lunch, I take the opportunity for a few words with the bassman and drummer while Johnny tunes his guitar and goes over some lyrics.

I asked Keith Yon how he felt about working with Johnny

Yon: 'It's a whole different world of music, like nothing I've ever been involved with. The audiences are different, obviously. I've been in quite a few bands, but none that have ever done very big gigs or anything, apart from one band called The Tribesmen. That's where I met T. We've been playing together for about three years now. Since The Tribesmen, we've been playing in jazz bands and doing different sorts of things … some poetry stuff, totally different to what we're doing with Johnny. We get to travel a lot with him, that's an advantage. You couldn't say Johnny was … easy … to work with. You just have to accept his moods.'

On the subject of travel, I asked Tony how he felt about playing Johnny's home town.

St Helene: 'New York? This is the first time I'll be working in the States. I've been as a tourist once, but this is something else. It's daunting because most of the musical standards are really high. It's sort of like bringing coals to Newcastle. But it should be OK, people come to see Johnny Thunders, y'know. When we played France I was really surprised just how big he is. They love the guy. He's very much the centre of what's happening. He has this aura that draws people to him – maybe it's his fatalistic attitude or something. Most of the time it's great. Mind you, when we played in … I think it was Berlin, someone threw a full can of beer which hit me. Perfect aim cos I was right at the back of the stage. I wouldn't mind so much, but when we were coming into Germany, the cops dragged me off the train and strip searched me. Overall, I'm really happy working with Johnny. For me, it's a brand new perspective. Everybody's got different parts to their characters that you don't always get a chance to use, you know? People are more comfortable being what they are – what they think they are – without endangering their environments. So sometimes I think it's good to step into another world.'

Johnny's health has shown little sign of improvement, and by the third day in the studio a bad cold has also caught up with him, that has his eyes hooded and his skin the colour of a 1931 Hollywood vampire. The afternoon's recording stops and starts around his coughing fits.

Over the months and years, Thunders has come to put a lot of faith in Christopher Giercke's ability to sort out any business or personal problems that follow the guitarist like a shadow, and when word gets to the studio that his manager may not be joining them for their New York homecoming, Thunders becomes morose and worried. It was Giercke that pulled Johnny from the mire of the lost-legend gutter and had since tried every way to make him understand that the first step of the artist is to respect himself. Once that is done, all that is left is the honing of the gift and its presentation to a public that has, more so in London and New York, almost always been prepared to recognise that a guitarist like Thunders can only be counted out when someone ties a tag to his big toe.

Johnny is sitting in a chair in the middle of the floor, head bowed and sombre in black, his boots are resting on his guitar case with the Cosa Nostra sticker across it.

Stiv Bators, small face almost hidden by an outsized pair of sunglasses, is waiting in the doorway to see what's going to happen next.

Mike Monroe stands just behind him, looking for all the world like a blank beautiful Roger Vadim creation.

At last, Thunders, the fragile devil in the flesh, gets to his feet and orders Monroe and Stiv to take their places behind the mike stands.

'One more time, guys, OK? "Try for Trash",' he requests, 'like th' old Dolls' song.'

Johnny raises his arm like a demented choir master as they obediently re-produce the harmony backing. Thunders lights another cigarette and winks: 'Boy. You guys really sound like th' alley cats, huh?'

Sometime later, with Johnny out of the studio on a periodical hunt for junk food, Henri-Paul, in a very dazed state, is wandering in circles trying to get his guitar part right. Tony and Keith try and offer the young Frenchman advice, as does the soundman, but then Johnny wanders in, rubbing his hands together and asking: 'What's been happenin'? Anythin' exciting?'

Someone plays him the tape. Thunders starts to light a cigarette and stops, the match halfway to the end. He sounds out his words slowly to make the meaning threateningly clear: 'Henri. What th' fuck is that? Do you wanna rewrite it or somethin'?'

'No Johnny …'

'OK. Then maybe this time you'll go and play it the way I showed you yesterday?'

Henri-Paul staggers back into the sound booth.

Stiv Bators raises his sunglasses and seems surprised that the light has al-most faded. The former frontman of The Dead Boys, and currently The Lords

Stiv and Johnny.
(*David Arnoff*)

Of The New Church, Stiv has long regarded Johnny as something of an inspiration.

Stiv: 'I met Johnny back in 1973 or something. The New York Dolls were playing in Cleveland, with Kiss as their support, and I got to meet him after the gig. What I really liked about Johnny was his attitude, you know? He had this spark in his eyes – I'd never met anybody so smart ass before. Everybody back then was so tame, and here was this crazy, real cocky little guy picking fights with these gigantic bartenders. I wasn't really in a band then – it was like, you know when you get into a rut and nothing inspires you? That type of scene. And then The Dolls came along and their record really fired me, made me wanna do something, you know? I was a real big fan of Johnny's, just through the papers, and he didn't let me down when I met him, the way a lot of people do when you get to meet them. The Dolls had broken up before I'd managed to get a band together, and I guess the next time I met up with Johnny was maybe about 1975, he came back to Cleveland with The Heartbreakers: just Johnny and Jerry and Richard Hell. It was great because all the audience had turned up dressed as Dolls fans, and then Johnny walks out with a DA haircut!

'We've known each other a while now. I even have his pink jacket that he wore on the sleeve of the second Dolls' album. I traded him for a pair of snake-skin shoes. Johnny Thunders is very important. People should respect that. I mean, I never told him this cos he's big-headed enough, but, a lot of the time, when you just seem to be spending your whole life slogging around bars and cheap dives, you need an inspiration, you need a dream or an image and Johnny gave it. It was just his general attitude – nobody else was like him. I remember one time when Cindy Lang, Alice Cooper's girlfriend, had followed the band to Cleveland, and we were walking down the street, going from one bar to an-other, and she's running after him with her shoes coming off all the time – she had these stupid high heels – and she's shouting, "Johnny. Johnny. Hey, Johnny, wait for me," and he doesn't even turn around to look, you know; just says like "Shut up, bitch."

'We don't see each other all the time, just sort of run into each other every so often. Before this, me helping out on these demos, I guess the last time I saw Johnny was in a bar in New York. He was attacking the drummer out of Tom Petty's Heartbreakers because they'd stole his name. Johnny Thunders is a rare breed. A very rare breed.'

The subject of the conversation sticks his head out of the recording studio and commands everyone to come in and listen to a playback of the embryo 'Crawfish'.

Thunders is half satisfied and straps on his guitar for a brief moment of im-provisation while chanting lyrics dealing with Mafia and murder. Mike Monroe attempts an accompaniment on harmonica while Stiv positions himself behind the drums. Keith Yon has almost decided on a suitable bassline when Johnny stops and tells the impromptu band he wants to try a version of Marc Bolan's song, 'The Wizard'.

Monroe raises his eyebrows and looks toward Keith Yon, who shakes his head, just as perplexed at Johnny's sometimes obscure musical tastes. Yon leaves the room, slightly nonplussed: 'Shit. I don't know what Johnny's playing half the time!'

The situation is resolved by the sudden arrival of Christopher, sweeping into the studio with a heavy black overcoat draped across his back and shoulders like a cape. He is briefed on events and proceedings and then ushers Thunders to one side for an instant business conference.

The last thin strands of daylight have long since vanished when Christopher Giercke sits down in the office. With the band finished and the technicians left

A new kind of racket.
(*Laurence Suaré*)

for home, the studio takes on an antiseptic silence. Christopher looks out of the window at the changing neon jigsaw below: the only time of the day when London looks picturesque to anyone, as well as tourists. He unwraps a cigar slowly and turns his speculative eyes to the tape recorder and sighs; more in thought of the scope of responsibilities than the prospect of recorded speech.

'You know,' he begins, 'the great task of any teacher is to eliminate himself from the situation. He must do it in such a way that he is always there from a spiritual point of view, in case he is needed, but something is lost if he is depended on too much.'

Do you think that perhaps the danger exists that you may be looking at the situation too sympathetically?

He raises a hand slightly and rotates it in that timeless gesture of equivocation:

'I hope not. I don't think so. You see, over the past three or four years, my absences have been very deliberate. I want to build Johnny's self-confidence; make him realise he can take care of situations on his own without any help from me or anyone. Johnny wants me to fly out to New York with him, but I am going to join him at the end of the week instead, to see if he can do it alone. I am very seldom happy – but I feel almost happy now. After he plays New York he'll rest up for a while, then the important thing is going after a record contract. We are going to have twenty-four copies of these demos made on Monday to send around. Everything must be done in stages.'

He flicks ash from one black sleeve, before continuing: 'You cannot ignore Johnny's problems. Detoxification, or trying for it, has terrible emotional effects on him. It's time to stop. You cannot go on smashing in all the windows, threatening to throw guitars out of windows, getting beaten up by the police. It is more dangerous than ever now, with him living in Paris, as the police are on a campaign to clean Montmartre of junkies. Everyone who uses these kind of drugs reacts to criticism in different ways. In The Heartbreakers, for instance, Jerry Nolan was the only one who could be honest about it. Jerry would say, "I will do my job, and a good one, but I will still take heroin." You have to respect that. He is honest about it, while Billy and Walter just lie, perhaps to themselves as much as anyone else.

'To deliver what is expected is not enough. Johnny has the responsibility not to present a fucked-up image to the world, it is very selfish. There is a big difference in heroin addiction and having a good time. In fact they have nothing in common at all. Liquor is the same kind of weird perversion, to drink until you fall over. I mean, Richard Burton and Peter O' Toole are great actors, but it's a similar kind of perversion in that everybody around them is made extremely unhappy to see it. They had a sense of accomplishment, as Lenny Bruce had, but it would be nice to keep it lighter. Much lighter. If there is a responsibility to be donated from them, it is to learn from their tragic downfall.'

Christopher rises to leave the studio, then pauses: 'You know, it's not really a management's task at all. It's a friend's task to develop his responsibilities to those around him.'

Now New York is waiting, Thunders and party are caught in that frustrating vortex of pre-travel chaos that always seems to descend at the last moment. It's just before eight in the morning and the floor is a maze of luggage and musical instruments. Johnny Thunders is dressed in a neat, black gangster suit with a narrow stripe running along the slender line of his frame. The home-town dates mean a lot to his personal prestige, and he wants to go back in style.

Downstairs the keys are returned to the desk and Johnny and Susanne join the others in the lobby. Christopher arrives and glances at his watch. The taxis ordered to take them to Heathrow are, of course, late. A phone call to the firm provides no satisfaction and Giercke slams the receiver down with an aggressive curse. Everybody piles outside to try and wave down passing cabs. The Maida

Vale air is shot through with thin shards of rain and no taxis are in sight. Thunders shivers forlornly and lights a cigarette. Everyone stands in a motionless group with their eyes fixed on the road. The whole scene is like a sloweddown sequence in a Peckinpah movie before the violence and the soundtrack returns.

Heathrow Airport is reached with a few minutes to boarding time left to go.

The band line up at the departure gate with passports ready. The blonde hostess gives Henri-Paul a crocodilian smile and tells him that his work permit has run out that morning.

Henri-Paul looks up at her with the wide-eyed disbelief of the perpetual misfortunate: 'What? It can't be ... it's in order.'

The hostess flashes a row of absurd dental work and continues in her official monotone: 'I'm afraid you must have made a mistake.'

Christopher pushes Henri-Paul to one side and calmly plucks his documents from the woman's hand and glances at them quickly before tossing them back on the desk before her: 'You are the one who's made the mistake,' he snaps. 'Check the dates.'

She is still forming a frustrated apology as Giercke guides Thunders and Co. through the gates and toward the plane.

Yukio Mishima Thunders. The cover of *Que Sera Sera*.

13
Que Sera Sera

The well-publicised Thunders' luck didn't desert him. Arriving back in the city just enough in advance of the dates to contract a throat infection which took away his voice, the guitarist was still well received for his home-town comeback for all of the four shows at the Irving Plaza. During the course of the concerts Thunders welcomed on stage, as guests, Walter Lure, Sylvain Sylvain, David Johansen and even the reclusive Arthur Kane, climbing up alongside Johnny long enough to show New York that he was still breathing after all.

A little while later, he mentioned that some of the difficulties he encountered weren't entirely related to his throat condition: 'I dunno … I went to New York to conquer it. I fucked up. I really fucked it up. Next time … eh …'

The disappointment of NY melted into an almost insignificant memory by comparison with his next move. Having promised to attempt another programme of detoxification, Susanne and Johnny took a flight to Stockholm. Brooding on the various setbacks that had afflicted his return to Gotham – a proposed opening spot with Dr John being cancelled, his voice going, the financial losses of the concerts – Thunders found solace in a bottle of Valium tens during the long journey. While the tiny blue tranquillisers that were once prescribed to harrassed housewives may appear innocous to the uninitiated, taken in excess the consequences are far from sedate. Through a Valium veil, nerves frayed to a hair trigger, speech slurred but not enough to disguise the insults, Johnny was rude to his girlfriend's family who had agreed to pick them up at the airport. After spending the night at Susanne's mother's place, he was moved to a hotel. Reacting to Thunders' drug-induced attitude, Susanne terminated the relationship.

Christopher Giercke, still in his Paris base, was well informed of the guitarist's movements but decided to stay in the shadows for a while to see if Thunders could manage to 'plan things; to see if he can fall on his own two feet. To keep giving Johnny support is perhaps the worst thing I could do for him right now – for that reason I think he should try and make out alone for a time.'

Confused and in a bad state of chemical depression, Thunders didn't take the time to analyse Christopher's actions, which he regarded as a form of betrayal, and resorted to the tested analgesic of releasing his hurt pride in accusations. With an almost paternal detachment, Giercke remained immune to any barbs that filtered across to him and Thunders found himself really 'so alone'.

By early May, he drifted back to London, briefly residing at Stiv Bators' empty apartment before moving on to Patti Palladin's. Hidden amidst the dishevelled grandeur of Patti's mock baroque living room, Johnny waved away her dog that's been sprawled across his legs, to search for some cigarette papers. 'I dunno how she finds anything in all this stuff.'

Some minutes later, he pulled them out from under the mound of blankets that he's been sleeping on. The first lost gypsy, Thunders was obviously unhappy, the effort he made to sound determined forced by pride rather than genuine belief in himself. Taking a small plastic bag from one of the two suitcases that are pushed into the corner, he spilled the contents onto the mattress. Fanning the various scraps of paper and phone numbers around like a cardsharp, he located an age-yellowed photograph of a very attractive young Latin kid with heavy black hair holding a large, carefully posed book before him. Johnny had remembered my request and brought it back from his mother's home in New York. I ask him how old he was then, and he tells me eleven or twelve. Brushing the ash from a joint across the front of his light blue shirt, he slowly falls asleep. The image in the photograph a warmer lifetime ago.

Leaving a trail of smashed up apartments, broken glass and burned spoons in his wake, Thunders swung between London and France. En route to finalising the edit of his latest movie, Christopher conceded that: 'Johnny isn't ready yet to start working too closely with anyone.'

For a short while, the guitarist stayed in an apartment block near Hyde Park but without a telephone in his room or change for the payphone he can't call up Chief, the man who he will eventually elect as road manager/personal assistant. A burly six-footer and English realist of the London rock 'n' roll circuit, Chief quickly discovered that 'taking care of business' also involved the guitarist moving into his cramped flat for a spell: a less-than-easy domestic situation in which to set up a series of dates.

Their relationship began in a period of confused adjustment to one another, and even though, eventually, the situation appeared to even out, it never did mature beyond a short-lived and tenuous association. Chief made the arrangements – Thunders played his own games.

Despite an initial run of gigs being blighted by cancellations and postponements, mainly due to work-permits not being sorted out in time, Johnny had seemingly gained strength from the previous month's slide, and a fragile stability was maintained. By the time Cosa Nostra reached Manchester on 4 July, the concerts had fallen into a more regular pattern. Although Johnny promised something special to celebrate American independence day at the Hacienda, by the evening he'd forgotten the date. The following morning, the band drove back to London, Thunders deciding en route that they should stop off in Hammersmith to check out the venue of that night's gig, the Clarendon Ballroom. Casting a dispassionate eye over the empty hall, the guitarist left the talking to Chief, who tells a member of the Clarendon's road crew that they'll do their sound check after the two support bands, Bone Orchard and Chelsea, have finished theirs.

Returning early evening, Thunders strides in wearing a billowing blouse with mosaic print, Chinese slippers and a faint scowl. In the main dressing-room, he learns that Cosa Nostra's equipment has been buried under Chelsea's, making it difficult to dig out in time for the sound check. Although he has little interest in the dull quandry, Johnny is instantly surrounded by the Clarendon's roadies, bitching about the necessity of doing the check. Gene October, Chelsea's frontman, adds his comments and receives for his trouble a steely glance from Thunders on his way out and a poisonously adamant refusal to share the dressing-room with them.

By night-time, the venue's tiny spare equipment room is heavy with a thick, grey net of herbal smoke: there are no lighting facilities, and, as none of the paint-stained ancient windows will open, T is just about to ram a fist through one for some fresh air, when Johnny arrives and motions the band to follow him. Cosa Nostra wind their way through the tightly packed audience and climb up on stage.

The theme from 'The Man With The Golden Arm' comes screaming out from the speakers to signify the start of the gig. Bouncers crouch on their heels side-stage, muscular ball-boys ready to fling any unwelcome trespassers back in the field. This evening's trouble, however, comes from more technical origins when, halfway through the set, the power cuts out. T maintains a steady beat until it's clear that the problem is going to hold out longer than Thunders' limited enthusiasm with the hecklers. He leads the band back once electricity is restored and they finish the set. Not a classic performance, but under the cir-cumstances ...

Cosa Nostra played the Marquee on Johnny's birthday before briefly parting company. After making an appearance at Dingwalls' 'alternative' Live Aid show, Thunders travelled to Canada for what should have been a solo acoustic tour: instead he teamed up with two of the guitarists from the Canadian band Teenage Head, and used Chief on drums.

West 3 Studios
Sitting around a small black and white television whilst picking at the remnants of lunch from the local fast food takeaway, Johnny, Tony and Keith have called another halt to the recording session's progress.

'Hey! "The Streets of San Francisco". Ahh ... I seen this one before. I been to North Beach y'know, the place is full of whores an' guys in purple an' yellow striped suits.'

Thunders is at West 3 to record his first studio electric album since *So Alone*, seven years earlier. Rather than position the band in their individual partitions in the studio and work systematically through the songs, Johnny periodically picks up his concentration from where he last threw it, straps on a guitar, and commits his music to tape in short bursts. Later, they listen to a replay of the backing track for 'Endless Party' and everyone is mildly pleased. Thunders slowly puts a match to a cigarette: 'It's supposed to speed up a bit towards the end ... OK ... leave it for a bit. Let's try "Short Lives".'

'Short Lives' (a song paradoxically close to most people's expectations of the composer himself) took up the majority of the afternoon. By teatime, Cosa Nostra are back in front of the television but watching Johnny instead, as he tries to roll a joint, the contents of which keep spilling onto the floor. Thunders gripes: 'Rizla Orange, man. Fuckin' disgusting'. Like goddamned schoolpaper or somethin'.'

Johnny looks up and sees the tape-recorder, then nods towards T: 'He wants to say it's the best thing in the world to play with a white musician, it's the best thing in the world ...'

Peering over the peeling papers in Johnny's lap, T laughs: 'You should have a chapter called "Johnny The Spliff Vampire' you know.'

Johnny leans right into the tape-recorder: 'Keith and T are both scumbags.'

T: 'We're learning from the greatest scumbag of all.'

Keith: 'We're serving our apprenticeship in scumbaggery.'

Johnny: 'You gotta be a scumbag for six months to play in my band. Then I accept you. T's time is nearly up, but Chief's gotta long way to go. Lotta dues to pay – you'll thank me for this one day.'

As the weeks passed the album began to pull together, various friends dropping by the studio to lend a hand, including Patti Palladin, Wilko Johnson, Stiv Bators and John Perry.

Despite *Que Sera Sera* being the most controversial of Thunders' albums at the time, his regular supporters either loving it or hating it, the album offered the most current view of his music, but not the most realistic. The songs carried the familiar topics with the same, sneering 'Fuck You' intonations, but the guitar was either too low or even occasionally filled in by one of the guests.

With *Que Sera Sera* completed and the start of a major tour in the offing, Thunders flew out to Stockholm to see if he could repair his relationship with Susanne, whom he was missing a great deal. Not long after his arrival, fate threw yet another punch at the star-crossed guitarist when someone was supposed to have slammed a car door on his left hand, fracturing it and leaving him unable to play for several weeks. The American tour was put back and a copy of the doctor's certificate sent out to the understandably suspicious promoters. However, talking to Thunders on the telephone in Sweden, he sounded healthy and in good spirits despite the 'accident', and looking forward to taking off on a short European tour with Cosa Nostra. They opened in Holland, before crossing over to Sweden and Finland, finishing in time for Christmas when Thunders once again returned to Stockholm.

In February, the Johnny Thunders US Tour of 1986 went ahead without any

'Mister Niggs Nolan':
J.T.
(*Marcia Resnick*)

further delays. The vast seven-week itinerary of club dates, strung out like a neon necklace around America, successfully fulfilled the anticipation of both audience and press as Thunders met head-on the rumours and reputation that his very stance generated. Cosa Nostra were hard and tight and J.T. was at a performing peak (unlike his last stateside jaunt), but the customary chaos was also a part of the man's legacy: three dates into the tour, Chief called it quits when they hit Boston, failing to complete his apprenticeship in scumbaggery. Half mad from lack of sleep and the rigours of working with Thunders, Chief devised his own redundancy payment, in lieu of what he perceived to be his rightful earnings, and made a shaky exit in the dead of night. The curse of the dead presidents (US currency) tailed the tour back to New York, where Keith and T accused Johnny and Chief's successor, Stephen Hoda, of pilfering the band's funds. Incensed, they threw Thunders' clothes out of the window of the Chelsea Hotel. Fortunately, he wasn't wearing them at the time. With the echo of their parting threats still ringing in his ears, the guitarist left the maelstrom for the sanctity of Stockholm.

After a couple of weeks rest and recuperation, Thunders resurfaced in

London alongside Jerry Nolan in early May, ostensibly to work on an album by Japanese rockabilly guitarist, Jimmy K. The project, which had been co-ordinated by Thunders' old friend Marc Zermati and Japan's premier rock journalist, Gaku Torii, prompted a cease-fire on Nolan and Thunders' separation. Despite all of the exacting interludes, rock 'n' roll's answer to Bonnie and Clyde worked best against the world rather than each other. Young Jimmy K. had high hopes that their credentials would rub off on him, but it wasn't the kind of thing that money could buy, even though the record company were making it an easy heist. With Johnny in the producer's seat and Jerry taking care of the drums, the opening stages of recording looked promising. Between takes of the album, *Trouble Traveller*, Jerry was happy enough to comment on his long and often volatile relationship with Johnny.

'Listen, if I had it my way – and Johnny too, I think, had it way down deep in his heart – we would always have played together, but certain things happened where we had to separate for a while, which is too bad, because we sure do work well together. We bring the best out of each other. Even socially, friendship-wise, we bring a lot of good out of each other, as well. Sometimes we bring bad out of each other too, but musically, we're really good for each other. It's more than just playing, it's creating.'

With Nolan's wife Charlotte acting as business administrator, Jerry and Johnny planned a fifty / fifty partnership, recruiting a new band that consisted of former Sex Pistol, Glen Matlock, on bass and guitarist Barry Jones, from The London Cowboys. An inaugural gig at Dingwalls was pencilled in for 13 May, with second guitarist, Matt Kellett, while Jimmy K. had been promised a cue at the encore. A relative newcomer to the trauma team but nonetheless dedicated, Gaku Torii liked to hand out a business card that simply stated 'Rock Is My Life' – a risky motto given the circumstances. Gaku: 'I stayed with Johnny and Jerry in a flat in Baker Street. It was absolute fucking hell. At the beginning of the recording sessions, Johnny was OK but he was getting stoned in-between. The record company began to get nervous and I ended up acting as middleman. In the end, Johnny produced the A-side of the album. One day Johnny and Jerry had a big fight in the studio, Johnny started telling Jerry what to do with the drums. Suddenly, Jerry blew up: "Mother Fucker – you don't know anything about drums!" Another day, Jerry hit Johnny with a wine bottle. Johnny was crying like a child, telling Marc Zermati he wanted to go back to Sweden immediately but there was a show to play at Dingwalls.'

Aside from all the ongoing strife, Thunders was edgy about Keith and T who had made it known that they would be at the venue. Holed up at the bar, it became clear that they didn't really intend to harm the guitarist, just freak him out a little and their tactics worked. Johnny was so sloppy on stage he's nearly seasick, and manages to forget about Jimmy K., who is waiting in the wings. After the gig, Thunders asked the author for her critical reaction, to

Johnny and Jerry. 'Two old queens': J.T. (*Marcia Resnick*)

which she responded with some trepidation 'Ohh … it was horrible!' While such a response might well have offended many artists, Johnny found it highly amusing, breaking the tension of the night, but it was a short-lived respite. Gaku: 'At the Dingwalls show I was waiting with Jimmy K. because he was supposed to join Johnny on stage for a couple of numbers but Johnny was stoned and forgot about it. Later Johnny vanished for the night but the rest of us went back to Baker Street. When we got there, Matt started complaining about something. Jerry said, "Fuck you, don't talk about Johnny like that" and hit him with a big flower pot. His head was bloody and the neighbour wanted to call the police. The whole thing was a bad experience but I understood that this was rock 'n' roll.'

Despite Jerry's earnest torment when it came to his relationship with Johnny, he held no truck with outside grievances from short-stay passengers, whatever the circumstances. The broken pottery and scattered soil from the decimated flower pot remained on the floor of the apartment, along with other accrued debris and damages until the party checked out, leaving the chamber maids to nod their heads in disbelief when they finally gained access. After briefly touching base in Sweden, Thunders and company flew to Tokyo where they played to enthusiastic audiences of over four and a half thousand, in just four gigs. In spite of all the terrible capers that punctuated Johnny's life, and the chemical instabilities, there was no one better on a good night and in that electrifying moment the slate was wiped clean, the bad gigs forgotten.

Although Gaku had been driven to distraction in London, he was more than pleased to hook up with Thunders on his home turf. While Johnny continually tested the limits of all around him, he possessed the ability to be uniquely endearing due to a genuine vulnerability. How one survived was up to the individual. Gaku: 'Johnny came back to Japan with Jerry and Barry Jones and Glen Matlock. He was very well and the shows were great. He also played a big hall in front of 3,000 people for television. The promoter of the event had been made an offer by some Japanese musicians who wanted to back Johnny, so he booked a studio but Johnny didn't want to rehearse, he said the musicians knew his songs. The promoter who was very straight got really wound up about it. Johnny did have to do a sound check at the venue but he didn't like the sound of the amp. The promoter had ordered a vintage Marshall that Johnny had already used at one of the gigs but, before the television show, his mood changed and we started running out of time. I told the promoter to take the amplifier away then I went to see Johnny in the dressing room. "OK, we'll find a replacement amp." We just brought the same one back. Then the promoter wanted to know which guitar Johnny was going to use. Johnny said the Les Paul Junior, which was like his arms and fingers. However, later that day, he was given five or six guitars by a guitar company, including a red Stratocaster. Just before the show, he changed into one of his pink suits and was looking at himself in the dressing room mirror when he gets the thought: "Pink suit, red Stratocaster, good for TV!" but he was on in ten minutes and the red guitar was back at the hotel. He turned round and asked the promoter where it was, you should have seen the guy's face!'

Through autumn the band continued to tour, but a two-week stint in Australia was marred when the bus rolled over. Once the dust settled, Johnny was the first to scramble out but Jerry broke his collar bone and had to take an unusually gentle approach to his drumming for the duration of the dates. In early November they headed for Spain with a new tour manager in tow. It had been an easy progression from working with The London Cowboys to taking care of Johnny but not an easy task, as Mick Webster discovered: 'Jerry introduced me to Johnny and the first tour I did was in Spain, with Glen Matlock, Nolan and Barry Jones. After that, on 1 January 1987, we went to the States. Johnny and Jerry had equal billing and Arthur Kane and Barry Jones were in the line-up. That was a good tour, from one side of the country to the other, right down to Miami. My job couldn't be classed as an ordinary tour manager – I was on twenty-four hours a day. When Johnny was awake, I was awake; when he needed to go somewhere, I had to be with him. Some of the places we went to, you wouldn't want to visit in your nightmares, they were so bad, but I had to get him back safely so he could do a show. He walked a very thin line. It wasn't my job to judge him, it was my job to look after him. When I first started working with him, he told me I could never stop him doing what he did; someone once tried and he turned it around on them, they were doing what he did inside of five days. Sometimes it was difficult to get him on stage, he'd be in the dressing room enjoying himself. He always made the audience wait until it was right to go on. The promoters would be creating havoc but Johnny knew how to time it, the audience would be keyed up and ready for him; it seemed to be like a part of the show. The guys who had booked the gigs would inundate us with calls at the hotel, especially in America. They would worry and things would get blown out of all proportion. We had a lot of problems getting work, we were always being accused of cancelling dates but the only dates that were ever cancelled were either scrapped because it was impossible geographically or somebody would book a gig and we hadn't been told about it. Some promoter would say that Johnny was playing and then collect the money on the tickets; that happened a lot. There was always this "is he going to show up?" routine, but it was pure nonsense.'

As tapes filtered back from the two-week US tour testify, the band were hotter than molten lava, Nolan clearing a steady path for Thunders' cascading chords, Kane and Jones creating a perfect balance. Although the majority of the gigs stuck to fairly familiar material when it came to the set list: – 'Pipeline' / 'Blame It On Mom' / 'Dead Or Alive' et al and a midway acoustic break – the sheer force of performance was truly exhilarating, breathing new life into a bunch of oft-paraded numbers. Unfortunately, the truce between Johnny and Jerry was broken by the end of the dates when money matters and concerns over a possible album soured the pitch. Thunders arrived back in London minus Nolan on 15 February, primarily to work on a single version of 'Short Lives' at Matrix studios. Somehow J.T. and the recording process just didn't get on well; being placed under pressure to deliver was an edgy business and he often preferred to goof off rather than just get down to it, finding distraction after distraction like a magician producing a million multicoloured handkerchiefs from a top hat. Two days later, on 19 February, he entered Remaximum Studios with Patti Palladin, Glen Matlock and J. C. Carroll on mandolin, to cut a cover of 'Que Sera Sera' as a late accompaniment to the album. Despite 'Que Sera Sera' making it as an afterthought, the results were fetching, if a little off the wall, Thunders adding his own touches to the song that Doris Day made famous:

> When I was just a little brat
> I asked my teacher what will I be?
> Will I be a mess?
> Will I have success?
> Here's what she said to me …

While the single was in production, the immediate future snapped into focus when Thunders and Palladin began to consider the logistics of making an

Acting out, Johnny tyakes a break during the filming of *Mona et Moi*.
(*Courtesy of Patrick Grandperret*)

On the film set of *Mona et Moi*, with actor Denis Lavant and the film crew.
(*Courtesy of Patrick Grandperret*)

entire album of covers as a dual venture. Likewise, Jungle Records worked out
the logistics of paying for such a project. Alan Hauser: 'They negotiated with
us to spend £20,000 on the album, which was a reasonable price. Out of that
they took a personal advance of £12,000, which only left £8,000 for the studio,
but they thought that was sufficient.' It ended up costing £40,000.

A hit list was drawn up consisting of material that had once been the

Mona (Sophie Simon) et Johnny. (*Courtesy of Patrick Grandperret*)

On the beach. (*Courtesy of Patrick Grandperret*)

signature tunes of artistes as diverse as Judy Garland, Mitch Ryder and Otis Redding, but this initial selection was eventually superseded by choice cuts from The Seeds, Roy Head, Natalie Wood, The Shangri-Las and Dion, amongst others. However, the project was held in abeyance when Johnny returned to Paris to resume filming at the request of director Patrick Grandperret, who had finally managed to find new backers for his movie. Although Grandperret's film took even longer to make than the entire *Godfather* trilogy, the director was tenacious and keen to get rolling after the considerable delay. Numerous plot and title alterations from *Go Back To Go* and *Personality Crisis* were eventually ditched in favour of *Simple Simon* – the story of a fan and his relationship with Johnny – but as the latest story line developed, the film took a different turn, metamorphosing into its final evolution *Mona et Moi*. Patrick Grandperret: 'The film took up five years of my life but just four-and-a-half weeks to shoot. *Simple Simon* was a little like 'Sid and Nancy' but as I got to know Johnny, I wanted a lighter dope angle with more humour. Johnny did not have a big part in *Mona et Moi* but his role is very important. He was very easy to work with, he didn't like to compromise but there were no problems because we were in agreement with most of the ideas. I would direct from sequence to sequence, the actors would make up their dialogue, we would rehearse, then shoot. After *Mona*, Johnny wanted to make a film about the life of his manager, Christopher – that was his idea. He wanted to play Christopher and direct. We would have to find someone to play Johnny but I'm sure he would have made a great director, he was visual and had very expressive taste.'

After filming the additional sequences for Grandperret's movie, alongside a young cast that included rising star Denis Lavant, Johnny detoured back to London to warm up for the covers album. The finer details were still up in the air, save for the title *Copy Cats:* part playground refrain and a distant echo of a 1962 Gary US Bond's tune. Later, Thunders told an American reporter from *Records* magazine:

> It's a project I always wanted to do ever since I heard the John Lennon album, *Rock 'n' Roll*.

However, recreating the jukebox of Thunders' and Palladin's childhood, the tunes that tumbled out of clubs that were still adult territory, the music that came from behind the door of a sister's bedroom, the whole formica-topped, milkshake-flavoured, tear-stained, hip-shaking, heartbreaking panorama, was a multifaceted concept, rather than a basic rock album. As rehearsals began with the core of players from the 'Que Sera Sera' single session, it soon became clear that the wide scope of differing styles required to pull off a project as ambitious as *Copy Cats* would need a far larger ensemble, a group of folks that could shake bones like Screaming Jay Hawkins and click heels for an authentic mambo. Eventually an impressive roll call of twenty-eight musicians contributed to the album but first they had to be mobilised. Thunders sent out signals to Nolan, but the drummer stayed in Sweden.

Copy Cats. Johnny
and Patti.
(*Leee Black Childers*)

Meanwhile, nobody seemed to know where to find guitar supremo, John Perry. Patti managed to track down a Spanish telephone number, through John's old girlfriend, and Alan Hauser called the Catalan coast. Perry, a seasoned veteran of such calls – well used to 'urgent' Thunders demands – didn't break his holiday, but returned at the end of the month. The former Only One made his entrance as one bunch of sessions, already underway at Falconer Studios in Camden, seemed to be going nowhere. 'When I arrived, I found an unusually despondent Johnny (even by his standards) sitting on the steps, well away from the studio with his head in his hands; disjointed snippets of Nowhere Music drifting down the corridor; the purified sound of Nothing Happening. John leapt to his feet, flung out his arms, hugged me, and asked: "Dfuckyabinman?" Never seen him so animated. Once inside, it was pretty clear that the sessions had been drifting for weeks – though nothing prepared you for actually hearing the tapes! Began to see why John had been so pleased to see me.

'Remember, *Copy Cats* is an album of covers, and if you intend to cover a song, it is a distinct advantage – some might say an essential – to know the changes. Of course, Johnny could blag his way through any song with his three chords and come up with something kinda presentable – or at least, something that sounded like him – but the method was useless for a band. Two guitars, bass, keyboards all playing different chord progressions …

'So the first thing was to jot down some charts. At least note the chords and mark where the accents fell. Far as I could tell there'd been musicians around for a fortnight, but nobody willing to take the roll of bandleader (least of all Johnny, who just wanted to be Dion, anyway). What did we do? I think we scrapped the lot and started from scratch – new band, new tapes. Quicker to lay down new tracks than patch up old ones. Sessions were fun from there on. John used to vanish then phone from callboxes saying the CIA were following him – mortal danger. Alan had *gotta* send over fifty quid in a cab *now*. Hard to see exactly how the latter would solve the former.'

As the album trawled through the past, lightly covering material from 1958–69, Thunders plunged the present darkly. Any stay in the same place for too long was always dangerous and in London, mounting cocaine psychosis overtook him. Alone at night he unravelled, the shadows assuming demonic proportions while his worst fears manifested when he imagined that he had been arrested and had to turn himself in for an early morning court appearance. Fortunately, he overslept and woke up a free man. While Patti Palladin continued to supervise *Copy Cats*, Johnny flew to Stockholm on 8 June to be with Susanne who was some seven months pregnant. As the summer burned up so did Thunders' throat when he returned to put his vocals on the album. Recording was briefly halted until the mystery affliction, that periodically affected his singing, cleared.

With all of the Phil Spector dimensions and details that *Copy Cats* entailed, the cast list expanded to include a horn section, Maribel La Manchega's castanet flourishes and Chrissie Hynde, whose backing vocals grace Patti's tender rendition of The Shirelles' classic 'Baby It's You'. Back in Sweden, Johnny dealt with his own version of the same theme, as he looked into the eyes of his new-born daughter, Jamie, for the first time. Jungle, meanwhile, held crisis talks over the album's rising budget.

For most of the autumn, Thunders stayed close to home, aside from a sojourn to Paris where he played two shows at the Gibus. With Patti Palladin at the helm, the album entered the mixing stages, while the biography went off to the printers. On 10 November 1987, the first edition of *In Cold Blood* was launched in a converted church. The (London) Limelight had a full congregation as Johnny performed a twenty-minute acoustic set to mark the occasion. Afterwards he pulled me into a smoky corner of the former joss house to show me some snapshots of Susanne and Jamie. He was happy. Such a simple statement, I wish I could have used it to describe him more often. He glowed with

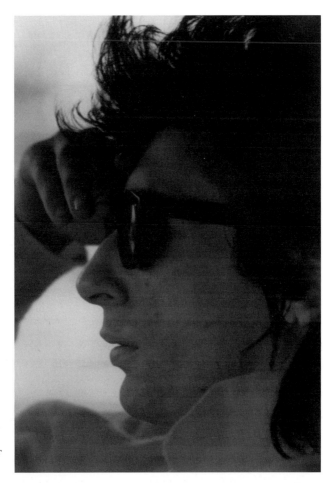

Through the
past darkly.
(*Courtesy of
Chris Musto*)

a poppa's pride and, whatever the downside of the guitarist's history, in theory he possessed traditional morals and was already fretting about Jamie's first date. With some concern, he detailed how he was going to tail the courting couple from a distance, just to be sure that his daughter was safe.

I signed off with a cautious optimism and an awareness of the fragility of such sentiments when it came to Johnny Thunders. Wishing him all the luck in the world seemed like a petty currency but it was the best that I could do.

(*Kazuhiro Kobayashi*)

14
Fate And Fatality

In the final descent of Johnny Thunders' life, he tried to pull back from the tail-spin, make some changes, but the ground was coming up too fast to meet him.

Amidst a build up of generally positive publicity and mounting interest in the release of *Copy Cats*, Thunders, accompanied by drummer Chris Musto, bassist Adam Pierson (ex Red Lorry Yellow Lorry) and Michael Thimren, played a truly disastrous gig at the Town & Country club on 2 December 1987. In a review of the event which appeared in *Melody Maker*, Carol Clerk, normally a Thunders' aficionado noted:

> I've seen Thunders clean, on-form and brilliant, I've seen him stoned and absolutely bloody awful, but I've never seen him like this, so listless, so tedious, so depressing.

And those were just the finer points. Once again, Johnny Thunders had fallen prey to the big gig syndrome; any place where the stakes were high, he got higher, then very low.

Although Chris Musto, who had hooked up with Thunders via Marc Zermati and Patti Palladin, had only just come on board for a short English tour, he quickly developed a protective streak towards the guitarist. Chris Musto: 'The third show of the tour was at the Town & Country club and it was a disaster. Poor old Johnny, he got in a real pickle. It was my first experience of "The London Syndrome". The day before the gig, Johnny decided to start losing his voice, it was an obsessive thing. At that stage he had a blank about London, as he did about New York, Los Angeles and Paris – most of the major cities. He knew he was going to be criticised because he was Johnny. His defence mechanism would go into overdrive and he'd end up in a mess. The emotional mess would start a day or two before then just speed up. Then there was the so-called "fans", the kind of people who would offer him a line of coke, thinking that they were being cool, but with Johnny's chemical makeup, it would turn into a psychosis. It was the worst thing for him, he would become a monster, especially under pressure. After two vitamin B12 injections, we got him on to the stage of the Town & Country club, and for the first couple of numbers, I felt confident, but then it just became shambolic. It was awful. Johnny was out there and he was an absolute mess, although he still looked great. He always had attitude. After the show, he realised what he'd done, the people who ran the club were appalled, he'd never be able to play there again. He'd effectively blown the major London venue circuit and I nearly left.'

Three shady guys: Chris Musto, J.T. and Stevie Klasson. (*Courtesy of Chris Musto*)

The debacle at the T & C, Johnny stumbling sightlessly in a self-induced delirium, marked a watershed. Although he was unable to reverse the insecurities that clawed away at his personal life, he began to make changes musically at least, which were eventually unveiled by the summer of 1988. Tired of the inconsistencies of pick-up bands and in-fighting with older compadres, Thunders recruited a group of relatively fresh-faced musicians. With only one trouble maker in the ranks, Johnny himself, he could be sure of a more stable environment. The kind of group that he had once mused over after the completion of *So Alone* in 1978, a rock 'n' roll revue, started to take shape. Only Chris Musto, who never did quit, remained from the previous year, while Thunders discovered nineteen-year-old guitarist, Stevie Klasson, playing at a biker party in Stockholm. Stevie: 'After the show Johnny came over, he wanted to know how I'd ended up in the band, and then he tried to trade me for my leather jacket. I invited him to this club I was running called the Pipeline and we ended up jamming until the early hours of the morning. Two weeks later, he came back and we played some more. He gave me his phone number and suggested that we get together. He hardly knew anyone in Sweden, he was mainly looking after Jamie while Susanne was working. About a week later he showed up at the club again, and asked me if I wanted to go on the road with him. Two days after that, he phoned me for my passport number.'

As far as the new line-up went, the only problem was the geographical distance between the musicians: London, Stockholm and New York, which made group gatherings a complex and costly manoeuvre. While Thunders, in his post *So Alone* reveries, had wanted three chick singers, Stephen Hoda's girlfriend,

Johnny, Susanne and
Jamie in Sweden.
(*Alison Gordy*)

Alison Gordy, a theatrical blonde bombshell in the Ursula Andress mode, more
than made up for the shortfall in numbers. Alison: 'My boyfriend introduced
us. We were round at a friend's house, Patti Palladin was there as well, she was
playing tapes of the *Copy Cats* album. I picked up a guitar and started singing,
then Johnny came over to see if we could do a duet and we sang a couple of
things. One tune that stuck out was what turned into "Birdsong". I said "That's
great, you should finish it." He was like "I'm working with it but I'm not sure
what I'm going to do with it." Then he played an alternative version, which was
a love song ["Some Hearts"]. He came back to New York in the early summer,
that was the second time we met up. We were in a cab and he said, "You want
to put something together?" He had a gig coming up at the Limelight. He asked
if I knew anybody else that could sing and I told him that my friend Jill
[Wisoff] could sing and play bass.'

The NY contingent of Thunders' new band was rounded off by the addition
of a convivial sax player named Jamey Heath, who joined Alison Gordy and Jill

Johnny and Jamie. (*Alison Gordy*)

Wisoff on stage at the Limelight on 24 July 1988, alongside drummer Jeff West and bassist Tony Coiro who frequently backed the guitarist in his home town.

In time Jamey Heath, the clean-living antithesis of the stoned saxophonist of jazz lore, traded sides, falling under the deadly spell that occasionally consumed people in Johnny's orbit, but it was an independent process. From a distance, demoralisation may be seen as a (perverse) form of seduction but Johnny Thunders was the most poignant anti-drugs statement that ever there was. Stevie Klasson in particular became aware of Thunders' later stance on drugs, which followed the line of 'do as I say, not as I do'. Stevie: 'He was always lecturing me about drugs because he knew that was why things hadn't always gone the way he wanted them to. One time, we were on tour and we got a little too drunk and wanted to get something to put up our noses to wake us up, so we went to this place but they didn't have the right thing, they only had heroin. I said: "Let's get some of that." He smacked me in the face as hard as he could, I hit the floor. For a month he lectured me every day about it.'

Johnny was fond of saying he was an entertainer, which downplays his musicianship, but the new band, which would by default earn the name of The Oddballs after Thunders jokingly used the phrase whilst explaining how different they all were to a journalist, afforded him the opportunity of a more mature approach. After all, the old way had been killing him in public. Neatly

(*Courtesy of
Amy Kosher*)

side-stepping the quandaries of grown-up rock 'n' roll – which often entails
confusing insipid with inspired, parody, or denial without style – Thunders remained an alluring and exciting performer. The occasional inclination to play
around with his vocal range became more pronounced as *Copy Cats* testified,
while his songwriting grew increasingly contemplative. Everyone looks for clues
– the veiled prophecy in the doomed artiste's last repertoire – but Johnny's is
more telling than most. Aside from personal concerns, whether it be the open
letter to the music press that is 'Critics Choice' (a.k.a 'I Tell The Truth Even
When I'm Lying'), the hurt bravado behind 'Disappointed In You' and the betrayal that infuses 'It's Not What You Say', Johnny began to address subjects
outside of his usual remit such as 'Children Are People Too', 'In God's Name',
(co-written with Patti Palladin) and the superb 'Help The Homeless'. The hu-
manity that he had tried to nullify by the anaesthesia of drugs, that he so con-
vincingly submerged as an all-seasons reprobate, surfaced gasping for breath,
especially on 'Society Makes Me Sad', which brings the heart to its knees. But

Born to Cry. (*Gary Trotter*)

could he get a major deal on the strength of the material? Could John the Baptist have kept his head? Naaah, behind the glass towers of the record corporations where manufactured does for real life and an outlaw is the ex-wife's mother, no one was about to reprieve the condemned man of rock 'n' roll. Still, he lived in some hope, although that faded too. Even Thunders' sublime adaptation of Dion's 'Born To Cry' from *Copy Cats*, failed to make any impression on its release in November 1988. Johnny knew all too well that his career would fare better in death and noted it for posterity in 'Disappointed In You', when he wrote: 'The only way you get respect is when you die.' From 1988 to his demise in April 1991, Thunders did what he had always done: took to the road.

Backed by The Oddballs, the gigs had a revue flavour, Johnny in his candy-wrapper coloured suits bringing a little considered showmanship to the party. Describing the vibe of the band to *Records* magazine, Thunders stated:

> It's sort of a sixties-ish Motown feel with my kind of sound. The madness
> is more controlled. I definitely think it's a part of me growing up.

If he had addressed his creativity, he was unable to do the same emotionally, despite his intentions. Chris Musto: 'He was a pleasure to work with and stylistically he left everybody to it. It was very varied on stage but basically it was improvised rock 'n' roll, to do that properly you've got to know what you're doing.

The only thing that irritated me about Johnny was his lack of self-respect, which was brought on by what he used to do to himself, that hedonistic approach was so frustrating. He gave the impression that he never analysed himself, but he did. He existed by his heart, he existed passionately. He did things first, then thought about them later. His desires were very basic, he wanted to be loved, he wanted to have a nice place to live, he wanted to be comfortable.'

The homelife that Johnny Thunders craved was attainable, but he couldn't diffuse the ingrained capacity for self-sabotage no matter how wretched the consequences. In January 1989, Thunders pulled the plug on a short Spanish tour, in a desperate attempt to salvage his relationship with Susanne. Sadly, he failed. The introduction of a baby into their lives irrevocably altered the status quo: Jamie came first and Johnny's lifestyle became more of a threat. Christopher Giercke: 'Susanne had a great love and gentleness for Johnny but at the point that she had a baby, the protection of the child became the all over importance. It was difficult enough to live with Johnny, than to live with Johnny and a baby. Susanne made the instinctive choice and Johnny could not understand that, consciously. The last weeks before they split up, I was in the Himalayas filming and Grandperret was shooting another film and I think he was left too alone. He eventually returned to New York which didn't stabilise things, but he did fall back on his feet.'

Johnny Thunders returned to Gotham with a weary finesse, bolstered by some enthusiastic local press and a flurry of home-town gigs, including two nights at the Beacon Theatre, supporting The Replacements on 30 and 31 March with The Oddballs. Back to familiar transient ways, Johnny crashed at bassist Jill Wisoff's place along with Stevie Klasson for a couple of months. Before she cracked from having Thunders as a house guest, Wisoff set up and paid for some demos but the results were disappointingly lacklustre. A second shot at capturing some of the new material also failed due to less than auspicious circumstances, when Thunders, accompanied by Jamey Heath, Stevie Klasson and film-maker Rachel Amodeo, travelled to Rochester, where an outfit called The Chesterfield Kings had organised some gigs and free studio time. Rachel Amodeo: 'The gigs were great but the recording didn't go so well. The Chesterfield Kings were big fans of Johnny's and when we arrived, they were like: 'Oh my God, my hero's here!' By the time the weekend was over, they weren't so sure. Basically, Johnny wasn't musically compatible with them, he played from the heart and they got impatient.' An attempt at 'Society' was scrapped due to some reticence on Johnny's behalf, but a version of 'Critics Choice' later surfaced on an EP alongside 'I'd Much Rather Be With The Boys' and a live cut of 'London Boys', after the guitarist's demise.

In Paris, Patrick Grandperret was finalising the details of *Mona et Moi*, which included the possibility of a soundtrack album in collaboration with Jungle. On his home turf, Thunders was once again blending into celluloid, at

Johnny in the role of Vito Napolitano, on the set of *What About Me*.
(*Courtesy of Rachel Amodeo*)

the behest of Rachel Amodeo who was making her directorial debut with *What About Me*, an account of the perilous existence of New York's street denizens, from the exiled to the outcast and homeless. Rachel Amodeo: 'I thought I would write a story about bad luck. I decided to base the situation in my neighbourhood park, Tompkins Square park, where a large homeless community developed, until the park was closed. I had already met Johnny once before when he was staying with a mutual friend called Patti Giordano, then one night I saw him doing an acoustic spot and realised that his music would be perfect for the film. I told Patti Giordano that I wanted to talk to Johnny about the soundtrack and he called right away and came over to see it. We became friends and I decided to write a part for him. The first role that came to mind was that of a priest or a gangster. I asked him if he had any ideas about it, and he said, "I think I should play your brother." Johnny was a natural actor, very professional and charismatic. When I asked Johnny what his character's name should be, he said, "Vito, because that's my son's name." He thought of Napolitano, as our last name. His character was very sincere in the film. Very true to his character in real life.'

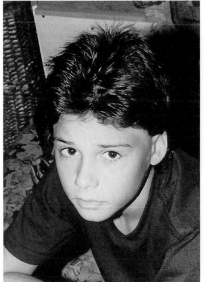 

Dino. (*Alison Gordy*)   Vito. (*Alison Gordy*)

The last message to a lost son was sent out like a flare in an unknown night.

While Johnny knew that Susanne would never bar him from Jamie, the fate of Vito and Dino, whom he had not seen in ten long years, haunted him. Indeed, he would always carry a small, time-weathered photograph of the boys taken at a party. When Emil Genzale passed away during the period when Thunders was still living in Sweden, the guitarist expressed regret that he had never gotten close to his father. For reasons outside of Johnny's control, it was now too late to break the second circle of separation that had originally begun in Michigan, when his wife Julie suddenly took off with Dino, still a babe in arms, and Vito. Johnny Jnr. was similarly whisked away. At first, Julie kept in touch with Johnny's family. Mariann Bracken: 'She contacted us and told us that due to Johnny's drug habit, she couldn't put up with him anymore. At the time we agreed, not knowing that her habit was as bad as his. She kept in contact for a couple of months, making us promise not to tell Johnny that we knew where she was. We complied with it, we told him we knew but weren't telling him unless he straightened out his act. One day we called the number that she'd given us but she'd left. Johnny tried looking for her; Jerry Nolan's mother had something to do with a tracing agency called Child Find. In one period of three years, Julie had eight different addresses. Johnny and I didn't see a lot of each other in later years, he was on the road, things like that, but he'd call me at least once a week; if he didn't have the money he'd call collect. He would tell me if he was depressed, he didn't think anybody cared about him. He would tell me he had nobody, no friends, he'd say, "All I have is you and Mom." The main

The Seventh
Veil.
(*Alison Gordy*)

thing that ate him up more than anything else was the fact he couldn't find Vito
and Dino. He didn't want to be a father the way his had been.' Julie did not let
the family know the whereabouts of Vito and Dino until after Johnny's death.

In early August Thunders flew to London to pick up his regular methadone
and Valium script from his private doctor, and sealed a deal with Jungle
Records. Skipping on the idea of a soundtrack album for *Mona et Moi*, Johnny
persuaded Alan Hauser to issue with *Bootlegging The Bootleggers*, as a retort to
all those that had profited from his work with illegitimate products, effectively
short-changing the guitarist. When Johnny Thunders didn't play, he didn't get
paid. *Bootlegging The Bootleggers* provided a short-term solution to his ongoing
financial instability and let's face it, he wasn't the kind of guy to bother with a
savings account. Between a selection of live tracks culled from 1985–1989,
Thunders narrates *Bootlegging* like a bouncy hybrid of Bugs Bunny and Louis

Armstrong. However, his introduction to the opening number, 'M.I.A.' points directly to his final destination, New Orleans. If he hadn't yet bought his ticket, he knew the direction.

Through the endeavours of an old friend of Johnny's called Abbijane, the guitarist took part in a rock 'n' roll charity pool tournament aimed at bringing awareness of the destruction of the rain forests. Attitude triumphed over technique when Thunders made it into the semi-finals, where he encountered David Johansen. At the celebrity bash afterwards, Johnny met a promoter who subsequently booked the band for two tours, the first of which kicked off in Winnipeg on 28 August. The Midwest jaunt, however, almost ground to a halt at the starting post when the tour bus was impounded by customs officers, who held Johnny at a hospital until the legitimacy of his methadone script was proved via a fax from Marc Zermati in Paris. Further difficulties ensued at the border when it was discovered that the non-US members of the band lacked the correct working papers. Alison Gordy: 'The Midwest tour was kind of a fiasco. We couldn't bring Chris and Stevie across the border so Jill and Jamey went off to Winnipeg with Johnny to salvage the gigs, which they had to do acoustically. Originally we were supposed to get $5000 but it ended up being $750, which they spent trying to get to Minneapolis. I was pissed off with Johnny. He had put me in a bad position because I was driving as we crossed the border and my license and reputation was now involved. Johnny wasn't in good shape either, just dragging himself around. He'd binged out and wasn't that together, although he did do a good show in Minneapolis. Jill and I weren't getting along either, so I told Johnny I was going back to New York. Johnny needed Jill more than me to finish the tour. He thought I was pissed off at him and that's why I'd left, but it wasn't. When they all got back into town, we went out for something to eat, and Johnny told me he'd been to Jill's apartment to collect some things and he had it out with her. Then we got a tour in California and Chris's friend Stuart [Kennedy] came over to play bass. We rehearsed once with Stuart, then off we went.'

The twelve-day West Coast tour began with a flourish on 13 October, amidst high hopes that Thunders would be able to hook a deal for the new material. Chris Musto: 'We played LA, which was great, packed out an old church, a well-known venue called the Second Coming. San Francisco went well but the funniest show was in San Juan Capistrano. Johnny completely forgot that the band were there. He kept stopping the numbers half way through to play acoustically. We walked off. By the time Johnny finished the set, there was about three people left in the club. He was standing on one of the tables with his acoustic guitar going "Name a song" to what was left of the audience, and they would call out, "Pirate Love" and he'd go: "Yeah, I ripped that off Bad Company. Name another one." It became this really funny routine of "Name a song, any song, and I'll tell you who I ripped it off from." Then he sang the

Johnny B. Bad. California. (*Jamey Heath*)

same song, twice. I started apologising to the manager of the club but the guy said "It's fantastic, bordering on genius," and yes it was but I was astonished he felt the same way, too. I can't say that the band weren't pissed off though. We were sitting down to breakfast, and at that time of the morning Johnny was probably the last person I wanted to see. He said: "What was it like last night?" I said "Where were you? It was like watching a one-man club act." "Was I funny?" '

Midway through the tour Thunders, like a poltergeist, began kicking up dust clouds of chaos in his wake; the promoter, who'd come along for the ride, retired early from the fray, while the windows of the band's hire van mysteriously shattered from the inside. Johnny's wide-eyed hypothesis on random acts of street malice failed to convince the aggrieved parties. Then, California was rocked by a massive earthquake. Caught between Long Beach and San Jose, Chris Musto wondered if it was a psychokinetic side-effect of the tour. When the tremors receded, the dates continued, sparking A & R interest from five different record companies. After going back to New York with the band, Thunders returned to LA for a benefit gig which he later mentioned in the course of an impromptu, unpublished interview with journalist Brian Paisley. 'At Thanksgiving, I did this benefit in Los Angeles with Clem Burke, Frank Infante and Will Sexton. We gathered $1000 and gave the money to a mission so they could buy turkeys. I went to the mission myself, and played three songs in front of a podium, with all these old people playing with their toes and stuff.

It was the scariest thing I ever did in my life. I've never been scared on stage. Ever. It's the most secure place. When I put this song out ["Homeless"] I want to dedicate all the money to soup kitchens because what goes on is such an injustice, especially in America, y'know it's one of the richest countries ...'

Thunders would probably have been better off staying on stage for the duration of his time in California. As usual, the guitarist's reputation drew the dark moths who clustered around him, whenever he stayed in any one place for too long. Back on junkie time, Johnny blew his hard-won amnesty with the majors.

On 24 January 1990, Johnny returned to London to see his doctor, before meeting with the languid Luca Mainardi. An Italian prodigy and former student of classical ballet, the native success of Mainardi's first album *Rock And Roll Clown* (1985) enabled him to lead an orchestra. Inspired by *Hurt Me* Luca tracked down Thunders through Jungle Records, and so began what was possibly the strangest of all of the guitarist's musical encounters. Luca: 'My music concentrates on different languages and cultures; I never ask anybody who plays with me to perform their usual stuff. A session was set up for Johnny at CTS Studios in Wembley. We spent the first night at a hotel where the French Institute used to book free rooms for me, and the staff always addressed me as "Maestro". That evening Johnny destroyed everything, he fell over and broke the sink in my bathroom, his own room was terrible. We had to creep out in the morning. I've never been back since. My next mistake was renting a flat in Maida Vale for us and a couple of my Italian friends, for two weeks. It became unbearable, my nerves were shot. The problem was that you never got any sleep. I always had the feeling that disaster was imminent. We had many arguments but the biggest came after I nearly stepped on a syringe that had been left on the floor. He apologised and said he wanted to talk to me alone, he was very sad because his mother wasn't well and of course not being able to see his children always played on his mind. Things got better once Stevie Klasson arrived. Stevie was very young, like Johnny's son, but sometimes Johnny was the son, it was a very tender relationship. Anytime Johnny was in the studio, you could never guess how he would be. When everyone else was ready, he wasn't; sometimes he'd fall asleep. He shook your concentration, but maybe that's not such a bad thing, and gave great performances out of nothing. He had a lot of good ideas, he wanted to sing bits of all the national anthems of the world – Italy, France, Japan. What was interesting for Johnny was the fact that we were doing something different. We did three songs, one of them, "Lydia", was about a girl that Johnny was in love with but she was in a relationship. When he did the song in the studio, he called her and played it over the telephone. The second song had the working title of "Lullaby", it developed from an improvisation, it's very Sicilian, very surreal, the lyrics are about his daughter, Jamie. The other song is a sort of mazurka, with a European feel, like Kurt Weill. It starts with four accordions, Johnny was thinking about Judy Garland, he says something like "One day they all turn away …" '

If Johnny Thunders was indeed thinking about Judy Garland, or even Janis Joplin who uttered similarly forlorn sentiments in 'Kozmic Blues' – 'Friends, they turn away' – he resorted to the same tactics as the fatal *femmes*, when he returned to his doctor within days of the last appointment, for a little something extra. Hoping to intervene before the guitarist could pick up yet another prescription for tranquillisers, Alan Hauser called the private practice, to no avail.

It wasn't really a case of Johnny falling into decline, rather his life finally caught up with him after he separated for good from Susanne. Thunders had always relied on others for stability because he had none of his own. On 3 February, the guitarist flew out to Paris for some dates at the Gibus and a recording session with Stiv Bators. Only the shows went ahead as planned. Something very bad manifested and it wasn't Stiv and his girlfriend Carolines' cat, Satan. While the rest of the musicians involved in the project – Sigue Sigue Spuntnik's Neal X, The Godfather's Kris Dollimore and Vom from Dr And The Medics – were left to their own resources, Dee Dee Ramone and Thunders ended up staying in Stiv and Caroline's apartment on Rue St Honore. For whatever reasons – perhaps the murky ownership details of 'Chinese Rocks' that Dee Dee Ramone has always alleged to be his – there was a growing hint of brimstone in the air. The sessions themselves, at which Thunders (barely) played guitar on two tracks, 'Two Hearts' and 'Ain't Got Nobody', were distinctly ill fated. It had not been a good idea to house the two New Yorkers under the same roof. Stevie Klasson: 'Johnny got pretty messed up over the Dee Dee incident. He said that Dee Dee accused him and Stiv of stealing some money, they told him they hadn't but Dee Dee smashed up Johnny's guitar, then poured a bottle of bleach into his suitcase. All Johnny had was his guitar and clothes, he didn't have an apartment; Johnny was so hurt by it, he took it badly. Much later he did get back at Dee Dee, in a club in New York called the Scrap Bar, which became one of Johnny's favourite haunts. He smacked Dee Dee on the back of the head as hard as he could with a beer pitcher, then the bouncer threw Dee Dee out.'

In the immediate aftermath of the Dee Dee incident, Thunders took refuge with one of his oldest friends in Paris, Octavio Cohen-Escali, whom he had known since the days of The Dolls. While Johnny was well below par, in the company of Octavio and his girlfriend, Isis, he rallied round some. Octavio: 'The night he moved in, he asked Isis to sing, then he suggested we do some more songs. We taped some of it at home, there was one called "Big Lips" which had French lyrics, then he worked a song around Isis called "Seduction" – he said he would have liked to have a string section in it – then there was one called "Discord Parfait" which means being in tune yet not agreeing.' Despite an arrangement to record the material on 15 May, with Neal X acting as producer, the plan never came to fruition. *Mona et Moi*, however, premiered at the Odeon cinema in Paris on 4 April, scooping the prestigious Jean Vigo prize. Now Johnny truly was a movie star, but broke as ever, he played two more gigs at the Gibus to boost his resources.

With a handful of acoustic dates scheduled in Ireland, Johnny looped back to England on 15 April 1990, where he was supposed to catch a plane to Dublin. The timing was crucial as the Dublin show was to be televised. Retiring to the airport bathroom to powder his face, which he did in the style of Jackson Pollock – liberally and messily – Thunders was brought to the attention of customs officers who mistook the loose powder for a narcotic substance and frog-marched him off for questioning. In all he was held for twenty-four hours and missed the first show. After completing what remained of the Irish gigs, accompanied by Jamey Heath, Thunders went to stay with Mick Vayne in Leeds before the English leg of the dates began. Mick had first met his hero in 1988, when his band The Vaynes supported The Oddballs on a six-week European jaunt. In 1989, Vayne again met up with Thunders when he was back in town for a British tour. With some prior medical training in his background, he grew increasingly concerned for the guitarist. Mick Vayne: 'While we were talking he nodded out, it got worse as the night wore on. I'd never known him to be like that before, he'd always been so lively. I realise now, when I look back, the more time he spent here, the more out of it he got. He was depressed, he'd been put on anti-depressants and they can be really heavy. He'd take far too many and forget how many he'd taken. He'd get into his pyjamas, lie on the sofa and watch videos night and day. He used to get out a lot of films that had something to do with drugs, like the John Belushi film *Wired* and that Richard Pryor movie where he's taking cocaine. One day, he wanted to go and look at a secondhand clothes shop I'd told him about. He was walking down the road with a big spliff, when he goes "Do you think I'm a bit more retarded than the last time you saw me?" "You are a bit." "I can't remember anything anymore, I can't remember what I'm doing, do you think I'm taking too much?" "Yes, I'd lay off the anti-depressants, they're not good for you, especially in the amounts you're taking them." "I'll starting cutting them down, one everyday." He was deteriorating; if you're going to come off heroin or methadone you need to do it properly. Later that same day, he said, "I think I'm going to die soon. If I die, I'll leave you my guitars." If he hadn't have died, I wouldn't have thought anything more about that conversation, it didn't seem to be serious.'

Vayne was called upon to play guitar for the remainder of the mini-tour, after Thunders fell asleep on his hand, trapping a nerve. On 11 May, Johnny flew out to Greece for three shows, returning to England for a further five days, before the start of another acoustic tour in Germany. It seemed as if each good-bye was becoming ever more poignant. Mick Vayne: 'I had to wheel Johnny

Amongst the
ruins.
(*Jamey Heath*)

through Heathrow airport on a luggage trolley, he'd fallen asleep. He gave me
this little portrait pendant of Christ, which I always wear around my neck. He
said it would keep me safe. He'd been to a Catholic shop with Gerard [Gerard
Famous, also formerly of The Vaynes] in Leeds. He had a big box full of
crucifixes and rosaries. He used to feel guilty and he believed that they would
somehow protect him. He also gave Gerard and myself a little saint thing rep-
resenting St Jude, made out of monk's robes. He said his mother made him
wear St Jude. St Jude is the patron saint of lost causes.'

Before he returned to New York, where a run of gigs had been set up by Amy
Koster, a friend of Jamey Heath's who worked for a management agency,
Thunders approached Alan Hauser to discuss a studio album. Like an elastic
Lazarus, the guitarist had once again bounced back, repaired by the constant
distractions of gigging. Although Jungle may have lacked the financial clout
that ensures billboard coverage and blanket radio play, they had always shown
support to their highest profile artist, especially in times of crisis, which was
often. However, Jungle were going through a rough patch, largely due to their
distributor Rough Trade's slide into bankruptcy, while sales of *Bootlegging The
Bootleggers* had been a little shaky. Despite his reservations, Alan Hauser mulled

over the pros and cons of taking Johnny Thunders back in to the studio. 'A number of things made us hesitant; the new band, even though they were a sta-bilising influence, were a six piece from different parts of the world, so logistically it would have meant the cost of flights and apartments for all of them. The situation with our distributor meant that we didn't have the re-sources to gamble. We also knew that whenever Johnny went into the studio, he seemed to think that the only way he could have a good time, and therefore make good music, was to be out of his head, which led to problems. However, he was very anxious to prove to us that he was cleaning up his act and indeed, he managed to, albeit only for a period of three or four months. Also, *Copy Cats*, which is an excellent album, had gone way over budget. Seeing that we were worried about finances, they proposed recording at a sixteen-track studio in New York to keep the budget low, but it was more of a demo studio. It wouldn't have done Johnny any favours to have tried that, it didn't make any sense. Much to our regret, we put the project on hold.'

On 3 June, Stiv Bators was hit by a car. Miraculously, he seemed unhurt, if a little dazed. After taking her spindly little beau home, Caroline wanted to call a doctor but Stiv shrugged off the suggestion. Aside from an odd sensation which he likened to an out-of-body experience, Bators reckoned that he was OK. Later that night, they retired to bed, where Stiv died in his sleep from internal injuries. On his next appearance in Paris, Alice Cooper dedicated 'Under My Wheels' to the former Dead Boy. Shaken by the news of Bators' sudden departure, Thunders began to get himself in order. The old rock 'n' roll resurrection routine was starting to wear as thin as Johnny himself. The bone structure that had made his face a pale canvas for photogenic shadows was be-coming a little too pronounced. Initially, the insidious aspect of illness was masked, possibly even to the guitarist, by all the years of drug use. Mariann Bracken: 'I think he was aware that he was sick but I don't believe he thought it was a medical problem. I feel he thought it was the drugs that were making him ill. If Johnny had a toothache he'd call me up, "What am I going to do?" He was like that with everything. Not long before he died he said: "I've got a lump on my neck, what should I do?" "Go to a doctor." He didn't go to doc-tors, he didn't believe in them, I think he was scared to go.'

When Receiver Records licensed *Live At The Lyceum*, the rights of which had in part reverted back to Thunders, he put the unexpected windfall to good use. On 3 September 1990, he checked into Hazelden, the world-renowned rehabilitation centre in Minnesota. Although there is another branch of Hazelden in NY offering similar services, Thunders sought help far from home. On his own turf, the guitarist had always been at the centre of a vicious circle, unable to resist the 'gifts' of those who got off on making him their drugged deity. Mariann Bracken: 'Johnny went into a rehabilitation centre. He called me one day and said: "I can't take no more." He had some friends [Heather, and Cathy Boruch] that were talking to him about it, he said that had triggered him off. The day before he went in, he stayed at our house so we could drive him to the airport. He was nervous, scared about what was going to happen, he wanted to start a new life. He called me from Hazelden the first night. He was in a lot of pain. He told me he knew that it was going to be hard but he was going to do it. He was in almost a month and we spoke at least two or three times a day. He took part in these sessions where you talk to people who have the same problem. He called me before one of them, it seems that they write things down about each other during the session. He was joking with me: "I wonder what they're going to write?" After he died we were going through some of his papers and we found the letters from the sessions. They all say exactly the same thing: "You're killing yourself about your children, you're not like your father, it's not your fault about the kids, you can't find them." He knew Susanne was a good mother. He loved Jamie. Johnny and Susanne had their problems, maybe they couldn't live together but he knew he never had to worry about his daughter. I know that Susanne loved Johnny and he loved her, it makes it even sadder that they couldn't get it together. At Hazelden, they recommended NA [Narcotics Anonymous] meetings but Johnny didn't believe in them, he wasn't for talking to a whole bunch of people. When he came out of rehab he was OK for a little while.'

Returning to New York, Thunders did his best to keep things together and settled into a one-bedroom apartment on 227 East 21st Street. It was the first time he had lived alone and the fact that his new abode was in spitting distance of a police station somewhat tickled the guitarist. On Friday 30 November, The Heartbreakers got together for a one-off gig at the (NY) Marquee, with the exception of Billy Rath who had forsaken rock 'n' roll for God, and was replaced by Tony Coiro from Walter Lure's band, The Waldos. Above all the night belonged to Jerry Nolan who had instigated the idea: 'I'd been wanting to do it for a long time. I'd wanted it so bad and it's a good thing it did happen because that was my last time playing with Johnny. I was so happy that night, I played so well. Walter and Tony said: "Boy, look at Jerry, look how happy he is." It was great and Johnny admitted it was too, that's all I wanted him to do, because he could be a scumbag, he could like it and say he hated it. I didn't want him to do that, I wanted him to say he liked it. He told Walter: "You know I hate to admit it but, fucking Nigs, what a show."'

As the Christmas lights came on in London, Johnny and The Oddballs regrouped for some European dates, kicking off with a gig at the Marquee on 21 December. Thunders was in good spirits, the benefits of his short stay at Hazelden still apparent. Gail Higgins Smith: 'Because we went through so many formative years together, even though there were a lot of months after the early years when we were apart, every time I saw Johnny, it was just like seeing him the day before. In the later times, it would really depend on the particular

Johnny and Gail. (*Courtesy of Gail Higgins Smith*)

night I saw him, how he would be. He would either be the old Johnny or some monster Johnny. I'm really glad that the last time I saw John was when he did that final show at the Marquee. That night he was exactly the John I knew when he was eighteen. I remember saying: "I heard about you being off the drugs." He said: "Oh Gail, you know me." "But you're so like the old John." "That's because I'm drunk and coming off the drugs I was on last night." But it was like seeing a glimpse of John that I hadn't seen in years.'

After the (London) Marquee show, the band travelled to Switzerland for a couple of gigs before Johnny and Jamey Heath headed off to Paris to play a five-night stand at the Gibus. Just as most people were thinking about their new year's resolutions, Thunders' gave up on his. Journalist Nick Kent, the *NME*'s former *enfant terrible*, ran into the guitarist as the clocks were striking the final notes of 1990:

> The last time I saw him though – Jesus Christ, I could hardly stand to look at John. You know in a bullfight how when the decisive dagger had been plunged into the neck of the bull and basically it's all over for the poor creature and it goes limp and cross-eyed before sinking slowly into the sawdust. Well, that's how Thunders looked on the night of New Year's Eve just as 1991 was being ushered in: limp and cross-eyed from all the torments he'd been visiting upon himself. – *The Dark Stuff*

Back in New York, the 'party' continued with all those who wanted to

The Wild One: Jerry Nolan. (*Phyllis Stein*)

absorb the rarefied air of getting high with Johnny Thunders. Realising that he
was going to have get out of NY fast if he was to survive, Thunders finalised the
plans he had been nurturing to go to New Orleans and start over. Stevie Klasson
was on standby to join him there, as was Jerry Nolan. The guitarist also got
in touch with Barbara Becker, a former artistic collaborator of Christopher
Giercke's, who was now managing Dr John in New Orleans. First however,
there was a handful of dates in Japan with The Oddballs to take care of, and a
recording commitment in Germany with punk band Die Toten Hosen (The
Dead Trousers) who were in the process of making a covers album of the spiky
classics of their youth, entitled *Learning English – Lesson 1.*

Before departing for Tokyo, Johnny met up with Jerry Nolan. Like
Thunders, the drummer had left Sweden and returned to New York. With the
help of his girlfriend, Phyllis Stein, whom he'd known since The Dolls, Nolan
had taken up the fight for self-conquest from old habits, but his pal wasn't far-
ing so well. Jerry Nolan: 'A lot of people look at Johnny and me like brothers
but it was more than that, it was more a father/son relationship. It's respect. I
take Johnny one hundred per cent for what he is and he takes me a hundred
per cent. That's based on trust. There were no two people closer. He could come
to my house and spill his guts, I'm talking about marriages, pregnancy, disease,
his wounds – help him to heal them so he wouldn't have to go to a doctor,
everything. But you know what? I couldn't do that to him, I couldn't spill my
guts to him but I accepted that. Johnny would come to me, show me all his
track wounds and know that I wouldn't tell nobody. It was the day before he
was supposed to go to Japan, there were a couple of things that I didn't know

Thunders in Japan for the last time. (*Yoshi Yuki Yuguzin, courtesy Chris Musto*)

what they meant, odd places for bruises to be, back, chest. I didn't find out until weeks later, that was the leukaemia. I started to talk him into forgetting the gig, I tried to tell him we had to go to the hospital. I told him I would have stayed, we would have got a private room, that I'd be in the room with him, or sitting just outside the door. I almost got him to do it, then he got scared. He just got scared of needles, doctors, hospitals, the whole bit. You may not realise this but most junkies are afraid of needles. I told him he was going to die. I said "Take care on this tour, you shouldn't be going anyway, you know that." Johnny had

The Oddballs; Johnny, Jamey Heath, Stevie Klasson, Chris Musto, Alison Gordy and
Stuart Kennedy. Japan '91. (*Alice Trezeszkowsky*)

this thing, when I would go on about his health, he would thank me for my
concern, then he would reach a point where he would say: "OK Jerry, you made
your point." We shook hands, his handshake was very weak. Then I hugged
him. I left Johnny on 14th Street and 3rd Avenue, the exact same corner where
I greeted Johnny for the first time after I'd auditioned for The Dolls. As I
walked down the street, I'm saying to myself: "I don't like the idea that I just
said goodbye to him in the same place as we said hello." By the time I got home,
I said: "He's not going to Japan, he'll never live if he don't go in the hospital
right now." That night he was supposed to go to Japan. He never made it. He
never made it the next day. He just made it the fourth day. He was going to call
me from New Orleans, I was going to go with him, he said: "Jerry we'll do it
fifty / fifty, just like we always did." '

A fragile Johnny Thunders set off to Japan on 30 March. Having previously
missed his flight to London, where he should have picked up his regular prescription prior to the dates, Thunders was taken to a hospital in Tokyo by Mick
Webster. Fearing for the guitarist's health, the doctors at the International
Clinic told him to pull the shows and return home. The gigs went ahead anyway, Thunders playing to adoring audiences in a country where he had long
been venerated. He was even chased down the street by a mob of flower-
wielding teenage girls. For Gaku Torii, who had not seen the guitarist in almost
three years, it was a chance to catch up: 'He was here for seven days, and I was
with him for most of that. The first show was in Tokyo, at the Power Station.
He looked tired, he was using an ordinary Les Paul Standard which he'd

borrowed from Stevie, but it was too heavy for him. He put it down and just sang. He was very bluesy, rootsey. The second gig was at Club Citta in Kawasaki, the third show was an acoustic with Stevie and Jamey at a club called the Anti Knock in Shin Juku. Steve Berlin, the saxophonist from Los Lobos, joined them on stage. Then he went in to the studio with a punk band called Ebi (Shrimp) to record one track, "Fucking Police". Later, me, Johnny, Stevie and Mick went to see Los Lobos play, but after half an hour Johnny said he was tired, so I went back to the hotel with him. He showed me pictures of Jamie, told me how pretty she was. I remember him saying that he didn't like living with women these days, he preferred drugs. He asked me if I wanted to manage him because I'd sorted out a deal for him. A Japanese company, Meldac, wanted him to do an album of covers from the sixties, material like Spencer Davis and The Yardbirds, with top Japanese musicians. They were going to call it *Johnny Thunders And The Gang Rockers*. He'd also asked me if I would organise an acoustic album deal for him, he'd even chosen a photograph for the cover and a title *Hurt Me More*. He started talking about wanting to make a record in New Orleans with Dr John. I noticed that whenever I was on the tour bus, he was playing Willy DeVille's *Victory Mixture* album which was recorded with Dr John. He dreamed about New Orleans and although I didn't want to manage Johnny, I did talk to the Japanese branch of WEA about his New Orleans idea, and they were interested.'

On 9 April Thunders, accompanied by tour manager Mick Webster, Jamey Heath and Stevie Klasson, visited Thailand for a couple of days rest and recuperation. Aside from picking up some custom-made silk suits, Johnny ventured into Jimmy Wong's tattoo parlour in Bangkok, with Stevie Klasson: 'I got a snake and an Indian Chief's skull done and Johnny got Jesus on the cross on his forearm. He didn't get any colours done on it, except for a little red on the black because he said the pain was too much. He was fascinated by religious symbolism. We were videoed while it was being done. After Thailand, we went back to New York. I got him a ticket to go to London. He gave me the keys to his apartment. His nephew Danny [Bracken] and I were to clean it up and pack his things, so he would be ready to go to New Orleans.'

After seeing his doctor in London, Johnny went straight to Germany with Mick Webster, where two acoustic shows had been set up in Braunschweig and Berlin, to cover the cost of the flights. After the gigs, they were collected in Cologne by Die Toten Hosen's frontman, Campi: 'For the album we decided to do an all-star version of "Born To Lose", with T. V. Smith, Cheetah Chrome, Dick Manitoba and Joey Ramone. When Johnny arrived he listened to the versions, then put his vocals on it. He was very tired, he didn't look so well but he really pulled himself together while he was in the studio. We recorded his guitar tracks in the toilet because he liked the sound in there. When we played it back we were happy with it but he wanted to do it again, he tried to do his best. On

J.T. and Campi from Die Toten Hosen. (*Courtesy of Campi*)

the other hand, he asked if we could do it tomorrow, he forgot that tomorrow he was leaving. He was pretty confused but aware of it, he even joked about it. After the session, on the way out to the car he said to Mick, "Let me drive." Everybody knew that he was not able to drive anymore. He didn't have a lot of power, he had to concentrate very hard all the time on what he was doing.'

Between two guitars, a suitcase and his saddlebags, Johnny had everything he needed for New Orleans; enough money from his work engagements to tide him over, a reserve of prescription drugs, and those shiny new silk suits. En route to catching his flight, Thunders dished out his loose change to the poor at a railway station in Germany before taking the train to the airport. Staggering with exhaustion, he was turned back from the departure gate by airline staff who wouldn't let him through until he had a medical. Mick Webster: 'After the medical, he was walking round the no-smoking area with the biggest cigar you've ever seen and he wasn't going to put it out for anybody. "To hell with them," he said. "If they want to get me out of here, they've got to come and get me." Finally we got to the gate. Normally at the end of a tour, it would be "See you in a couple of weeks." This time he held out his hand, he'd never done that before. I got a really strange feeling but I didn't want to think about it. When I got home, I must admit I was pretty worried.'

From the moment Johnny Thunders vanished beyond the departure gate on 22 April 1991, he acquired two shady companions, strange fate and bad luck, that seemed to dog his every move. At a stop-off in Chicago, the guitarist called up Mariann Bracken to say he had lost his ticket. The family wired him some money for a new one but it was never collected. Arriving in the Big Easy, a taxi

(*David Arnoff*)

driver dropped him at St Peter House at Burgandy and St Peter Street, between 9.30 and 10 p.m. The desk clerk on duty, Lesley Carter, later told the *New Orleans Metro* newspaper that Thunders had been 'dressed all in black from head to toe and he was sweating. At one point, I was afraid he was going to fall on me. He wasn't obnoxious. He looked real white, like a Geisha girl.' After checking into room 37, the guitarist had a quick mooch around Bourbon Street. Returning to the guest house he called Stevie Klasson who passed the phone number on to Thunders' sister. Mariann Bracken: 'We talked when he got there. We must have spoken for fifteen minutes or so. He sounded great, he told me how much he loved it there, how there was singing in the streets. He said he'd done well in Japan and Germany and even joked that he might have to pay income tax for the year. He never made it. He told me I wasn't going to have to pay a mortgage anymore. All the time he was in The Dolls he used to say: "Someday, I'm going to pay your mortgage." '

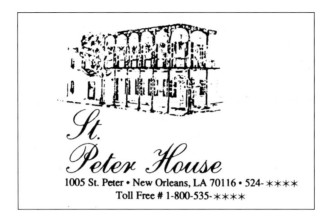

After talking to Stevie and Mariann, Johnny became disconnected from all that was familiar. What exactly happened in those final fraying hours as he slipped over the horizon will always remain inconclusive. However, it would appear that Thunders' presence in New Orleans triggered a surge of activity in the drug-dealing community. In his weakened state, the guitarist was easy prey for any passing opportunist.

Sometime that evening, Johnny made the acquaintance of brothers Mike and Marc Ricks who were staying in the neighbouring room. After smoking a couple of joints, all three visited a bar in the French Quarter, then returned to the guest house. The brothers apparently crashed out only to be woken by a series of jolts, like a fight without voices, coming from Thunders' room. Around eight in the morning, the hotel receptionist called Johnny about the noise. He asked if he could come and talk to her. Nothing was ever heard from the guitarist again. At approximately 3.30 that afternoon, cleaner Mildred Coleman knocked on the door of room 37. When no one replied she let herself in with her passkey and found Thunders curled up under the dresser, amidst a scene of disarray. Whether Johnny had been fighting with someone or struggling to stay alive has never been ascertained.

On the street, across from his apartment, Willy DeVille happened to be strumming his guitar when a police car ruined the picturesque scenario of an afternoon in the Big Easy, as it pulled to a halt outside the St Peter House. A resident of New Orleans, DeVille watched the activity with a dispassionate distance until the hotel manager asked him if he knew who Johnny Thunders was. Formerly of New York, DeVille regularly booked business associates into the St Peter and was acquainted with the staff. After officials from the coroner's office left with the body, a nervous hotel employee asked him to accompany her into room 37.

There are more inconsistencies surrounding the death of Johnny Thunders than the circumstances around the demise of Marilyn Monroe. Without hard

fact the terrible speculation began: Thunders had been spiked with acid, rob-
bed, murdered, left to die by a person or persons unknown, New Orleans
flotsam that seeped in like a tide and dissipated by daylight. There is no way of
assessing what grains of truth may have been lost in a miasma of rumour denser
than a Louisiana swamp. What is known is that room 37 was totally trashed and
most of the guitarist's possessions stolen, including his passport, makeup, lyrics,
silk suits and shoes, yet it wasn't treated as a crime scene. His saddlebags were
sent home empty. Not only did his family have to come to terms with his death,
they also had to deal with an unresolved situation, as Johnny's niece, Chrissy
Bracken, noted: 'If it had been in New York it would have been treated as a
homicide case, in New Orleans this was just a Johnny Doe who was doing
drugs. They didn't realise how much press and all the hassle they were going to
get. There was a syringe in the toilet, the police threw it away, they didn't test
it. They said no alcohol was found but they interviewed a bartender who said
that Johnny had a drink with him. Alcohol stays in the body for a long time.
We're never going to get the answers. Why were there empty packets of
methadone? He'd just come back from London to get it.'

Ultimately, Johnny Thunders arrived in New Orleans exhausted and in poor
health; whatever went down sealed his fate in a particularly wretched manner.
Like Billy Murcia some eighteen years earlier, many people, including the
media, assumed that Thunders died from a suspected (expected) drugs overdose. Although the New Orleans Coroner's Office commented upon the 'pres-
cence of methadone and cocaine', they were a contributing factor, but the
quantities found were far from lethal. However, in the terminology of the
autopsy, death was still drug related. In a letter to Alan Hauser clarifying the report, Coroner Frank Minyard noted that: 'Under ideal circumstances, tests for
Hepatitis C and HIV would have been performed ... the doctor performing the
autopsy did not feel strongly enough about either condition to order the tests
to be performed.' One wonders what exactly constitutes 'ideal circumstances'
for an autopsy. Concluding his explanation of the report, Minyard also mentioned the advanced spread of malignant lymphoma (a form of leukaemia) and
stated: 'I believe he was in a seriously weakened condition as a result of this
malignancy and that this contributed very strongly to his death.'

Johnny Thunders returned home for the very last time. With his death an
era ended. Mariann Bracken: 'The funeral was unbelievable. The church, St
Anastasia's, was packed. There was over a forty-car procession and so many
flowers and floral pieces, guitars, hearts. There were more people than anybody can imagine. Steven Tyler was there, Deborah Harry sent flowers, so did
Motley Crue and Aerosmith. The fans came from all over, they were very nice,
respectful. My husband said in one row there was a man with a $500 suit on
and at the end of the row there was a girl with an earring in her nose and
tattoos. Some of the people left little things next to Johnny in the coffin, a

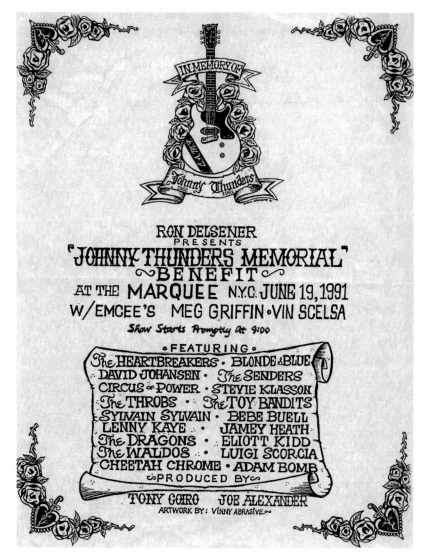

picture, a prayer card, a guitar pick … at first we were going to take them out but then we decided to keep them there. Johnny had so many people that cared.'

Somehow Johnny's partner in crime, Jerry Nolan, made it through the funeral: 'I don't remember bits of it, it was very dreamlike, I don't know why. I'm usually very clear headed but it didn't flow, it was strange. This is what I thought I would do to my friend: I would kiss him hello, leave the room and talk to everybody, then I would go back and kiss him goodbye. That's what I did.' Johnny Thunders was buried on Monday 29 April 1991, in St Mary's Cemetery, on the outskirts of Queens. He was thirty-eight years old.

Jerry Nolan took his friend's death extremely hard. After a period of mourning, he slowly began to surface. He participated in a memorial gig at the NY Marquee on 19 June, in Thunders' honour, that included Patti Palladin, members of The Oddballs, The Heartbreakers and The Dolls and other New York notables. The event raised $19,000 for Johnny's children, Vito, Dino and Jamie. As the summer gained momentum, Jerry started restoring a 1972 Triumph motorbike that he had originally discovered in Sweden. With a prior owner who had overcome a drug habit by diligently customising the bike, the Triumph became a talisman of hope. In August, the drummer visited London accompanied by Phyllis Stein. The first thing he did when we met up was to show me a copy of the 16 July edition of the *Village Voice* containing an impressive nine-page memoir entitled 'Beyond The Valley of The Dolls: A Guided Tour From Elvis to Sid' by Jerry Nolan with Doug Simmons. Not always the easiest of people to please, Nolan fixed me with one of his great cute 'n' tricksy grins that fleetingly obliterated all the loss. He hoped that the article would lead to a book or even a movie. The onset of winter put paid to all that.

Phyllis Stein: 'When we returned to New York, we started to concentrate on Jerry writing his book. We were given the names of literary agents and we were going to speak to a rock biographer. Jerry had also been working in the studio with his friend Greg Allen. Being in the studio was good for Jerry, as was a role in Rachel Amodeo's movie. He was upbeat and positive about the future. He kept telling me that he was finally really happy. In the beginning of November we thought he had come down with the flu and migraine headache. He was very sick. The doctors told me he had bacterial pneumonia and meningitis. They were giving him antibiotics and told me he would recover. Jerry was in the hospital about three weeks when he suffered a major stroke which left him in really bad shape, irreparably damaged. The reality was that he would never be able to leave that hospital alive. He was ill for another eight weeks and died on 14 January 1992 from complications. I had called Mariann that evening to ask her to help me with funeral arrangements. As if by telepathic communication, within two hours of that conversation, Jerry died. When Johnny died, Jerry asked Mariann that if anything happened to him, could he be buried next to Johnny. So yeah, he's buried right near Johnny. They're close and that's what Jerry would have wanted.'

Distant Drums. The Late Great Thunders and Nolan. (*Ian Dickson / Jungle archive*)

Johnny Thunders Discography
by
Freddy Lynxx

THE NEW YORK DOLLS

Title		Year	Label	Catalog	Country	Notes
Trash (Mono) / Trash (Stereo)	7"	1973	Mercury	DJ-378(73414)	US	Promo P/ S
Jetboy / Vietnamese Baby	7"	1973	Mercury	6052 402	UK	No P / S
Jetboy / Vietnamese Baby	7"	1973	Mercury	6052 402	Por	
Personality Crisis / Personality Crisis	7"	1973	Mercury	DJ 387	US	No P / S
Trash / Personality Crisis	7"	1973	Mercury	6052372	Sp	
Personality Crisis / Trash	7"	1973	Mercury	63414	US	
Personality Crisis / Trash	7"	1973	Mercury	6052732	Sw	
Jetboy / Vietnamese Baby	7"	1973	Mercury	6052 402	Neth	
Stranded In The Jungle / Don't Start Me Talking	7"	1974	Mercury	6052655	Sp	
Who Are The Mystery Girls ?/ Stranded In The Jungle	7"	1974	Mercury	6052 615	UK	No P / S
Stranded In The Jungle / Who Are The Mystery Girls ?	7"	1974	Mercury	73478	US	Promo No P / S
Stranded In The Jungle / Who Are The Mystery Girls ?	7"	1974	Mercury	6052 615	G	
Stranded In The Jungle / Who Are The Mystery Girls ?	7"	1974	Mercury	SFL-1855	J	
Babylon / Human Being	7"	1974	Mercury	6837207	F	
Looking For A Kiss / Who Are The Mystery Girls ? + Somethin' Else (Live)	7"	1974	Trash	TR-001	US	Reissued In 1982
Jetboy / Babylon + Who Are The Mystery Girls ?	7"	1977	Mercury	6160 008	UK	No P / S

Title	Size	Year	Label	Cat. No.	Country	Notes
Bad Girl / Subway Train	7"	1978	Bellaphon	BF 18608	G	
Personality Crisis / Looking For A Kiss	7"	1978	Bellaphon	BF 18576	G	
Pills / Down, Down, Downtown	7"	1984	Fan Club	NYD 1	F	Clear Vinyl
Pills / Down, Down, Downtown	7"	1984	Fan Club	NYD 1	F	White Vinyl
Personality Crisis / Subway Train	7"	1985	Antler	DOLLS 1	Neth	Picture Disc
Looking For A Kiss / Bad Girl	7"	1985	Antler	DOLLS 2	Neth	Picture Disc
Rehearsal & Live EP	7"	1989	NYD	NYD 101	US	
Rehearsal & Live EP	7"	1989	NYD	NYD 101	US	Red Vinyl
Lonely Planet Boy / Babylon (The Rough Mixes)	7"	1998	Sucksex	SEX 15	F	
Bad Girl / Chatterbox (Live 1974)	7"	1998	Sucksex	SEX 17	F	
Doll House Live In LA	10"	1988	Lipstick Killer	JUNK 74	US	Boot. Pink Vinyl
New York Tapes 72/73	10"	2000	Munster	MR 167	Sp	220 Grs Classic Vinyl
Personality Crisis + Looking For A Kiss / Subway Train + Bad Girl	12"	1982	Kamera	ERA 013-12	UK	
Personality Crisis / Subway Train	12"	1985	Antler	DOLLS 1	Neth	Picture Disc
Personality Crisis / Subway Train	12"	1985	Antler	DOLLS 1	Neth	3diff. Color
Looking For A Kiss / Bad Girl	12"	1985	Antler	DOLLS 2	Neth	Picture Disc
Looking For A Kiss / Bad Girl	12"	1985	Antler	DOLLS 2	Neth	3diff. Color
Personality Crisis + Looking For A Kiss / Bad Girl + Subway Train	12"	1990	See For Miles	SEA 3	UK	
The Early Years Live	12"	1990	Receiver	REPLAY 3011	UK	Blue Vinyl

Title	Format	Year	Label	Catalog	Country	Notes
New York Dolls	K7	1973	Mercury	MCR 4-1-675	US	
Too Much Too Soon	K7	1974	Mercury	MCR 4-1-1001	US	
Lipstick Killers	K7	1981	Roir	A-104	US	
Red Patent Leather	K7	1984	Fan Club	FCK 007	F	
Night Of The Living Dolls	K7	1985	Mercury	826 094-4M-1	US	
New York Dolls	LP	1973	Mercury	6398 004	F	Inner Sleeve
New York Dolls	LP	1973	Mercury	SRM-1-675	US	Inner Sleeve
New York Dolls	LP	1973	Mercury	6338270	UK	
New York Dolls	LP	1973	Mercury	6338270	Sp	
New York Dolls	LP	1973	Mercury	6336280	Neth	
New York Dolls	LP	1973	Mercury	RJ-5103	J	
Too Much Too Soon	LP	1974	Mercury	SRM-1-1001	US	
Too Much Too Soon	LP	1974	Mercury	6338498	UK	
Too Much Too Soon	LP	1974	Mercury	9100 002	F	
Too Much Too Soon	LP	1974	Mercury	63 38 498	Sp	Diff. Back Cover
Too Much Too Soon	LP	1974	Mercury	6338 498 1	Aus	
Too Much Too Soon	LP	1974	Mercury	RJ-5135	J	
Too Much Too Soon	LP	1974	Mercury	6463064	Neth	
New York Dolls Double LP	LP	1977	Mercury	PG210 -9100 002	F	Bestanthologie
Very Best Of New York Dolls	LP	1977	Mercury	6641 631	UK	Gatefold
	LP	1977	Mercury	RJ-7234	J	

Title	Format	Year	Label	Catalog	Country	Notes
Dallas 74	LP	1977	Smilin' Ears	7707	US	Bootleg
New York Dolls	LP	1982	Mercury	6336 280	N	
Too Much Too Soon	LP	1982	Mercury	6463 064	N	
New York Dolls	LP	1984	Mercury	SRM-1-675	US	Back Cover Black
Too Much Too Soon	LP	1984	Mercury	SRM-1-1001	US	Reissue
Live In Paris 12/23/73	LP	1984	Thunders	NEW 01	F	Bootleg
Trash (Don't Take My Life Away)	LP	1984	Desdemona	DES 2013	F	Bootleg
Red Patent Leather	LP	1984	Fan Club	FC 007	F	4 Diff. Color
Night Of The Living Dolls	LP	1985	Mercury	826094-1M-1	US	
Rock Legend aka Too Much Too Soon	LP	1986	Mercury	6463 029	A	Diff. Sleeve
New York Dolls & Too Much Too Soon	LP	1986	Mercury	PRID 12	UK	Gatefold
Dizzy Dolls	LP	1988		N.Y.D. 72/74	I	Bootleg
Looking For A Kiss	LP	1989	The Company	G.F. 46	US	Bootleg
Lipstick Killers	LP	1990	Danceteria	DAN LP 038	F	
7 Day Weekend Double LP	LP	1991	Brigand	LIP 73	US	Bootleg
Teenage News	LP	1998	Munster	MR 135	Sp	Color Vinyl + poster
New York Dolls	CD	1987	Mercury	832 752-2	US	
New York Dolls	CD	1987	Mercury	832 752-2	G	
Too Much Too Soon	CD	1987	Mercury	834 230-2	US	
Too Much Too Soon	CD	1987	Mercury	834 230-2	G	
New York Dolls/ Too Much Too Soon	CD	1987	Mercury	33PD-422	J	

Title	Format	Year	Label	Catalogue	Country	Notes
Red Patent Leather	CD	1988	Fan Club	FC 007	F	
Classic Tracks	CD	1988	Counterpoint	CDEP14	UK	4 Track Mini CD
New York Dolls	CD	1989	Mercury	23PD110	J	
Too Much Too Soon	CD	1989	Mercury	23PD111	J	
Lipstick Killers	CD	1990	Roir	88561-5027-2	US	
Lipstick Killers	CD	1990	Danceteria	DANCD 038	F	
Super Best Collection	CD	1990	Teichiku	TECP-28513	J	
Red Patent Leather	CD	1990	Teichiku	TECP-25234	J	
New York Dolls	CD	1991	Mercury	PHCR-6043	J	
Too Much Too Soon	CD	1991	Mercury	PHCR-6044	J	
Seven Day Weekend	CD	1992	Receiver	RRCD 163	UK	
Live 1975 Red Patent Leather	CD	1992	Restless	7 72596-2	US	With Bonus Tracks
Live 1975 Red Patent Leather	CD	1992	Receiver	RRCD 173	UK	With Bonus Tracks
Paris Burning	CD	1993	Skydog	62 256-2	F	
Paris Burning	CD	1993	Meldac	MECR-25023	J	Diff.Back Sleeve
New York Tapes 72/73	CD	1993	Skydog	62 257-2	F	
Evil Dolls New York Tapes 72/73	CD	1993	Meldac	MECR-25025	J	Diff. Cover Sleeve
Paris Le Trash	CD	1993	Triple X	51116-2	US	Same As 'Paris Burning' But with 4 Bonus Studio Tracks
Rock 'n' Roll	CD	1994	Mercury	314522129-2	US	
Rock 'n' Roll	CD	1994	Mercury	522 129-2	G	
Rock 'n' Roll	CD	1994	Mercury	PHCH-1327	J	

Title	Format	Year	Label	Catalogue	Country	Notes
Too Much Too Soon	CD	1994	Mercury	PHCR-4241	J	
Lipstick Killers	CD	1996	Danceteria	RE 104CD	F	
Paris Burning	CD	1996	Teichiku	TECW-20369	J	
Evil Dolls New York Tapes 72/73	CD	1996	Teichiku	TECW-20370	J	
Teenage News	CD	1997	Red Star	RS-7006	US	
Dawn Of The Dolls	CD	1998	Fab Discs	CD-0001	US	
Hootchie Cootchie Dolls	CD	1998	Solid	CDSOL-0016	J	With Lyrics; 13 Songs Sample
Street Trash New York Dolls / Heartbreakers	CD	1998	Recall	SMDCD 207	UK	A Shitty Version Of 7 Day Weekend (Only 12 Songs+ 2 From Escape Studio)
I'm A Human Being (Live)	CD	1998	Receiver	RRCD 260	UK	Live In Vancouver
Live In Concert, Paris 1974	CD	1999	Castle	ESM 734	UK	
The Glamorous Life (Live)	CD	1999	Big Ear Music	EAZ 4022	US	
The Glam Rock Hits	CD	1999	Cleopatra	CLP 0465-2	US	
New York Tapes 72/73	CD	2000	Munster	MRCD 167	Sp	
A Hard Night's Day	CD	2000	Norton	CED279	US	

THE HEARTBREAKERS

Title	Format	Year	Label	Catalogue	Country
Chinese Rocks / Born To Lose	7"	1977	Track	2094-135	UK
Born To Lose / Chinese Rocks	7"	1977	Track	ZBTR 7020	I
One Track Mind / Can't Keep My Eyes On You (Live) + Do You Love Me	7"	1977	Track	2094-137	UK

Title	Format	Year	Label	Catalog	Country	Notes
One Track Mind / Can't Keep My Eyes On You (Live) + Do You Love Me	7"	1977	Track	2094-137	G	
It's Not Enough / Born Too Loose	7"	1978	Track	2094-139	N	
It's Not Enough / Let Go	7"	1978	Track	2094-142	UK	
All By Myself (Live) / Milk Me (Live)	7"	1979	Max's	D.T.K. 213-45	US	
Get Off The Phone (Live) / I Wanna Be Loved (Live)	7"	1979	Beggars Banquet	BEG 21	UK	
Chinese Rocks (Live) / All By Myself (Live)	7"	1982	Jungle	JUNG 1	UK	
Get Off The Phone / All By Myself	7"	1984	Jungle	JUNG 14	UK	3 Diff. Color Sleeve
Get Off The Phone / All By Myself	7"	1984	Jungle	JUNG 14P	UK	Picture Disc
Born To Lose / It's Not Enough	7"	1984	Twins	T 1702	Sp	
One Track Mind / I Wanna Be Loved	7"	1984	Twins	T 1705	Sp	
Chinese Rocks EP	7"	1985	Jungle	JUNG 20	UK	
Pirate Love + Going Steady / Blank Generation + Hey Baby(Flight)	7"	1989	Nowhere	J 01	F	Release As The Junkies
Chinese Rocks (Live) / Get Off The Phone (Live)	7"	1996	So Alone	SEX 6	F	
Chinese Rocks / Born To Lose	7"	1999	Jungle	JUNG 62	UK	Pink Vinyl
One Track Mind / Can't Keep My Eyes On You + Do You Love Me	7"	1999	Jungle	JUNG 63	UK	Lilac Vinyl
Live At Mothers	10"	1998	Munster	MR 140	Sp	Pink Vinyl

Title	Format	Year	Label	Catalogue	Country	Notes
Vive La Revolution+ L.A.M.F. outtakes	10"	1999	Munster	MR 148	Sp	Double 10ó
Chinese Rocks / Born To Lose	12"	1977	Track	2094-135	UK	
Born Too Loose / Chinese Rocks	12"	1977	Barclay	740 502	F	Glossy Cover With Fingerprint Sleeve
Vintage 77	12"	1983	Jungle	JUNG 5	UK	
Get Off The Phone / All By Myself + Pirate Love	12"	1984	Jungle	JUNG 14X	UK	
Chinese Rocks EP	12"	1985	Jungle	JUNG 20T	UK	
Chinese Rocks EP	12"	1986	SMS	SP12-5285	J	
L.A.M.F.	K7	1977	Track	3191-118	UK	
D.T.K.L.A.M.F. Revisited	K7	1984	Jungle	FREUD C4	UK	Double-play K7
R.I.P.	K7	1984	Roir	A-134	US	3 Tracks Demo With Richard Hell
L.A.M.F. The Lost 77 Mixes	K7	1994	Jungle	FREUD C 044	UK	14 Songs
L.A.M.F.	LP	1977	Track	2409 218	UK	
L.A.M.F.	LP	1977	Track	2409 218	N	
L.A.M.F.	LP	1977	Track	2409 218	G	
L.A.M.F.	LP	1977	Barclay	940552	F	
L.A.M.F.	LP	1977	Track	ZPLTR 34025	I	Promo White Label
L.A.M.F.	LP	1977	Track	2409 218	Nor	
Punk Mix / Rock Mix Special	LP	1978	Barclay	HS69	F	Born To Loose DJ Comp.

Title	Format	Year	Label	Catalogue	Country	Notes
Live At Max's Kansas City	LP	1979	Max's	D.T.K. 213	US	
Live At Max's Kansas City	LP	1979	Beggars Banquet	BEGA 9	UK	
Live At Max's Kansas City	LP	1979	Atlantic	50 630	F	
Live At Max's Kansas City	LP	1979	Beggars Banquet	INT 146.521	G	
D.T.K.	LP	1982	Jungle	FREUD 1	UK	
D.T.K.	LP	1982	Jungle	FREUD 1	UK	White Vinyl
D.T.K.	LP	1982	Jungle	FREUD 1	UK	Red Vinyl
D.T.K.	LP	1982	Jungle	FREUD P1	UK	Picture Disc N°281
D.T.K.	LP	1983	SMS	SMS25-5046	J	
L.A.M.F. Revisited	LP	1984	Jungle	FREUD 4	UK	
L.A.M.F. Revisited	LP	1984	Jungle	FREUD P4	UK	Picture Disc
L.A.M.F. Revisited	LP	1984	Jungle	FREUD 4	UK	Pink Vinyl
L.A.M.F. Revisited	LP	1984	Jungle	FREUD 4	Nor	
Live At The Lyceum Ballroom 1984	LP	1984	ABC	ABC LP2	UK	
Live At The Lyceum Ballroom 1984	LP	1984	Lolita	5023	F	
D.T.K.	LP	1985	Jungle	JUN 6009	Gr	
D.T.K.	LP	1985	Twins	T 3011 (L)	Sp	
L.A.M.F. Revisited	LP	1985	Twins	T 3003	Sp	

Title	Format	Year	Label	Cat. No.	Country	Notes
Live At The Lyceum Ballroom 1984	LP	1985	SMS	SP25-5188	J	
Live At The Lyceum Ballroom 1984	LP	1985	AMD	AMDLP 7101	Sw	
Live At The Lyceum	LP	1990	Receiver	RRLP 134	UK	
Live At Mothers	LP	1991	Fan Club	FC 95	F	
What Goes Around	LP	1991	BOMP	BLP 4039	US	Red Vinyl
What Goes Around	LP	1991	BOMP	BLP 4039	US	Black Vinyl
L.A.M.F. The Lost 77 Mixes	LP	1994	Jungle	FREUD 044	UK	Gatefold
Pirate Love	LP	1996	M.I.A.	M.I.A. 002	F	
Pirate Love	LP	1998	M.I.A.	M.I.A. 002	F	Blue Vinyl / Blue Cover
Pirate Love	LP	1998	M.I.A.	M.I.A. 002	F	Blue Vinyl / Red Cover
D.T.K.L.A.M.F. Revisited	CD	1986	Jungle	CD FREUD 4	UK	
Live At The Lyceum Ballroom 1984	CD	1989	ABC	ABCD 2	UK	
Live At The Lyceum	CD	1990	Receiver	RRCD 134	UK	
Live At Max S Kansas City	CD	1990	Beggars Banquet	BBL9CD	UK	
Live At Mothers	CD	1991	Fan Club	FC 95 CD	F	
What Goes Around	CD	1991	Bomp	BCD 4039	US	
Live At The Lyceum	CD	1993	Teichiku	TECX-25435	J	
Outracks L.A.M.F.	CD	1993	Skydog	62250-2	F	4 Tracks
L.A.M.F. Another Takes	CD	1993	Meldac	MECR-18002	J	Same As Above With 2 Bonus Tracks
Vive La Revolution	CD	1993	Skydog	62251-2	F	

Title	Format	Year	Label	Catalogue	Country	Notes
Vive La Revolution	CD	1993	Meldac	MECR-25019	J	
L.A.M.F. Revisited	CD	1994	Receiver	RRCD-190	UK	
D.T.K. Live At The Speakeasy	CD	1994	Receiver	RRCD-191	UK	
L.A.M.F. The Lost 77 Mixes	CD	1994	Jungle	FREUD CD044	UK	
L.A.M.F. The Lost 77 Mixes	CD	1997	Jungle	FREUD CD044	UK	With A Limited Edition Vintage '77 CD
Live At Max's Kansas City 79	CD	1995	Roir	RUSCD8219	US	
L.A.M.F. Another Takes	CD	1996	Teichiku	TECW-15368	J	
Vive La Revolution	CD	1996	Teichiku	TECW-20367	J	
Street Trash New York Dolls / Heartbreakers	CD	1998	Recall	SMDCD 207	UK	Live At The Lyceum 1984
The Very Best Of Johnny Thunders	CD	1999	Teichiku	TECW-21861	J	Johnny Thunders & The Heartbreakers
Vive La Revolution+ L.A.M.F. Outtakes	CD	1999	Munster	MRCD 148	Sp	
Dead Or Alive	Video	1985	Jungle	JVD1	UK	
Dead Or Alive	Video	1990	Jungle	JVD1	UK	Different Sleeve

JOHNNY THUNDERS

Title	Format	Year	Label	Catalogue	Country	Notes
Dead Or Alive / Downtown	7"	1978	Real	ARE 1	UK	
You Can T Put Your Arms Around A Memory / Hurtin	7"	1978	Real	ARE 3	UK	
In Cold Blood (Studio) / In Cold Blood (Live)	7"	1983	New Rose	NEW 14	F	

Title	Size	Year	Label	Cat. No.	Country	Notes
Proud To Be Pirate EP	7"	1983	Cheese	SMILE 001	Sw	Live with Living Dead + Studio with Gang War
Hurt Me / It's Not Enough + Like A Rolling Stone	7"	1984	New Rose	NEW 27	F	
Short Lives + Cool Operator / Endless Party + Tie Me Me Up	7"	1986	Twins	T 1759	Sp	
Short Lives	7"	1986	RDL	DISCO FLEx N°3	Sp	Promo Flexi Disc
Que Sera Sera / Short Lives	7"	1987	Jungle	JUNG 33	UK	
Ain T Superstitious / Midnight Hour	7"	1987	Scatterbrain	SR-04	US	
Live At The Speakeasy London 1978	7"	1993	DTKP	NDR 01/02	F	Gatefold Bootleg
Interview + Life Goes On / As Tears Go By	7"	1996	Sucksex	SEX 7	F	
Daddy Rollin Stone / Leave Me Alone	7"	1996	Sucksex	SEX 10	F	
Countdown Love (A by Johnny)/(B by Jerry)	7"	1997	Sucksex	SEX 13	F	
The Fireball EP (5 Songs)	7"	1999	Sucksex	SEX 20	F	
The Thunderbolt EP (4 Songs)	7"	2000	Sucksex	SEX 21	F	
In Cold Blood	10"	1998	Munster	MR 142	Sp	Double 106
Hurt Me	10"	1998	Munster	MR 143	Sp	Purple Vinyl
You Can't Put Your Arms (Long Version) / Hurtin	12"	1978	Real	ARE 3	UK	Pink Vinyl
You Can't Put Your Arms (Long Version) / Hurtin	12"	1978	Real	ARE 3	UK	Yellow Vinyl No P / S
You Can't Put Your Arms (Long Version) /	12"	1978	Real	ARE 3	UK	Blue Vinyl No P / S

Hurtin

Title	Format	Year	Label	Catalogue	Country	Notes
Diary Of A Lover	12"	1983	JEM	PVC 5907	US	
In Cold Blood (Mini LP)	12"	1984	New Rose	NEW 31	F	
Que Sera Sera / Short Lives + I Only Wrote This Song For You	12"	1987	Jungle	JUNG 33T	UK	
Too Much Junkie Business	K7	1983	Roir	A-118	US	
Diary Of A Lover	K7	1983	PVC (JEM)	PVCC 5907	US	Double A Side
Hurt Me	K7	1984	New Rose	ROS K 26	F	
Que Sera Sera	K7	1985	Jungle	FREUD C9	UK	
Station Of The Cross	K7	1987	Roir	A-146	US	
Bootlegging The Bootleggers	K7	1990	Jungle	FREUD C30	UK	
So Alone	LP	1978	Real	RAL 1	UK	
So Alone	LP	1979	Pathe Marconi / EMI	2C 068-62717	F	With Sire Label
So Alone	LP	1983	Warner	WB 56 571	G	Reissue
In Cold Blood	LP	1983	New Rose	ROSE 18	F	
Pipeline	LP	1983	Rocking Rebel	RR 01	Sw	Bootleg
Wanted Dead Or Alive Reward $10	LP	1983	Zombie	C.U.N.T. 001	Sw	Bootleg
So All Alone	LP	1983			Sw	Bootleg
Hey Man Where Is My Guitar?	LP	1983	Subway	SUB 077	Sw	Bootleg
Cosa Nostra Never Sleeps	LP	1984	Spectra	SR 7E 190683	Sw	Bootleg

Title	Format	Year	Label	Cat. No.	Country	Notes
Hurt Me	LP	1984	New Rose	ROSE 26	F	
Play With Fire	LP	1984	Unique	198-40404/5	UK	Bootleg
Hurt Me	LP	1985	SMS	SP25-5197	J	
There's A Little Bit Of Whore	LP	1985	New Rock		Sw	Double Bootleg
Schneckentaenze	LP	1985	Modern Beat		G	Bootleg
Que Sera Sera	LP	1985	Jungle	FREUD 9	UK	
Que Sera Sera	LP	1985	Jungle	FREUD 9	Uk	Pink Vinyl
Que Sera Sera	LP	1985	Aim	AIM 1007	A	
Que Sera Sera	LP	1986	Twins	T 3031	Sp	
Que Sera Sera	LP	1986	SMS	SP25-5272	J	
Que Sera Sera	LP	1987	Jungle	FREUD P9	UK	Picture Disc
Lucky Strike Back	LP	1988		JT-6781/2	J	Double Bootleg
The Johnny Thunders Album Collection	LP	1988	Jungle	JT BOX 1	UK	3 Lp S + 126 + Badge + Poster Collection
Stations Of The Cross	LP	1989	Danceteria	DANLP043	F	Double LP
Too Much Junkie Business	LP	1989	Danceteria	DANLP044	F	
Bootlegging The Bootleggers	LP	1990	Jungle	FREUD 30	UK	
Bootlegging The Bootleggers	LP	1990	Jungle	FREUD 30	UK	Clear Yellow Vinyl
In Cold Blood	LP	1991	New Rose	ROSE 18	F	Reissue In Red Vinyl
Chinese Rocks	LP	2000	Get Back	GET 49	I	
Hurt Me	CD	1986	New Rose	ROSE 26 CD	F	
Que Sera Sera	CD	1986	Jungle	CD FREUD 9	UK	With 2 Bonus Track

Title	Format	Year	Label	Catalogue	Country	Notes
In Cold Blood	CD	1989	New Rose	NEAT 5CD	F	5 Track Mini CD
Live In Japan	CD	1989	J.A.P. Inter.	JAPD-18	J	
Bootlegging The Bootleggers	CD	1990	Jungle	FREUD CD 30	UK	
Too Much Junkie Business	CD	1990	Danceteria	DANCD044	F	
Stations Of The Cross	CD	1990	Roir	8856r-5028-2	US	
In Cold Blood	CD	1990	Teichiku	TECX-25232	J	
In Cold Blood	CD	1991	New Rose	ROSE r8 CD	F	
Saddest Vacation Act.1	CD	1991	Meldac	MECR-30023	J	
Saddest Vacation Act.2	CD	1991	Meldac	MECR-30024	J	
Hurt Me More	CD	1991	Meldac	MECR-30025	J	
Live In Japan	CD	1992	Century	CECC 00473	J	Reissue
So Alone	CD	1992	Sire / Warner	9 26982-2	US	
So Alone	CD	1992	Sire / Warner	7599 -26982-2	G	
So Alone	CD	1992	Sire / Warner	WPCP 4927	J	
Stations Of The Cross	CD	1992	Danceteria	DANCD043	F	
Have Faith	CD	1992	Fan Club	FCD 109	F	1rst Issue
New Rose Collection	CD	1992	Teichiku	TECX-25377	J	
Have Faith Live In Seinen-kan 88	CD	1993	Century	CECC-00609	J	
Chinese Rocks (Ultimate Live Collection)	CD	1993	Anagram	CD GRAM 70	UK	
Live Crisis	CD	1993	Mogul	MNR 003	G	Bootleg
Sticks & Stones	CD	1993	Totonka	CD PRO 7	US	Bootleg

Title		Year	Label	Catalogue	Country	Notes
Stations Of The Cross Revisited	CD	1994	Receiver	RRCD 188	UK	With Bonus Tracks
Que Sera Sera	CD	1994	Jungle	FREUD CD 049	UK	Reissue. Different
Add Water And Stir	CD	1994	Essential	ESD CD 226	UK	
Hurt Me	CD	1995	Dojo	DOJO CD 217	UK	Reissue
In Cold Blood	CD	1995	Dojo	DOJO CD 221	UK	Reissue
Countdown Love	CD	1995	Weeping Goat	WG 034	NZ	Bootleg
Johnny On The Rocks	CD	1995	Nightlife	N-048	J	Bootleg
The Best Of Johnny Thunders	CD	1995	Teichiku	TECW-23012	J	
Have Faith	CD	1996	Mutiny	60023 80005-2	US	
Have Faith Live In Seinen-Kan 88	CD	1996	Essential	ESM CD 453	UK	
The Studio Bootlegs	CD	1996	Dojo	DOJO CD 231	UK	
Internal Possession	CD	1996	Sonic	SRCD0020	UK	
Diary Of A Gypsy Lover	CD	1996	Sonic	SRCD0030	UK	
Fuck Off Marquee	CD	1996	Drug Party	FOM 838	J	Bootleg
Belfast Rock	CD	1997	Anagram	CDM GRAM 117	UK	
Saddest Vacation Act.1	CD	1998	Solid	CDSOL-0011	J	Reissue
Saddest Vacation Act.2	CD	1998	Solid	CDSOL-0012	J	Reissue
Hurt Me More	CD	1998	Solid	CDSOL-0013	J	Reissue
Live In Sweden 1984	CD	1998	Solid	CDSOL-0014/15	J	With Syl Sylvain (2cd)

Title	Format	Year	Label	Catalog	Country	Notes
One For The Road	CD	1999	Hit Parade	HP005	US	Bootleg
The New Too Much Junkie Business	CD	1999	Roir	RUS CD 8248	US	
Sad Vacation	CD	1999	Receiver	RRDCD 009 Z	UK	Same As Live In Sweden 1984
Born Too Loose	CD	1999	Jungle	FREUD CD 60	UK	Double Cd Compil.

JOHNNY THUNDERS & PATTI PALLADIN

Title	Format	Year	Label	Catalog	Country	Notes
Crawfish / Tie Me Up	7"	1985	Jungle	JUNG 23	UK	
Crawfish / Tie Me Up	7"	1985	Jungle	JUNG 23P	UK	Picture Disc
She Wants to Mambo / Uptown to Harlem	7"	1988	Jungle	JUNG 38	UK	
She wants to mambo / Uptown to harlem	7"	1988	Accord	101657	F	
Baby It's You	7"	1988	Twins	T1829 SN	Sp	One sided /Promo
I Was Born To Cry	7"	1988	Twins	T1830 SN	Sp	One Sided / Promo
He Cried	7"	1988	Twins	T1831 SN	Sp	One Sided / Promo
I Was Born To Cry / Treat Her Right	7"	1988	Jungle	JUNG 43	UK	
Crawfish / Tie Me Up + Crawfish (Bayou Mix)	12"	1985	Jungle	JUNG 23T	UK	
Crawfish / Tie Me Up + Crawfish (Bayou Mix)	12"	1985	Twins	T 1217	Sp	
She Wants To Mambo / Uptown To Harlem + Love Is Strange	12"	1988	Jungle	JUNG 38T	UK	
I Was Born To Cry / Treat Her Right + Can't Seem To Make You Minez	12"	1988	Jungle	JUNG 43T	UK	
Copy Cats	K7	1988	Jungle	FREUD C20	UK	

Title	Label	Year	Format	Catalog	Country	Notes
Copy Cats	Accord	1988	K7	101654	F	
Copy Cats	Jungle	1988	LP	FREUD 20	UK	
Copy Cats	Jungle	1988	LP	FREUD 20	UK	Yellow Vinyl
Copy Cats	Twins	1988	LP	T-3083	Sp	
Copy Cats	Accord	1988	LP	101651	F	
Copy Cats	Restless	1988	LP	7 72326-1	US	
Copy Cats	Citadel	1988	LP	CITLP518	A	
Copy Cats	Jungle	1988	CD	CD FREUD 20	UK	
Copy Cats	Restless	1988	CD	7 72326-2	US	2 Songs Missing

GANG WAR: JOHNNY THUNDERS & WAYNE KRAMER

Title	Label	Year	Format	Catalog	Country	Notes
London Boy + I'd Rather Be With The Boys + Endless Party + Just Because I'm White	Zodiac	1987	7"	NR 17006	US	Bootleg / Red Or Blue Vinyl
Gang War	De Milo	1990	LP	DM0003-1	US	
These Boots Were Made For Fighting	M.I.A.	1996	LP	MIA 001	F	Bootleg
These Boots Were Made For Fighting	M.I.A.	1996	LP	MIA 001	F	Blue Vinyl
Street Fighting	Meldac	1993	CD	MECR-25026	J	
Street Fighting	Skydog	1993	CD	62258-2	F	
Live At The Channel Club	R.E.R.	1995	CD	RER 9001-2	US	
Street Fighting	Teichiku	1996	CD	TECW-20371	J	
Crime Of The Century	Sonic	1996	CD	SRCD00050	UK	

MISCELLANEOUS

Justin Love

Title	Format	Year	Label	Cat.	Country	Notes
Pony Tail / No Love	7"	1981	Casino	CA-002	US	Johnny Produced Both Track & Co-Wrote 'No Love'

Jimi Lalumia & The Psychotic Frogs

Title	Format	Year	Label	Cat.	Country	Notes
Greatest Hits – Live	K7	1984	Rather Rude	#100	US	2 Songs with Johnny

Michael Thimren

Title	Format	Year	Label	Cat.	Country	Notes
For A Few Dollars More / Ain't My Friend	7"	1984	Sword	SWA S 001	Sw	Produced By Bill Rath. Johnny Plays on a Side

John Waite

Title	Format	Year	Label	Cat.	Country	Notes
Mask Of Smiles	LP	1985	EMI	2403861	F	Johnny Plays On 'No Brakes'
Mask Of Smiles	LP	1985	EMI	108349	Arg	Johnny Plays On 'No Brakes'

Two Saints

Title	Format	Year	Label	Cat.	Country	Notes
King Of NYC / Are You Living	7"	1986	Euphoria	ESS-034	US	Johnny Wrote Side B

Hanoi Rocks

Title	Format	Year	Label	Cat.	Country	Notes
Pills / Gloria	7"	1988	Space Faggots	4 850115	UK	Orange Cover / N°392 Autographed By Johnny

Shinya Ohe + Johnny Thunders

Great Big Kiss/ I Can't Help Myself +1	12"	1988	Vice	15EC-103	J	Johnny Sings 'Great Big Kiss'

The RC Succession

Covers	LP	1988	Kitty	28MS 0185	J	Johnny Plays On 'Eve Of Destruction' & 'Secret Agent Man'

The Nomads

Fire And Brimstone / Beyond The Valley Of The Dolls	7"	1989	Amigo	AMS 174	Sw	Johnny Plays Lead Guitar On B-side
Fire And Brimstone / Beyond The Valley Of The Dolls + Solitary Confinement	12"	1989	Amigo	AMMS 503	Sw	
All Wrecked Up	LP	1989	Amigo	AMLP 2017	Sw	Different Mix Than The 7" & 12"
All Wrecked Up	CD	1989	Amigo	30738	Sw	

Jimi Lalumia & The Psychotic Frogs

Twist And Shout / Boys	7"	1991	Beat This!	NR-1878I	US	Gold Vinyl

Johnny Thunders & The Chesterfield Kings						
Critic's Choice / I'd Much Rather Be With The Boy + London Boy	7"	1992	Junkie	JUNKIE 007	J	Bootleg

EBI						
EBI	CD	1991	WEA	WCM3-12	J	Johnny Plays On 'Fucking Police'

David Johansen						
The David Johansen Group Live	CD	1992	Epic	ZK 53218	US	Johnny Plays On 'Babylon'

Freddy Lynxx						
No Pleasure Thrills	LP	1996	Sucksex	SEX 5	F	Johnny Plays On 'As Tears Go By'
No Pleasure Thrills	LP	1996	Sucksex	SEX 5	F	Blue Vinyl
The Courageous Cat	CD	1997	Sucksex	SEX 9	F	Different Mix Of 'As Tears Go By'

Johnny Thunders & The Reign						
Zippered Up Heart *	7"	2000	Norton	49-091	US	

Tracks on the accompanying Johnny Thunders CD

1 'BORN TO LOSE' (THUNDERS) VIRGIN/EMI MUSIC
Recorded Essex studios 20/2/77 – 'After-Curry' Mix

2 'IT'S NOT ENOUGH' (THUNDERS) VIRGIN/EMI MUSIC
Recorded Ramport Studios 1/6/77 – 'Mix 3'

3 'LET GO' (THUNDERS/NOLAN) VIRGIN/EMI MUSIC/JUNGLE
MUSIC/LEOSONG
Recorded Ramport Studios 10/6/77

4 'ONE TRACK MIND' (LURE/NOLAN) JUNGLE MUSIC/
LEOSONG
Recorded Advision Studios 10/9/77

5 'BABY TALK' (THUNDERS) VIRGIN/EMI MUSIC
Recorded Advision 15/9/77

6 'PIRATE LOVE' (THUNDERS) VIRGIN/EMI MUSIC
Recorded Ramport Studios 7/6/77 'Mix 4'

7 'A LITTLE BIT OF WHORE' (THUNDERS) JUNGLE MUSIC/
LEOSONG
Recorded West 3 Studios August 1985 'Alternate Mix'

8 'CHINESE ROCKS' (RAMONE/RAMONE/RAMONE) WARNER
CHAPPELL MUSIC
Live version recorded 27/10/84 at The McMordie Hall, Queens University,
Belfast

9 'STEPPING STONE' (BOYCE/HART) SCREEN GEMS/EMI MUSIC
Live version

10 INTERVIEW – Recorded 22/8/84 for DOA video

Tracks 1 to 7 plus interview included courtesy of Jungle Records
    Tracks 1 to 6 alternate mixes from 'L.A.M.F. – the lost '77 mixes'
    Track 7 alternate mix from 'Que Sera Sera', FREUD CD049
    Special thanks to Alan Hauser
Tracks 8 and 9 included courtesy of Johnny Thunders Estate

BORN TOO LOOSE – THE BEST OF JOHNNY THUNDERS
(FREUD CD 60)

Disc 1 Tracks

1 Born To Lose
2 Chinese Rocks
3 It's Not Enough
4 You Can't Put Your Arms Around
   A Memory
5 Pirate Love
7 Diary Of A Lover
8 Born To Cry
9 One Track Mind
10 I Only Wrote This Song For You
11 Crawfish
12 Little Bit Of Whore
13 Hurt Me
14 M.I.A.
15 Society Makes Me Sad (live)

Disc 2 Tracks

1 London Boys
2 Too Much Junkie Business
3 Great Big Kiss
4 Chinese Rocks
5 Get Off The Phone
6 All By Myself
7 I Love You
8 I Wanna Be Loved
9 Countdown love
10 Blame It On Mom
11 Personality Crisis
12 You Can't Put Your Arms …
13 Eve Of Destruction
14 Like A Rolling Stone
15 Like A Rolling Stone
16 Hurt me
17 Diary Of A Lover
18 Sad Vacation
19 Pipeline
20 I Can Tell
21 A Little Bit Of Whore
22 Talking 'Bout You
23 Too Much Junkie Business / Pills
24 Gloria

This album, as well as 'L.A.M.F. – the lost '77 mixes', 'Que Sera Sera', 'Bootlegging The Bootleggers' and 'Copy Cats' with Patti Palladin are available from all good record shops or by internet shopping at www.jungle-records.com

Johnny Thunders CDs available through Cherry Red Records

JOHNNY THUNDERS – CHINESE ROCKS -
THE ULTIMATE LIVE COLLECTION
(CDGRAM 70)

Tracks:

1   Pipeline
2   Countdown Love
3   Personality Crisis
4   Little Bit Of Whore
5   M.I.A
6   Stepping Stone
7   Alone In A Crowd
8   Endless Party
9   Copycat
10 Don't Mess With Cupid
11 Born To Lose
12 Too Much Junkie Business
13 Chinese Rocks
14 Pills

The albums on this and the next page are available through all good
record shops and also through the Cherry Red mail order service on
00-44 (0)207-371 5844 (phone) 00-44(0)207-384 1854
or infornet@cherryred.co.uk (E mail)
Cherry Red Website: www.cherryred.co.uk

JOHNNY THUNDERS - BELFAST ROCKS
(CDMGRAM 117)

Tracks:
  1   Pipeline
  2   Countdown Love
  3   Personality Crisis
  4   LittleBit Of Whore
  5   M.I.A.
  6   Too Much Junkie Business
  7   Talk About You
  8   Chinese Rocks
  9   Copycat
 10   In Cold Blood
 11   Alone In A Crowd
 12   Eve Of Destruction
 13   You Can't Put Your Arms Around A Memory
 14   Sad Vacation
 15   Born to Lose
 16. Stepping Stone
 17   Pipeline
 18   Chinese Rocks
 19   Chinese Rocks (again)

For more information, the virtual spirit of Johnny Thunders can be found in the Cyberlounge at:
    http://home.echo-on.net/~ifftay/thunders.htm

For access to a fanzine and other Thunders-related items, write to:
    Mr Vujan
    130 Rue de la Republique
    92150
    Suresnes
    France

For a 20-year day-by-day diary of Johnny Thunders, plus shopping, news and info, visit the Jungle Records website at:
    www.jungle-records.com

For mail order on Jungle Johnny Thunders products write, with an S.A.E. or I.R.C., to:
    Jungle Post
    62 Chalk Farm Road
    London
    NW1 8AN
    United Kingdom

Also available from

CHERRY RED BOOKS

Indie Hits 1980–1989
The Complete UK Independent Charts
(Singles & Albums)
Compiled by Barry Lazell

Indie Hits is the ultimate reference book for alternative music enthusiasts. Indie Hits is the first and only complete guide to the first decade of Britain's Independent records chart, and to the acts, the music and the labels which made up the Indie scene of the 1980s. The book is set out in a similar format to the *Guinness Hit Singles* and *Albums* books, with every artist, single and album to have shown in the indie charts over the 10-year period being detailed. The first Independent charts were published by the trade paper *Record Business* in January 1980, by which time they were well overdue. By that time, Mute Graduate, Factory, Crass, Safari and Rough Trade were just a few of the new breed of rapidly expanding labels already scoring hit records. They were

www.cherryred.co.uk

producing acts like Depeche Mode, UB40, Toyah, The Cult, Joy Division and Stiff Little Fingers, all to become major international sellers. Later years brought the likes of the Smiths, New Order, Erasure, The Stone Roses, James, The Fall and Happy Mondays (not to mention Kylie and Jason!) – all successful and influential independently distributed hitmakers. The A–Z section details every chartmaking 1980s indie act and all hit records in a detailed but easy-to-reference format. Also included are complete indexes of single and album titles, an authoritative history of the origin and development of the Indie charts during the 1980's, listings of all No 1 singles and albums with illustrations of rare original sleeves, print ads and other memorabilia of the period plus a fax 'n' trivia section including the artists and labels with the most chart records, the most No. 1s and the longest chart stays. If it was in the indie charts of the 1980s, it's in here!

Paper covers, 314 pages, £14.95 in UK

Cor Baby, That's Really Me!
(New Millennium Hardback Edition)
John Otway

Time was when John Otway looked forward to platinum albums, stadium gigs and a squad of bodyguards to see him safely aboard his private jet. Unfortunately it didn't happen that way. A series of dreadful career decisions, financial blunders and bad records left Otway down but not out. This is his true story in his own words. It is the story of a man who …

- has never repaid a record company advance in his life
- once put on a benefit concert for his record company after they had cancelled his contract
- signed himself to the mighty Warner Bros label simply by pressing his own records with the WB logo
- broke up with Paula Yates telling her it was the last chance she would get to go out with a rock star

This book is Otway's hilarious yet moving account of his insane assault on the music industry, a tale of blind ambition and rank incompetence, and a salutary lesson for aspiring musicians on how not to achieve greatness. But if the John Otway story is one of failure, it is failure on a grand scale. And it makes compulsive reading too!

Hardback, 192 pages and 16 pages of photographs, £11.99 in UK

Also available from

CHERRY RED BOOKS

All the Young Dudes
Mott the Hoople and Ian Hunter
The Biography
Campbell Devine

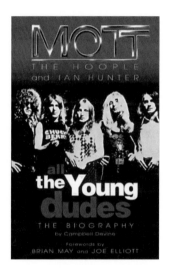

Published to coincide with the Sony 3-CD anthology of their music, *All the Young Dudes* traces Mott The Hoople's formation, their work with David Bowie, their rise to international stardom and beyond, including offshoots such as Mick Ralphs' Bad Company, Mott and British Lions, plus Hunter and Ronson's solo careers and collaborations with Van Morrison, Bob Dylan and Morrissey.

Devoid of borrowed information and re-cycled press clippings, this official biography contains new, sensational and humorous inside stories, controversial quotes and an array of private and previously unpublished views from the band, embellished with comprehensive appendices including discographies and session listings.

The author has collaborated with Ian Hunter and all of Mott's founder members, Dale Griffin, Overend Watts, Verden Allen and Mick Ralphs – who have provided their own anecdotes and photographs to illustrate and enhance the project. There are further personal contributions from Luther Grosvenor, Morgan Fisher, Stan Tippins, Diane Stevens, Muff Winwood, Ray Major, John Fiddler, Blue Weaver and Miller Anderson.

This biography will be welcomed by both the committed and casual rock reader, and by all Dudes, young and post-young!

Paper covers, 448 pages and 16 pages of photographs, £14.99 in UK

'This book is by far the most comprehensive work on the subject, and could well be the best book written about any band.'

– Adrian Perkins on his Mott web page

Also available from

CHERRY RED BOOKS

Embryo
A Pink Floyd Chronology
1966 – 1971
Nick Hodges & Ian Priston

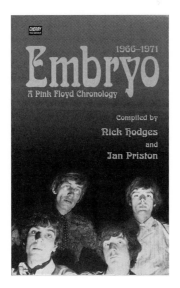

What exactly happened in 'The Massed Gadgets of Auximenes', 'Games For May' and 'The Committee' and what were Pink Floyd up to in Studio 3 at Abbey Road on 1 June 1967?

'Embryo: A Pink Floyd Chronology' is the most fully comprehensive and in-depth study of the early work of the Pink Floyd that has been compiled to date. An archetypal labour of love, the chronology draws together details of rare recordings owned by collectors, concert ads, tickets, obscure posters, unseen photographs and long-lost reviews, into a high-quality tour of the band's day-to-day work up to their first epochal work 'The Dark Side Of The Moon'.

Beginning with an evaluation of the Floyd's first tentative steps towards their concept albums – a genre which they went on to make their own, and continuing through a painstaking commentary on the development of the band's concert, film, studio and television work, the detail of this book will achieve and surpass the high standards that Pink Floyd collectors demand.

'Embryo' also explores the solo history of the band's first enigmatic and often misunderstood leader Syd Barrett. Correcting mistakes made previously by others, the book additionally represents a fully equipped and up-to-date research resource which is made easily accessible by a detailed index and chapter-by-chapter notes. 'Embryo' is a must for every serious fan.

Paper covers, 302 pages and photographs throughout, £14.99 in UK

CHERRY RED BOOKS

We are always looking for any interesting book projects
to get involved in. If you have any good ideas, or indeed manuscripts,
for books that you feel deserve publication, then please
get in touch with us.

CHERRY RED BOOKS
a division of Cherry Red Records Ltd
Unit 17, Elysium Gate West,
126–8 New King's Road
London SW6 4LZ

E-mail: iain@cherryred.co.uk
Web: http://www.cherryred.co.uk